Late Bloom

Late Bloom

New Lives for Women

Luree Miller

PADDINGTON PRESS LTD
NEW YORK & LONDON

To the memory of my mother-in-law,
Mary Merhar Miller,
whose long life affirmed
the strength and resilience of women

Library of Congress Cataloging in Publication Data
Miller, Luree.
Late bloom.
1. Middle aged women – Biography. I. Title.
HQ1123.M48   301.41'2   78–25983
ISBN 0 448 22687 1 (U.S. and Canada only)
ISBN 0 7092 0517 1

Filmset in England by SX Composing Ltd., Rayleigh, Essex.
Printed and bound in the United States

Designed by Patricia Pillay

IN THE UNITED STATES
PADDINGTON PRESS
Distributed by
GROSSET & DUNLAP

IN THE UNITED KINGDOM
PADDINGTON PRESS

IN CANADA
Distributed by
RANDOM HOUSE OF CANADA LTD.

IN SOUTHERN AFRICA
Distributed by
ERNEST STANTON (PUBLISHERS) (PTY.) LTD.

IN AUSTRALIA AND NEW ZEALAND
Distributed by
A.H. & A.W. REED

Contents

For permission to quote the lines of poetry on the following pages, the author and publishers thank:

PAGE 29: *The Complete Poems of Marianne Moore.* Copyright © 1969 by Marianne Moore. Reprinted by permission of Viking Penguin Inc. PAGE 215: Reprinted from "From an Old House in America" from *Poems, Selected And New*, 1950–1974, by Adrienne Rich, with the permission of W. W. Norton & Company, Inc. Copyright © 1975, 1973, 1971, 1969, 1966, by W. W. Norton & Company, Inc. Copyright 1967, 1963, 1962, 1961, 1960, 1959, 1958, 1957, 1956, 1955, 1954, 1953, 1952, 1951, by Adrienne Rich.

Author's Note

Books – least of all this one – seldom spring fully developed from the writer's mind, like Athena did from the head of Zeus. Janet Marqusee, my publisher, first urged me to write about the lives of some late-blooming women I mentioned to her. She felt an affinity with them because she had been a full-time, seven-day-a-week mother of five children until she joined her husband as the co-publisher of Paddington Press and began working in an office rather than in her kitchen. Then I discovered that Janet, like the women I interviewed for this book, is a perennial, blooming in every season of her life – as a mother, an artist and a community leader, before she became, in her forties, a full-time publisher.

Readers of my previous book, On Top of the World: Five Women Explorers in Tibet, *encouraged me also, by pointing out that, to them, one of the most interesting aspects of those five Victorian women was that they were in their middle years before they set out on their remarkable adventures.*

And so many friends and relatives spurred me on with their enthusiasm for the subject that I cannot begin to thank them all. Throughout the writing, Catherine Carpenter, my editor, helped keep me to my topic with her wise and gentle suggestions.

My greatest debt of gratitude, however, is to the women who allowed me to write about their lives. Self-effacing as they all are, they eventually consented to talk about themselves in hopes that their stories would be helpful to other women. Their trust in me was a solemn obligation. I know that in these short profiles I could not do them full justice. I know also that, for many of them, seeing their stories here in print will be painful, for they are private people, not accustomed to a public scrutiny. My admiration and gratitude to them is increased by this knowledge.

My own private "support system" continues to be my family: Blair, who found me a little bright-orange, second-hand Honda to give me the mobility I needed; Stacy, who gave me criticism and sent me quotations I used; Scott, who typed, edited, and commented on the entire manuscript; and Bill, my critic, who takes me out to dinner and remains my mainstay of thirty-two years. Without them the writing of this book would have been longer and harder, and not nearly as happy an experience as it was.

Foreword

A woman who is over fifty, as I am, may wonder how she sprinted so quickly into her second half-century. And once there, across that great dividing line between youth and age (which may be at forty or forty-five or sixty-five, depending on how hard life has been or which race you are in), she is surprised to find that life is not over, after all, as she supposed it would be when she was bounding through her springtime. She is not all washed up – burnt out after thirty, as Freud, in a misogynistic mood, proclaimed women were.

If we had paid attention to the lives of all the women around us, we would have known long ago that Freud was wrong. Multitudes of women have proven that maturity is a time of doors opening for them: doors into themselves to find a talent or an interest that they did not have the time to notice before; or doors opening out, into the world they either dared not, or could not, enter before. A hundred years ago, Elizabeth Candy Stanton looked around at her friends and succinctly noted that "the hey-day of a woman's life is on the shady side of fifty."

This book is an account of women who, in their middle years, found the strength and the creativity to change and to grow and to shape their own lives: women who became late bloomers. It is a confirmation of what I have always known: that women are resilient and flexible and multifaceted. Like most basic truths, it was too close to home for me to give it much credence. But the evidence had always been there that women can bloom after thirty. It was manifest in the lives of ordinary women: my grandmother, my mother, my aunts, my friends, and their friends.

These are their stories, all true, told in their own words. It is not a sociological study or survey; the average is not here. I do not believe in the average woman. We all are uncommon. Yet not as different as we may have thought when we were younger. I know of no life that has not been scarred by deep pain or tragedy, and none that has not been touched by joy. We all stumble and sprint through life, searching for meanings, and for ways to stay sane. The women here have found answers that work for them. Circumstances and temperaments made it easier for some than for others to make new beginnings, or to find what they wanted to do, and do it, for that is what blooming is – being true to oneself.

Under the surface differences, there is a sameness in women's lives, and these women's stories encompass, I believe, a broad enough spectrum of experience for any woman to find parallels with her own circumstances and sentiments. Human nature is fairly constant. The way we look at it is what changes.

Less than half the women in this book feel comfortable with the word "feminist." They feel it too often is used as a pejorative label and they reject facile tagging of complex attitudes. But all are pro-women (which does *not* mean anti-men). And all acknowledge that their lives have been changed by the women's movement. Some are directly involved in it, some have caught fire from its sparks. Proof of the positive disposition all of them have toward feminist issues is the fact that they were willing to take the time from their busy lives to talk for many hours about an issue vital for women: how to balance the demands placed on them with what they feel to be their personal needs. In hopes that it would help others, they were candid and open about that crucial period when they faced the certainty that they alone, in the most fundamental sense, were responsible for their own lives – lives which they saw – looking back over their shoulders at their grandmothers – chances were, would be very long. Several women said that they wanted to record their experiences for their daughters, so that they might profit from their mothers' mistakes and take heart from their triumphs. We all are daughters.

I did not intend to obtrude so much in this book, but I have never been able to maintain a scientific detachment toward other people. Before I know it, I'm saying, "That's right!

I've felt that way, too." Personal validation, particularly in matters concerning women, rings with more truth for me than sets of statistics.

My doctor handed me a cautionary list of all of the disabilities that descend on women after menopause. I handed it back. Expectations have a potent influence on our physical and mental health. I would rather know more about the rich lives of older women than limit myself to his charts. These women are real, and who knows what biases affected the selection of his data? All around me are vigorous, interesting, useful and radiant late bloomers I believe in.

Part One
Survivors with Style

"The will to survive is so alive in us women."

COLETTE
The Evening Star

Women in My Family

During the nineteen thirties when I was in high school, my mother went back to college. She had an eight o'clock class five mornings a week at the University of Washington. So did my brother, Watson. He drove to the university in his old 1925 Model T Ford roadster without a top. Since he had very little money for gas, he figured out a route by which he could coast almost all the way from our house on a steep hill to the Engineering College on the lower campus about three miles away. A lot depended on the traffic lights. My mother rode with him, but her classes were in the art department on the upper campus, so she jumped out of the roadster when Watson crossed University Avenue and turned down toward Engineering. If the light was green on the avenue, she had to make a quick exit so that she would not break the roadster's momentum. Watson never slowed down much for her. None of us did – my father, my brother, or me. We expected her to keep up, and she did.

More and more often we found Mother in the basement sculpting instead of in the kitchen cooking. All of us were changing. Watson was home less. My interests were shifting from baseball and ice-skating to the school newspaper and yearbook. My father did more of the grocery shopping and often cooked our dinners. "Your mother," he explained, "is coming into full bloom."

Mother's artistic talents I knew had been recognized when she was a young woman. Her teacher encouraged her to go to Berkeley to study at the University of California, a heady prospect, she said, for a country girl from Idaho. To earn the money to go, she taught school for several years in the little towns of White Bird and Stykes.

The hard work expected of her as the oldest girl between two boys on her father's homestead did not enamor her of rural life. When she could be spared, she worked for wages, cooking and washing dishes at the few scattered ranches in the mountains between the Snake and the Salmon rivers, so that she could go away to school, beyond the eighth grade. When she was seventeen years old, she put her clothes into a saddlebag and rode her horse down from the mountains to catch a train north to Lewiston, Idaho, to attend the state normal school, where she received her teaching certificate in 1913.

One summer she met my father at a teachers' institute. He had a law degree from the University of Missouri and had practiced in Oklahoma, "helping steal rich oil land from the Indians," as he used to tell us, until his idealism overcame his acquisitiveness, and he headed west to find a new life. When he began teaching school in Ferdinand, he used to ride over to White Bird to court my mother. Then, when she left for California, he jumped on her train; as they crossed the Rocky Mountains he persuaded her to choose him instead of art. Several years after they were married in 1916, they moved to Seattle, where he attended the University to study for a Master of Arts in education. For awhile Mother managed to take classes too, by leaving Watson, who was about six years old, in a grassy, wooded patch beneath her classroom window. Three years later I was born. Increasingly my mother's creative energies were diverted to painting rooms and furniture, tailoring and dressmaking, gardening and canning fruits and vegetables. She worked through a long cultivation period before she came into full bloom.

I was older than my mother had been when I returned to the University. My children were grown and I was nearly fifty. But it never occurred to me that I might be too old to learn new skills quickly. When Mother was sixty-seven years old I had taught her in three weeks to drive a car. She and my father had moved to the suburbs, far from public transportation, and she soon realized that if anything happened to him (he was six years her senior), she would be stranded. Her motivation was high and my visit was short, so we concentrated. My husband found her a snappy little 1954 green Ford sports coupe and for the next ten years she sped up and down the steep hills of Seattle at such a clip my brother and I feared for her life.

Mother's younger sister, my Aunt Luree, was a speeder, too.

She still lived on a ranch in Idaho, and her son worried over the way she cruised down the straight, flat highways at eighty miles an hour, pulling a horse trailer hooked to her old Ford. She had decided to ride in the rodeos that were beginning to be held at night like baseball games, and about as frequently. For her it was a way to get out of the house: she was a recent widow and very lonely. Aunt Luree had ridden in rodeos when she was younger, but like Mother, she had let her husband drive their car. After he died, she wheeled the old Ford around the fields until she got the hang of it, then took off down the road and never missed a rodeo within a hundred-mile radius. She bloomed too. The summer of 1964 I took my ten-year-old daughter to the Night Rodeo of Caldwell, Idaho. When Stacy saw her great-aunt ride into the brightly lit arena at the head of her riding club, the Payette Valley Possettes, she climbed onto the railing to cheer for her. Aunt Luree sat straight as an Indian chief on her beautiful chestnut mare. In one hand she held her reins; in the other she steadied the flagstaff for the blue silk banner of the Possettes.

Aunt Luree still affirms her future by putting things that she might be able to use someday in her "Put-Thing Room": a hooked rug, a pair of soft old leather chaps, some long-fringed shawls, heaps of riding trophies and ribbons, pieces of unfinished needlepoint and crewel, some yellowed tatting, stacks of straw hats, and a rocker she is going to strip and refinish. For me life is too peripatetic to keep such a roomful of possibilities. My husband's work keeps us moving. Up to now I have spent most of my married life setting up our household in different countries, finding or helping establish schools for our children, learning bazaar Hindi, and cooking unfamiliar foods, then packing up and moving on. So I keep a Futures Notebook, small and loose-leafed, that fits into my purse. On planes over the Pacific, in pedicabs in Asia, on the Calcutta Mail, the old Orient Express, and on ships crossing the Atlantic, I have been jotting down notes for my future: ruminations about the books I want to write. A need for long-range planning is in my bones.

From my family I have learned that women live a long time, a good part of it as widows. I have a picture of my grandmother when she was ninety, astride one of Aunt Luree's prize-winning horses. Little Grammy (she was a scant five feet tall) was a widow for about fifty years – from her late forties until she died at ninety-six. Hard work and early privation did not shorten her life; the traumas of separation, ostracism, and death did not destroy her buoyant spirit. "To your spunk, Louisa," my father always said as he raised a glass of her dandelion wine. "My thanks to you," she would answer in her Swiss dialect.

Little Grammy's family in Switzerland had been converted to Mormonism by missionaries from the Church of Latter-Day Saints. They sent her, when she was ten years old, with her sister who was eight, in the custody of friends, to America. It was seventeen years before she saw her parents again. Crossing the Atlantic Ocean in a small steamship was so terrifying to her that she would never consider returning. She and her sister rode the train to the end of the line at Casper, Wyoming, then climbed into a horse-drawn wagon for the rest of the journey to Montpelier, a Mormon settlement in southern Idaho, where they worked as household helpers for their board and room. When Louisa eloped at nineteen with Grandfather Watson, a United States deputy marshal sent to investigate charges of polygamy among the Mormons, she was cut off from the Church – taken from her sister and friends, once again a stranger in a strange land.

My grandfather took her to Oregon, where he drove a stagecoach, then up into the meadows and yellow pine forests of western Idaho – to the jumping-off place, Little Grammy told me – too far from market to raise cattle. Instead Grandfather raised horses to sell to the United States Army Cavalry, and he led pack trains into the silver mines at Buffalo Hump. Little Grammy learned to raise gardens and animals and children, and how to cope by herself, for often she was alone on those remote ranches, in a time when Indians still triggered fear. In that far corner of the West, her talent for healing the sick was highly valued by her distant neighbors who came to her with their broken bones and snake bites and strange fevers. She had gentle healing ways. On the high Joseph Plains she eased herself out of her saddle to give birth to a premature baby with only Grand-

father to help her. She outlived that daughter, two sons, and her husband. In 1950 when she was eighty-two years old, Little Grammy took her first airplane ride, alone, to San Francisco, to see my first-born baby. She was escorted off the plane by an admiring steward, a tiny, erect woman in an extravagant black hat and a bright red coat, beaming with pride – for herself and for me. We endure.

Recently women have started reclaiming their past and demanding to know why they have been left out of history. They are demolishing the old assumptions that only men do things important enough to record and to write about. And they are exposing the oppressive conditions under which most women have lived their narrow lives, enclosed in a domestic sphere, cut off from the larger male world of power and success. But in this painful rereading of our past, I do not want to undervalue the heritage of quiet strength that binds me to my grandmother and mother and Aunt Luree. There were multitudes of women like them: not famous or what society labels as successful, but resilient and enduring, who, despite the difficulties in their lives, cultivated their own true selves. These women found a deep joy in what they did well. Quietly they nurtured the gifts that they had. Eventually their talents took them beyond the small circle of their family lives and they developed a dimension of their own so that when they were older and their years of family service ended, their lives were not bereft of meaning. Certainly they knew pain and grief; in other circumstances they might have been happier and more fulfilled. But given the thin soil that they had, they managed to grow and blossom and come to full bloom.

Today more women are adding to their lives a flair, a touch of style, and a creative mode of living that older women seldom have been credited with. Their settings are important to them; they choose and arrange them with care. They do not live weighed down with leftovers from earlier periods of their lives. Their selected treasures are harmonious and unobtrusive amid the evidence of their current activities. They are carrying on a rich but largely unrecorded tradition of women who know how to live well. Vibrant, joyous, magnetic, and outgoing, these survivors are women with style.

1. Hope from the Midwest
HOPE SMITH DAUGHERTY

"Difficulties, opposition, criticism – these things are meant to be overcome, and there is a special joy in facing them and coming out on top."

MADAME V.L. PANDIT
in *The Envoy Extraordinary* by Vera Brittain

Hope Smith Daugherty was fifty years old when she left Manhattan, Kansas, to come to Washington, D.C., as National 4-H Program Leader for teens and young adults under the Science and Education Administration of the United States Department of Agriculture. She had been a widow for four years. The USDA informed her that she would have a single person's moving allowance. "Look," she told them, "I may be coming alone, but I think, act, and move as the head of my family. I have all of this stuff that I will not leave behind. My piano and all of it comes with me. It is part of my home and I do not live in two rooms."

As she told me this, Hope's dark brown eyes glinted with a mixture of amusement and determination that sent a wave of recognition through me. Hope is my first cousin. She has my father's look: Smith eyes. Usually they shine with good humor and a hint of mischief that charms people into not noticing that force of will: the Smith camouflage for high purpose and great self-discipline is a disarming folksy manner. I sensed immediately that Hope carries on the tradition. She put her arms on the table, her slightly scooped nose and laughing mouth twitching with the effort to look serious while her eyes danced with triumph. "When you become a widow, you do not immediately think of yourself as single," she said. "So they all conferred back there in Washington, and in the end they moved me as a family." She had won her first round with the bureaucracy. Now we sat at her treasured old cherry dining room table that was her mother's. It just fit into her attractive new three-bedroom house with a huge yard, which she found by computer and bought in one afternoon, in Arlington, Virginia, just across the Potomac River from the District of Columbia.

Hope is a handsome, clear-skinned, healthy-looking woman with thick, curly gray hair and dark eyebrows, who bounces rather than moves, and who animates her rapid conversation by making fluid gestures with her beautiful, well-groomed hands. We probably played together on our grandparents' big wheat farm near Carrollton, Missouri, when I came from Seattle with my parents to visit during the blistering hot summer of 1932, but neither of us remembers the other one. There were so many cousins. Grandma and Grandpa Smith had ten children, eight boys and two girls. My father was the eldest boy and Hope's father was the next eldest. Mine went west as a young man and hers stayed on in the heartland of America. Hope Alice was born in Piggott, Arkansas, on July 8, 1920.

From our farm-reared fathers we both learned that we are lucky simply to be here, alive, standing more or less upright, that complaining is self-defeating, and that a sense of humor is the best survival tactic there is. Hope's dad was the consummate storyteller; he molded life into one tale after another. "And he had common sense like you wouldn't believe," Hope added. Next best was Uncle Jewell, we decided, who laughed so hard in the telling that we never did hear the end of his stories. Next was my dad, who specialized in anecdotes about city slickers being outwitted by country bumpkins. The eight Smith boys were sons of the earth and proud of it.

"And I'm Midwest to the core," Hope declared. "I grew up thinking that, politically speaking, both coasts were full of a kind of idiot. The North was too cold to worry about and the South had to be the dumbest ever. Thinking that way makes it nice. You love where you are living."

Yet Hope has been moving all her life, from her tightly knit family in Kennett, Missouri, where she grew up, to larger cities and wider circles, mostly in Missouri, Texas, Oklahoma, and Ohio, as the wife of a biochemist and the mother of two daughters. Through all her changes of fortune, she has retained her rural, matter-of-fact manner that is as open as the farm fields that her father, a crop insurance salesman, taught her to pay attention to. One of her most vivid memories is the tongue lashing that he gave her when he overheard her giving a flip answer on the telephone to a farmer who called him about his wheat crop that had been destroyed by hail. "Those tender little plants, beaten to the ground – a family's livelihood lost," he admonished her. "You listen now, and you show consideration and sympathy." She lives by that lesson: people are individuals as vulnerable as wheat under hail, and deserving of kindness.

For a long time her husband, Jack, almost made her forget how vulnerable to the forces of nature everyone is. Six feet two inches tall, with a good physique, Jack gave her the impression of being indestructible. He was a powerful swimmer who relished cutting through the ocean waves in the Gulf of Mexico off the Texan shore; he went scuba diving and played handball regularly until a heart condition slowed him down, then caused his death at the age of forty-nine. The last two years before he died he was in pretty bad shape, with great ups and downs, but enough ups to keep on teaching. When he lay hemorraghing internally, fighting for his life, in the Baptist Hospital in Oklahoma City, Hope sat outside his intensive care room studying for her Master of Arts comprehensive examinations.

"So I wasn't thrown out on my own, cold turkey," she said. "Long before I could face it, I must have known how ill Jack was. I eased back into the working world."

She can use the word "ease" because it was not Jack's illness that made her stop short and decide to make a change. This reassessment came after about fourteen years of marriage when Jack was secure in a teaching position at prestigious Rice University in Houston, Texas, where he associated with some of the top men in his field, and loved his work. "In those days our goal was *his* career," she explained. "That was the thing in my era. It goes back to the college ideal: if you get a nice husband and two children, you are perfectly happy. I know that I was happy, but I also know that I was fitting into that mold that makes you say that you are perfectly happy. You've got this nice Ph.D. husband. Of course you have worked like the devil to help him get it, but that's expected too. While he was getting his doctorate we were operating on peanuts, but that was part of the game. We knew where he was going. I never griped. If you had my mother and dad you didn't go around with a long face. My mother didn't believe in migraine headaches or nervous breakdowns.

"From 1940, when I was married, until 1954 I stayed home all of the time. I always knew that you could handle the home and kids with part of you; you didn't have to have the whole thing there. But it was also the era when you didn't take a full-time job. It has just occurred to me, looking back now, how I filled my two girls, Lynn and Beth, with the same idea that they should defer everything that was theirs – that same mold of husband first. I was so blind."

But looking back ruefully is not Hope's style; in a moment she was laughing again. "You should have seen me then. The girls were about nine and twelve. I had done it all: PTA, Brownie leader, Scout leader, choir director, room mother. I was on everybody's list. I was an active member of the Presbyterian Church and the Music Club, played in two bridge clubs, and was being pressured into joining the Garden Club. I just knew that I was a sitting duck whenever the phone rang. There I was at home – available. My neighbor Shirley was in the same fix. She was an excellent home economist; her kitchen always smelled of baked ham, chocolate cake and permanent wave lotion. She gave permanents to all of her neighbors. And she was as frustrated as I was. Calls would come in mostly between ten and twelve in the morning. The working mothers couldn't do any of it. We could get out our station wagons and pick up all of the kids. Often I would leave the house just to get away from the phone."

Eventually Hope did go to one meeting of the Garden Club.

The discovery that flower judging was a complete, serious state in life for some people, with no little laughs to aerate the soil, made something inside her snap. "My whole life," she thought, "can never depend on how I cut a stem."

The same evening a number of parents called Hope asking her to take their daughters to the Girl Scout supper because they couldn't get them there early enough. As she remembers, one little girl came tripping out to the car, her mother walking behind her holding a martini glass in one hand and a cigarette in the other, an annoyed look on her face. "You're just a little bit late, aren't you?" she scolded Hope. "Our guests are about ready to arrive." When Hope returned the little girl from the Scout supper, her parents' party was in full swing. "And I got to thinking," Hope confessed, "am I really doing any good with all of this? Being the unpaid everything?"

She decided that she was not. An unstructured life leaving her vulnerable to every request, worthy or not, had strung Hope out to the limits of her patience. Saying no is never pleasant and she seldom could. So when the principal of the local elementary school asked her if she would fill in for a teacher who had just left and finish out the school year teaching the third grade, Hope happily said yes. She had a teaching certificate and had taught for one year before she married. In Hope's generation women who were practical, or whose parents felt they should have a way of earning their living "just in case," usually studied for a degree in education. Hope was no exception. Even though music was her passion, she attended the teachers' college at Cape Girardeau (now Southern Missouri University), perched high on a bluff above the Mississippi River about one hundred miles north of her home and one hundred miles south of St. Louis. "No alternatives occurred to us," she shrugged. "We were just about as isolated in Kennett as anyone could be and still be part of the ongoing world." Her one chance to major in music when she won a scholarship to Arkansas State College in Jonesboro, Arkansas, was vetoed on social grounds by her mother, who had been educated at Miss Woodward's School for Young Ladies in Frankfort, Kentucky, and still harbored certain prejudices against Arkansas. Besides, her father pointed out, a person cannot make a living with music.

"If I had known where to go, or had anybody to help me when I left college," she speculated, with a twinge of regret in her voice, "I might have gone to Kansas City where the Starlight Theater was forming, or to the Municipal Opera in St. Louis, and sung in the chorus of some of their productions." Then with a flick of her wrist she swept away her castle in the air, "Oh, well, getting back to teaching felt good. The school hours and the summer vacations were the same as the girls, so there were no problems on that score."

Absorbed in his own work, Jack did not have any reservations about Hope's teaching. It did not cause any dislocation in their family life and he tended to view it as temporary. When her girls grew up and asked her how she had worked out her relationship with Jack, Hope answered that they had never really talked it over, she was too much a product of the times. Jack had known she had a mind and treated her accordingly. They had met at Cape Girardeau: Jack sounded the pitch in the acappella choir. He was a minister's son, used to seeing a marriage as a working partnership. They sang in the church choirs wherever they went, and at Rice University they organized a Gilbert and Sullivan company. Music and sports were the twin pivots of their active social life. "Football was the big name of the game in the Southwest," Hope recalled. "We went to all of the games and the attendant parties." It was a time of dinners on the lawn of their big house, barbecues every weekend, trips and camping in the summers. Fifteen good years. "I loved the flow of the South," Hope's voice was soft and humming. "I loved the pace." Then in a brisker voice, "But I can't for a minute tolerate the dripping magnolia and women who faint. They do a whole lot of sham in their relationships, men to women. They're not really honest with each other. A lot of chauvinism still passes for courtesy."

Then came what Hope called the "iffy" years: "If Jack is O.K. we can go to the game or visit sister and her husband in Cincinnati." He gave up teaching to become head of biological research at the Civil Aeromedical Research Institute at Will Rogers Field near Oklahoma City. "Now my age was an asset," Hope said. She was forty-one and perceived as a settled, stable matron. She got a job teaching sixth grade. They bought their dream house even though Beth was married and Lynn away in college. But growing in Hope's mind was an ominous feeling that she might be left alone in that large house. She could not put it into words. She and Jack never discussed it. Instead she shifted into high gear – a practical, coping device that many women resort to under stress – intense, productive activity. She began to study for her M.A. Then another opening occurred and Hope moved into it: a French teacher and curriculum coordinator was needed for a high school in a town nearby. Jack was in the hospital for a checkup when she went for her interview.

"Well, Hope, when did you teach French?" they asked her at her bridge club. "I haven't," she replied. "When I told them I was going to Moore High School in the fall, it was just as if I had exploded a bombshell," Hope laughed at the memory. "Our bridge club stopped playing for about thirty minutes while we discussed the pros and cons of Hope driving up to Moore. 'Hope Daugherty, have you *ever* taught French?' 'No, but I had four years of Latin in high school and majored in French and English in college.' There were so many little feelings about my duty to be close by so I could dash home when Jack came back from the lab. Later one good friend dropped by, ostensibly for a cup of coffee. Finally she got to the point: she and her husband had discussed it and decided that I really was biting off a little too much at this point." Hope grinned. "But it was a marvelous feeling to get out of the mold and try something new."

Nobody had told Hope that teachers' salaries were negotiable when she went up to Moore for her interview. She stumbled onto the fact because she was thinking of Jack back in the hospital, hesitating and weighing the advantages and drawbacks of taking on this new job. "I would tell women today," she said with emphasis, "to get to salary first thing. Look 'em in the eye and talk about it. I think any employer respects you more than if you beat around the bush and try to act as if you're doing it for youth and mankind."

A subtle shift was taking place in her and Jack's relationship: she was beginning to feel the stronger of the two. "I knew in my bones that the best thing I could do was push to the limits of my capabilities. I could have settled back and had a good medium-level life no matter what," she shrugged. "Jack had a good insurance program."

Instead she decided to try for her Ph.D. It was her lifesaver.

"At first I was scared to death and thought I ought to go home and crochet something," she recalled. "But after a couple of years teaching French I identified with Peggy Lee's song, 'Is That All There Is?' It was mostly my own apprehension that I had to get over to apply in the first place. It's no big deal when you get into it. Men talk a big game, but you have to learn not to let it overwhelm you. Learn to see through it. Higher education is full of men who are ABDs. All But Dissertations. It's part of the brotherhood.

"To me it was a great release when I admitted to myself and everyone else that I wanted to go on to get my doctorate. I was a student about twenty years too soon, though. In those days a middle-aged woman didn't apply for grants. I whomped out for everything, taking evening and summer classes, at first, then full-time for the last year. Jack was very supportive from his bedside, as it were. I've often seen women capable of doing so many things and then have someone whom they really care about say to them, 'Oh, you can't do *that*!' It must be terrible to come home to someone who is nonsupportive.

"Culturization!" she exclaimed as she bounded up to get us more coffee. "That's why it took me so long to admit that I wanted a Ph.D. One of my professors defined a woman in graduate school as one who hadn't found a man to keep her, or if she had, had lost him." Hope grimaced wryly. "There's always someone to put a woman down – you know, that devastating assumption that you can't really do it, that vague putdown."

Late as it was, she finally had committed herself to what she really wanted to do. When she was forty-six years old, she was accepted into the doctoral program at the University of Oklahoma. "Listen," she said with a flip of her wrist, "graduate school is a state of mind. You build confidence by increments – a nod here, a smile there. You need just a little bit of success before you are bold enough to try anything new – if you don't want to stay in the same rut forever.

"If you have a sinking feeling or feel left out, you'll quickly find seventy people to agree with you. Stay away from them and don't give over."

Then in a very short period of time a combination of events radically changed the life of the Daughertys. On a plane returning from Boston, Hope glanced over at Jack looking out of the window, saw him fish for his handkerchief, and noticed a trickle of blood coming from his nose. She rushed up the aisle for the stewardess. The pilot got permission to land. An ambulance was waiting. Though neither they nor the doctors knew for certain, it was the beginning of the end. Jack moved to a less strenuous position at Purdue University. His aged and ailing parents came to stay with him in the house he and Hope bought in Indianapolis. Money began to dwindle rapidly. Hope stayed behind at the University of Oklahoma to complete her degree. "A little like war-time," she remembered. "A year alone, making all of the decisions." For a moment she stared out of the window, then turned back to me. "Until now I don't think I ever put it into words before, but I sat there one morning in the office of the dean of education at the University of Cincinnati and accepted the job he offered me before I said anything to Jack." Even in retrospect, Hope was surprised at herself – so unquestionably had she consulted her husband before making any decision. So imperceptibly had her confidence built, her character changed.

When Jack died in February, 1969, Hope Daugherty was an assistant professor of educational psychology.

That Jack would die before they did had never occurred to his parents. Hope had to act for them as well as for herself. It was a quick growing-up experience: for twenty-eight years she had deferred to Jack's judgment in all mechanical and financial matters. Now the business of urgent decision-making carried her through the initial trauma of his death. Her girls, her sister Elizabeth, and brother-in-law sustained her through that spring. "Wrapped in a cocoon of love and concern," she said. "So I was still not on my own. I was making decisions, but if they didn't work I still had somebody to fall back on." One night she went for coffee with some of her students after her night class at the downtown campus. About midnight when she returned to her apartment the telephone was ringing. "Mother, where *have* you been?" came Beth's worried voice from across Cincinnati. "I've been calling you since 10:15!"

"Little things like that spur you on," Hope chuckled. So when, through a mutual friend, someone from the Kansas State University called to tell her they were interested in hiring a person who could teach psychology part-time and work with 4-H groups part-time, once again she was ready to go. "And I didn't have to be a horse specialist or poultry expert to do 4-H work. We talked for an hour. I felt so energized!"

Then came one of the biggest wrenches of her life. She saw her furniture into a moving van, got into her car and drove, alone, across the flat farmlands, fifteen hundred miles west from Cincinnati to Manhattan, Kansas.

"When you move to a new place with a presentable husband, it is readymade," Hope discovered. Alone it is entirely different. For a while it was miserable; she kept a diary for the first time in her life. All the single, staid home economists closed in on her. Here was one for their ranks. They met on Sunday mornings at the Pancake House or in each other's homes where they competed in serving fancy crepes. Each one had a dog and cute stories to go with it. Hope countered with accounts of her grandchildren. At first she laughed, then she got angry. Typically, she took action. She put it to a friend at the university: "Look, Alice, I've got to level with you. I don't fit into this crowd. It's your dog and my grandchild. Your plan for a vacation, mine for when I can see my family. No – huh-uh! That's not for me. But I want to stay their friend. Can I manage that?" She did.

And she made new friends – on her own for the first time in her mature life. Those two years in Manhattan are a treasured memory. "Then why would you want to put another layer between yourself and humanity by going to Washington?" a young man asked her. "You've been so great here in Kansas."

Because, as Hope would have tried to explain to the young man if he really had wanted an answer, when a person teaches the same courses over and over, she loses a little bit of whatever it is that makes it exciting in the first place. Stretching herself, solving new problems, is essential to Hope's self-esteem and the mainspring of her ebullience. "Whenever my job becomes mechanical or a chore," she said, "then you can be darned sure that I am going to stop doing it and try something else."

It is not the same for everybody, she is quick to agree. Some people are sustained by routine and security. "In the long run," she declares, "it seems to work out that most people generally do what they really want to do."

As 4-H Program Leader, Hope travels to fifty states, Guam, the Virgin Islands and Puerto Rico. As a traveling woman, she resents being shunted to the smallest, darkest tables in restaurants and the second-best rooms in hotels. She carries a small calculator in her purse and tips accordingly. She will not linger over the slights or hurts that have come her way as a woman, particularly as a woman alone, but, she assures me, she has embraced feminist thought all along. More and more she is becoming part of a feminist network, not just in Washington, but everywhere she goes. "I just feel that we get more points made if everybody is feeling good about it," is her philosophy. "Of course I don't mean for a minute," she is quick to add, "that you should compromise any of your morals or principles. But," she grinned, "for the first time in history it is great for a woman to be fifty. We're no longer supposed to look like Lana Turner; we don't have to hide our age anymore."

How does she cope? Just getting up in the morning is coping, she believes – the first success of the day. Congratulate yourself. Build from there in small increments; they add up. A good cup of coffee. The morning newspaper. Thursdays are harder, she admits; there is no bridge column.

The smile lines around her eyes crinkled, she flourished her hand in a little drumroll and I knew that another story was coming. This was it: the first day that she reported to work at the U.S. Department of Agriculture, Hope caught a bus from Arlington, Virginia, to the District of Columbia and got off at the South Building where eight thousand people work and where there are miles of corridors. Wedged into an elevator, she thought, "Hope Daugherty, you *have* arrived. You're in the city, and you're in government." Cheerily she sang out a heartfelt "Good morning!" Total silence. She might as well have been alone in the middle of the Mississippi.

But every six weeks or so my irrepressible cousin from Kennett, Missouri, repeats her friendly greeting. Sometimes these days she gets an answer. It cheers me up to think of her out there making her points. People are beginning to notice that Hope Daugherty is a professional woman with responsibility who will not for a minute let her rank rob her of her essential warmth and humanity.

2. A Mentor in London
MARY GRANT

"I May, I Might, I Must"
"If you will tell me why the fen
appears impassible, I then
will tell you why I think that I
can get across it if I try."

MARIANNE MOORE

For about three years Mary Grant was my mentor, although
I am sure that she was unaware of the role I cast her in. Had
she known, she would have denied being an ideal exemplar
of an older woman living a rich and good life of her own
making. But for me, the knowledge that she had built this
life from very modest beginnings was particularly bracing
because I met Mary at a low point in my own life.

She reminded me of a wren when I first saw her: small, neat,
and quick-moving. Her profile was regular, her blue eyes
bright, her smile warm. Always tastefully dressed and soft-
spoken, with a wisp or two of white hair escaping from the
loose bun at the nape of her neck, Mary looks like a respectable British matron who might be meeting a friend for an
afternoon of tea and shopping. But more than a quarter of a
century ago, when she was nearly fifty years old, Mary
answered a newspaper advertisement that changed her from
a complacent housewife into a dedicated volunteer worker
with the Family Planning Association of the United Kingdom.
"It was odd," she recalled, with a little laugh. "I was singu-
larly un-community-minded at the time. But the local birth
control clinic advertised for helpers and I thought it quite a
useful thing to do. It did not seem 'do-gooding' to me. But
nobody at all whom I knew was concerned with family
planning; it was not very popular. I just went into the clinic.
They rather liked the look of me and thought I might be most

useful as Chairman, a voluntary position. I had a certain standing in the town.'' The town was Darlington, in Durham, in the north of England, and her husband was a managing director of a construction firm there.

When I asked her what had prompted her to take that step out into the world, Mary shook her head: "Just an impulse. I'm an impulse shopper, too.'' It is not in Mary's temperament to be introspective. She does not remember any agonizing over whether she should or should not become involved with the Family Planning Association. They asked for help and she simply answered the call. I, on the other hand, remember exactly why I responded to a similar advertisement years later in London, and thus met Mary.

It was a dismal December morning in 1969. I had pushed back the breakfast dishes and spread the London *Times* out on the kitchen table. With something akin to panic, I flipped past the news and entertainment sections to the job advertisements. It was still dark, and raining outside. England is surprisingly far north and I was in a slough of melancholy brought on by the weather and an overwhelming sense of uselessness. My sons and daughter were in high school and college, so I saw little of them except with their energetic friends against a background of overamplified Rolling Stones records. Much of the time that I spent with my husband was in the company of comparative strangers: journalists, television producers, and diplomats, all of whom were highly informed, by sources I was not privy to, on delicate subjects such as the Common Market, the situation in South Africa, and the internal politics of the BBC.

I needed a life of my own.

What delusion made me think that I would find it through the classified sections of the newspaper I cannot imagine. But it was a reflex action: whenever I was frustrated with the way my life was going, I would coffee-stain the help-wanted columns searching for that nonexistent job that would solve all my problems – a search for a unicorn if there ever was one, since in those preliberation days foreign service wives were not allowed to work overseas except as teachers of English or in American schools. But the ad I saw that day circumvented the U.S. Foreign Service restrictions because it was for a voluntary position – for an experimental program being set up by the Family Planning Association.

"It was something quite pioneering then," Mary recalled: an information bureau that she helped initiate and then directed. It was in three tiny rooms opening directly onto a busy street in the garment district of London. One big window was filled with large purple and yellow signs reading: "Sex Problems? Confidential Help. Walk In. No Appointment Necessary." The rationale was that many people had problems they were too shy to discuss with either the doctors or the nurses at the FPA clinics. Sympathetic as the professional staffs were, their white medical coats or uniforms and their educated accents tended to intimidate patients. People also were inhibited by the lack of an adequate vocabulary to describe their often vague worries. In the informal setting of the Information Bureau, with just one sympathetic person who was neither a doctor nor a nurse, they might be able to express their anxieties. And since sexual difficulties generally are overt expressions of other problems, many people could be helped once their problems were defined, by referrals to organizations dealing with financial, legal, or other areas of common concern.

Largely because I was an American with a classless accent and old enough to look as if I had some experience, Mary selected me to be one of the five volunteers for the Information Bureau. Each of us was responsible for keeping it open one day. Monday soon became the most exhausting and exhilarating day of my week. With Mary we visited the organizations we would be referring clients to, such as the Citizens' Advisory Bureau, the James Pringe Venereal Disease Center, and the Pregnancy Advisory Service. We learned who were the key people at each place and elicited their support. Then she sent us around to train for a time in the different departments of the FPA as well as in crowded clinics such as those in Islington and Hammersmith. Eventually I was able to cope with the geography of boroughs and counties to determine what advice and help clients could obtain locally. At last my ear became attuned to working-class accents and I picked up a whole new vocabulary. But in the subtle skills of dealing with people none of us could match Mary. With a sixth sense she always knew what was troubling a person; often I asked her to come in to talk with clients who were making no sense to me. Bobbing her head in a characteristic gesture, she would tap the table with her pencil, helping a distraught woman conjure up the words she wanted, or soothing a frightened, aggressive man. With a stern, "Now see here!" she could thwart a bully. And she taught me to talk to strangers about sex without stammering and turning scarlet. How I admired her composure!

With typical American inquisitiveness, I wanted to know all about her. Peering over her gold-framed half-glasses Mary said, with the renowned British sense of privacy, "You're barking up the wrong tree."

Yet in no way does Mary give an impression of being remote. She is warm and approachable, and has a sense of whimsy I find delectable. We have exchanged silly poems, explored art galleries, walked in Bloomsbury, and drunk mulled wine at Shakespeare productions in Regent's Park. We share an enthusiasm for Jane Austen. Mary introduced me to Victorian writers such as Charlotte Yonge, and she gave me a print of wildflowers in a field by Gustav Klimnt that I treasure because it is as bright and gay as she is. But we have never spoken to each other about our intimate affairs. Confidences sometimes can, I have discovered, overload a friendship with a heavy sense of obligation. "Quite right!" I can imagine Mary saying. With her I share an unspoken understanding, a comfortable and comforting friendship.

Mary can talk without tiring about the FPA, but she saw no point in talking about herself until I explained that her example might inspire other women to see what might be done in the field of volunteer work. "Ah," her face lit up with a wide smile. "I didn't start it at all until I was practically fifty. But the point is that work of this sort is specially suited to anyone older in that she can make use of any personal experience she has had earlier in her life. It helps her to understand what people are putting across. This may not be reflected in words, but it certainly is reflected in attitudes, and it comes across to the people involved."

But what sort of background gave her such an empathy for other people?

"Well," Mary began hesitantly, "My mother, who was from the north of England, married a Polish student when she was twenty-one and went back to Poland with him, where, apart from her marital position, I think that she was supremely happy. She liked the sort of life which was completely foreign. I was born in Warsaw in 1902 and my sister was born a year and a half later. After about six years of marriage, my mother left her husband and came back to England with us two small children and a Polish-speaking peasant girl to look after us. We were never told why she left. She had a small income, a settlement from when she was married, but it was very small. I think that she thought she would get more support from her family here. In Warsaw someone might have said, 'Come on and live with us, dear. How delightful to have the children.' Well, in Durham they didn't say that. People aren't in a position to do that. So I grew up in furnished rooms, or other people's houses, near people who didn't want small children. I was never noisy and I always had to fit in.

"Mother's money had come from a mortgage on a house in St. Petersburgh as it was called then. Then, in 1914, during the First World War, the money stopped coming in. Not a penny piece came. We lived in rooms through the war. My mother's eldest brother was very kind and let her have money. She got low-grade clerical work – when she could."

To receive a scholarship to Leeds University, Mary had to become naturalized. She had a Polish name and a bit of the tradition from her mother. "I bitterly resented this naturalization," she said. It took a certain birthright away from her. But she had no choice. When she graduated from the university she taught school for a time. "Then I married, and I always thought how lucky I was to have a husband and some children, and while not a lot of money, a reasonable income, and a house, and so on. It is all comparative."

From this point on, Mary led an extraordinarily quiet life. "Throughout the Second World War, with the blackout and all, I rarely went out except for household shopping," she said. "I read a lot, did a certain amount of hand sewing, and kept the house and children. I had a boy between Stephanie and John, who died as a small child. Then, just before the war, we took over a refugee girl, a Jewish girl from Berlin, who was with us for five years. My mother was with us a good deal too, so during those years it was really housekeeping and cooking for six."

"Yes," she repeated, "I was quite un-community-minded. I had been tied not only with children, but a husband who was away perhaps two nights a week. When he was at home he was working. I was never restive about this because, as I told you, I was brought up very quietly."

In 1945 the war ended. Mary was forty-three. Soon after that her son went away to school, but it was not until her daughter left, too, that Mary began going into the Darlington FPA clinic one afternoon a week. "Initially I went into family planning work," she told me, "thinking how very unfair life is: this talk of equal opportunity for the sexes when women are liable to become pregnant whether they want to or not, as they certainly were until the present generation." In those days there were not many clinics. The one paid worker had a large area to cover, so Mary, who worked as a volunteer, at first just one afternoon a week, was left a good deal on her own to make decisions. At Stephanie's half term at school in London, Mary went down to visit her and took the opportunity to look into the headquarters of the FPA. "I was very, very struck with the caliber and the congeniality of the people who were there," she recalled. "They said they would give me every support during these difficult times. We had financial problems and dreadful premises. Our clients were called 'poor patients' in those days."

Mary's greatest problems were with the Medical Officer of her district. He made no connection between the high rate of infant mortality in his area and a general lack of birth control information. Mary's eyes flashed at the memory. "He should have been doing something about it!'' She fought against small harassments: the sign for the FPA clinic constantly being taken down; refusal by the hospital to allow the bulky contraceptive supplies – heavy cartons of condoms, diaphragms and creams – to be delivered or stored at the hospital; no phone for patients to make appointments; no payment-free premises. Mary did not crave the role of a champion for women. No urge for excitement sent her out in search of battles to wage. After nearly a quarter of a century as a wife and mother who almost literally stayed inside of her house, she was uniquely self-sufficient and content. She read, sewed, and cooked. But she was pulled into a world that she had never known before; irrevocably she entered a maelstrom not of her making, caught up by her sense of outrage that women were denied information or help in caring for themselves.

The women who came to the Darlington clinic were shy and apologetic, generally ignorant and sometimes desperate. Many of them had problems that were extremely aggravated due to their inability to control their own reproduction. "I remember a working class mother,'' Mary said, "with a sixteen-year-old haemophilic son. She faced the problem of having someone with him constantly. I didn't ask her how she had avoided other pregnancies up until she came to us, but she felt she had to justify coming in for birth control information.''

These women and children touched Mary deeply. "A family planning doctor couldn't do very much then for the patients in a ten-minute session,'' she recalled, "but the doctor was sympathetic or she would not be giving her services to the FPA. And the very fact that the doctor said to a woman with a problem, 'This isn't unusual. It very often happens,' then the woman would not think of herself as abnormal or a monster.'' Increasingly Mary appreciated the value of family planning services. At the same time she recognized a considerable opposition to them. To counteract this she hit upon an ingenious strategy.

"It is no good to go out and tell groups that they ought to have family planning services,'' she said. "I don't think that is awfully convincing. I think it is much more convincing if anybody who seems fairly balanced, is of a certain age, and respectable, is prepared, when she is asked, 'What do you do with your free time?' or 'What are you interested in?' to say, in a few sentences, without pushing it, that she is working toward free and comprehensive family planning services."

To be sure that she was asked those questions by a significant number of influential people, Mary, the former stay-at-home wife, began to join organizations like a membership addict. She became a member of the committee of management of a teacher training college and of an approved school for delinquents, the director of the local Red Cross, a governor of a secondary modern school and she helped establish a branch of the National Council of Women. At committee meetings she would place her FPA diary in a conspicuous spot on the table so that members would ask her questions about it. Nothing revolutionary: just a steady picking away at prejudice which often can undermine resistance more effectively than a head-on assault. "The very fact that I had had an isolated life made it easier," Mary explained. She never had depended on group approval. "Quite soon," she said, "out of a dozen or so members of our local chapter of the National Council of Women, four or five became family planners. Through contacts we got pressure on the appropriate committees in town and soon had premises for our clinic in a proper local authority welfare clinic." Her tactics were beginning to work.

There were nine FPA clinics in the north of England when Mary first started. Ten years later there were thirty. As secretary she organized an annual meeting for the Northern Federation. "We would gather at Scarborough," she remembered fondly, "which is a pleasant watering place. It was quite an outing for all of us to come for a couple of nights to a hotel."

Then in 1963, after a little over ten years of volunteer work, Mary left the North and moved to London. Several years earlier her mother had died, and her husband's nagging illnesses finally were diagnosed as multiple sclerosis. "So really, if I had been shut up in a house at that point," she declared, "it would have been very dim indeed." When getting around London in taxis began to be too difficult for her husband, she drove him around in a little Austin. During his appointments she would nip into the central office of the FPA to lend a helping hand. Understaffed as they always were, they appreciated Mary's help two or three times a week. "And I stayed on in the flat," Mary said, "after my husband went into a nursing home. I still had the little car then, and I used to drive out to Roehampton, where he was, just outside of London, four or five times a week. And I got to going into the central office rather more often. It all fitted in very well."

First the director asked her if she would verify the clinic addresses and assign each clinic a number. "Then," Mary chuckled, "he said, 'What about a telephone inquiries service to answer questions about clinic services?' It meant my finding people who were prepared to come in for half a day to answer calls and be reasonably accurate and reliable. The next step was the Information Bureau. And that," she said to me, "is where you fit in."

True, I did fit in – enthusiastically for the first six months, stimulated by the newness of it all. Then the work began to wear me down. After a particularly difficult day when clients crowded in with more than the usual problems – pregnant teenagers themselves as immature as infants; aggressive, ignorant boys on the dole who feared they were impotent; frightened husbands whose wives, ill after an eighth or tenth child, were denied birth control information by their doctors – I felt like calling it quits. It was a volunteer job and it was not worth the emotional exhaustion it cost me.

At five o'clock Mary put her head in the door to ask if I wanted to walk up Wigmore Street to have a cup of coffee. We sat outside a crowded cafe, and, more belligerently than I meant to, I challenged her on the worth of volunteer work – taking jobs away from other women, "do-gooding" and dilettantism – being lady bountiful, who could afford not to be paid. "Quite right in some areas," she agreed. "What we say is 'ladies in flowered hats.' Those sorts turn up very much at Conservative party conferences, and on committees. They might work very hard. But they are not prepared to work in one direction nearly full time. The point is that where there is a need for a service and women work hard for it, in the long run you are creating jobs. The antenatal clinics," she stirred her coffee vigorously, "the child welfare centers, to name only two started by volunteers. And the FPA, of course, which eventually was able to employ doctors and nurses on the recognized pay scale. Often this helps women doctors get back into professional life. They might have children and can't get work for two or three afternoons or evenings a week, which they can in a FPA clinic. They could work that way until the children are older and they are able to go into full practice.

"Clearly, the women who make contributions in voluntary organizations on the whole can't be the younger ones because most certainly nowadays they are not only concerned with their families, but many are wage earners as well. So increasingly you tend to get older women. There has been a tradition of work done in this country," Mary continued earnestly, "by voluntary organizations that are built up to quite a useful form, then handed over to the government. FPA clinic service should be largely taken over by the National Health Service. But the battle is never completely won." Then her face brightened. She told me about a committed volunteer who started out almost single-handedly – Elizabeth Kaye, who initiated the National Cancer Control Campaign to assure every woman of a smear test. "So you see," said Mary, "identifying problems, offering help, and educating the public often is work that only volunteers like you can do." Her argument was unassailable, and her luminous smile and clear blue eyes were as irresistible as an English garden after a summer rain. There was no longer any question of my abandoning her, the Information Bureau, the whole good work. I stayed at the Family Planning Association another two and a half years, until I left London.

A few years later I returned on a visit, anxious to see Mary again. It was a beautiful summer day. Afternoon sunlight shone down the long narrow street where she lives, its glow mellowing the solid red-brick row of Victorian buildings, those imposing edifices with white-pillared porticoes now gone slightly shabby. Mary stayed on here after her husband died. She likes the location. "It's a very good area for keeping up," she said. "It's convenient for anyone coming to London who needs a bed. It is near Victoria Station and it is very pleasant having this space. I wouldn't like to be shut up in one room." There is space in the apartment for her children and grandchildren to stay with her. "Who do you have for renters now?" I inquired, knowing that she rented her two bedrooms and had converted her dining room into a charming bed-sitting room for herself – a typical arrangement many European widows favor. Student lodgers can become surrogate families if one wishes, and the rental income supplements small pensions. "A few years ago I began to run out of personal contacts for long-term renters," Mary replied. "So I placed an ad in the newspaper. A young Ghanian businessman came round and he's been with me ever since. He is an ideal lodger. Short-termers occupy the other room."

We had tea and talked about how, in the early 1970s, we had climbed long flights of stairs in a condemned building, searching for one of the first women's centers, then came away with posters, pamphlets, and renewed enthusiasm for the women's movement. Then I told her that I had just enrolled in the university, at the age of forty-eight, to study for my master's degree; and that probably I would not have had the courage to do it if I hadn't learned, in my three years working with her at the FPA, that, at a place separate from my home, I could accomplish an enormous amount of work in a few hours. "How relieved the children must be," Mary responded. "Now when they go off on their own affairs, they won't have to worry about you, home alone worrying about them." I had to laugh; I had never thought of it that way.

Then Mary took me out on her small balcony to see her unicorn – a plaster-of-Paris creature about the size of a fawn, painted gold, reclining amid pots of red geraniums and ivy. "It is rather nice, don't you think?" She patted the unicorn's head. "My sister-in-law, Madge, made it for me. She belongs to the Community of St. Mary the Virgin. I have none of her faith, but I couldn't imagine anyone I feel more congenial with, or anyone else with whom I can talk such nonsense. In a way Madge is a late developer also. She is in her seventies and only recently took up sculpting. She does it on odd days when the convent can spare her."

Mary paused to peer over her glasses at me. "I suspect," she said with a trace of a smile, "you'll learn how to manage, too."

If she hadn't been British, I would have hugged her.

3. An Inspiration in Seattle

ERNA BOUILLON

"In a word, I am always busy, which is perhaps the chief reason why I am always well."

ELIZABETH CADY STANTON
Diary entry, 1900

To have reached the age of eighty-five years intact, with her zest for life undiminished, is a triumph that Erna Bouillon relishes. An impression of invigorating tenacity and a great will to survive emanates from her, evoking in me an instant affection. "Go talk to Mrs. Bouillon," my sister-in-law, Ellen, had said. "Her story is an inspiration. She has been surprising and delighting us for years."

Erna Bouillon lives in a high-rise retirement home in Seattle on the east side of Green Lake, where I learned to swim long before people crowded its beaches as they do now. On the eighth floor, in her two-room apartment, exquisitely decorated in blues, purples, and whites, we draw up Louis XVth chairs, opposite a breakfront full of Meissen china, and settle down for a long conversation. At eighty-five, nothing about Erna is rigid or passé. Her eyes shine behind fashionably tinted glasses, her voice is vigorous, her hair short and curly. Trim and erect, she wears a striped dress with a chiffon scarf and open-toed sandals. But the most remarkable accomplishment of this attractive woman is that she began her career at the age of sixty.

When Erna Weeks, as her name was then, decided to become a student again, she was fifty-eight years old. She went to San Francisco and began to flourish. Not that her life before that had been unhappy; on the contrary, it was full of sunshine. She does not deny experiencing her full measure of pain and her share of tragedy, too, but those episodes have been dealt with, overcome, and now, with the prerogative of age, she prefers to remember the joyous times.

Born into a large, prosperous, and loving German family in San Antonio, Texas, in 1893, Erna Meerscheidt adored her father and loved her mother. Her father, a benevolent patriarch who believed in education (he had studied for eight years in Heidelburg), regularly trouped his family, often including nieces and nephews, off to Europe. Under his tutelage they examined exhibitions in art galleries and museums and absorbed the historic atmosphere preserved in manors and castles. At the impressionable age of thirteen, Erna, with her two sisters, attended an exclusive boarding school for a year in Germany. The elegance of the aristocratic life to which they were exposed, combined with the beauty she saw in Europe, so influenced Erna's aesthetic sensibility that she developed a flair for design and decorating – a talent she had no time to nourish until she was at the age when most people are considering retirement and a slower pace of life.

At the completion of that school year abroad, Erna's father moved his family to Seattle, then a pioneer town in the far Northwest, where, he had determined, the vegetation was the same and the rainy climate as salubrious as that of the Black Forest of Germany. The extreme heat of Texas had given Erna's mother migraine headaches, and, she felt, caused the death of two of her babies. In Seattle, Erna attended the newly established University of Washington. Shortly after her graduation as a home economist in 1916, she achieved the goal of every girl in her class by marrying a suitably eligible young man with a promising future. In predictable fashion, they had four children. One, a son, died when he was thirteen, shortly after she and her husband were divorced. Although not related, the two losses were concentrated into a short period of her life. "Mr. Weeks was good to the children," she maintains, "but when there were problems or trouble, he just left." Their youngest child was eight when he left for good.

For eighteen years Erna lived in the same big house in the university district of Seattle, raising her children, working for the YWCA and other civic organizations, and occasionally walking across the tree-filled campus to take a course in psychology or literature. One by one the children went off, to Alaska, New York, overseas. And she was alone. "All I had to do was cook for myself," she recalled. "The house stayed clean." Child support was finished, her financial future stringent. "So one day," as she put it, "I got the idea that this was crazy. I had worked my head off all of these years on civic boards and never earned a cent. Why not learn something that would pay me?"

"I was stumbling around, wondering what to do," Erna recalled, "when interior decorating occurred to me because I had helped so many of my friends decorate their houses." Friends had admired the decoration of Erna's home and trusted her judgment in the selection of colors, the choice of fabrics, and the arrangement of furniture. "So I was doing all of this work for them," she said, "and of course, they weren't paying me. I just did it because they were my friends. And I thought, well, what can I do? Decorating came to my mind."

Erna's nature is to act, so as soon as she had an idea of the direction she would take, she called the University of Washington to inquire about returning to study for an appropriate degree. As she remembers the conversation, Miss Foote, the head of the art department, asked her how old she was. "Well, I'll soon be fifty-eight," Erna replied. "Why, at your age four more years of college would be ridiculous," Miss Foote declared. "You would have to repeat a lot of courses you have already had. Now you just go down to Rudolph Schaeffer's School of Design in San Francisco and in two years you can get a diploma."

Following this good advice, Erna moved with alacrity. She applied and was accepted by Rudolph Schaeffer. Immediately she wrote back asking him to rent a room for her: "I had to have someplace to go when I got there. I wasn't going to spend money on a hotel." Then she sold her house and moved what furniture she kept into an apartment she rented with her oldest daughter.

"Was it hard to sell the house?" I asked her. "Not then,"

she said. "We had moved around so much in my childhood I could do it. But years later when I went back to show it to someone I loved, and found it had been torn down, I burst into tears and cried and cried. I wanted to go through it just one more time."

Moving into a collegiate atmosphere at the School of Design was, to Erna, like slipping back over all those years to the world of art she had known and loved in her childhood. Her old drawing skill that she had as a girl came back to her although she had not drawn since she left boarding school in Germany. Even though they were nearly forty years younger, the students at the School of Design accepted her completely. Her enthusiasm for art is so intense now there is no doubt that it was equally contagious then. With a ripple of laughter she told me that when she finished a drawing the students would take it to frame for her with balsa wood – "all they had," she said. "They were so good to me and never made me feel my age." Even now a note of incredulity creeps into her voice: "Do you know, those young matrons who would come up from the Peninsula or across from Marin County, just to take a course in color from Rudolph Schaeffer, would invite me to their homes for a party. They would provide transportation, coming and going. That's how good they were to me. They took me right in and we had a lot of fun."

Erna lived in a small residential hotel on First Street where breakfast and dinner and one meal on Sunday were provided, but she had no place to make sandwiches for lunch at school. So, before she hopped on a cable car clattering up Telegraph Hill, she bought a grapefruit, some crackers, and cheese. "That was my lunch every day for a whole year," she said. "The students used to laugh at me: 'Here she comes with her grapefruit.'" The classes on aesthetics and the history of design enthralled her. She drew and built models of rooms with the interior decoration to scale. Once every week she and a young friend, "nineteen at the most," would walk up Post Street through Chinatown together. Socially and intellectually Erna's first year at the School of Design was a thorough success. But at the end of the term she told Rudolph

Schaeffer she was not coming back for the second year. "I can't afford it," she said. "And do you know what?" She fixed her eyes on me. "He said, 'I want you back here. I want you in my school and I'm giving you a scholarship.'" Erna flourished her hand in the air. "So back I went!" In June, 1953, just two weeks short of her sixtieth birthday, Erna Weeks graduated from the School of Design.

Certified as an interior decorator by her diploma, Erna returned to Seattle. She had rented her apartment to students, so she had no place to live. Happily a friend of a friend recommended her as a house-sitter in a home in Laurelhurst, an affluent residential area. "I had no money, so it came in very conveniently," she said. "The owners were going on a two-month vacation. They left all the food for me and everything I bought was to be charged to them." Living in a beautiful house which, nevertheless, could be improved according to Erna's now well-trained sense of decoration, gave her an inspiration. She offered a plan to the owners in compensation for their generosity: while they were gone she would rearrange their furniture and make other small changes. If she thought they needed some new pieces, she would suggest to them what they should be. Whatever apprehensions she had about the boldness of her plan are forgotten now. What she remembers is how delighted the owners were when they returned and saw the changes she had made in their house. They praised her to their friends and her career was launched. The wife of the president of the University of Washington gave Erna her first job, redecorating the President's Mansion in Washington Park, a huge undertaking stretching over many months.

Had Erna Weeks been a young woman fresh out of college, nobody would have trusted her with such an important assignment. Her age was a definite asset, she is certain, not only in the eyes of her clients, but from the viewpoint of the workers she depended on: upholsterers, drapers, carpenters, and carpet layers. With characteristic foresight she had invited some of them to the house in Laurelhurst when she was staying there, to show them the standards she aspired to on the chance that they would do business together later on, as they did. The couple who made custom draperies appreciated the fact that Erna had hung a lot of drapes in her lifetime. "I worked right along with all of them," she declared, "and never had a complaint from customers or workmen." Her younger colleagues with younger clients had trouble collecting their fees. Erna's customers paid promptly.

She has a clear memory of the places she decorated and is particularly proud that now, nearly twenty-five years later, the principal pieces she installed in both the President's Mansion and the Gamma Phi Beta Sorority House are still in the same spots where she had placed them, and that the furniture has been recovered in almost the same fabrics and colors that she selected. "I felt a twinge of satisfaction," she confessed, "that my work had been good, liked, and durable."

One of the first things she learned from Schaeffer was never to take a job she was not paid for; a rule she broke only once, learning to her dismay how right he was. The customer who does not pay feels no compunction against removing a piece placed by the decorator and substituting one of his own, thereby ruining the whole effect. Yet the same person will say the decorator did the arrangement, thus inadvertently undermining her reputation.

For ten years, from the time she turned sixty until she was just over seventy, Erna Weeks, decorator, was so busy she did not have time to print a card. Then, what was a friendship blossomed into love and Victor Bouillon asked her to marry him. She was faced with a choice between marriage and a career; not for an instant did she harbor the illusion that the two were compatible.

"I knew that an elderly man (Victor was seventy-three) did not marry a woman and let her have something else on her mind," she declared. "I knew that if I married Victor I would have to make him the important thing in my life. I would have to give up my decorating. In decorating I would go to wholesale houses and come home at night with swatches of fabric and put a sample on the sofa, another on a chair. Then I would shift my furniture around something like the arrangement in the house I was decorating. I would look and look at them, then say to myself, 'That piece isn't right. I'll go back to the wholesale house first thing tomorrow because now I know what to look for.' I would have a seven o'clock dinner and take all of the rest of the evening looking. I knew that wouldn't work after I married Victor. I knew I would have to drop it. So I dropped it."

In her seventieth year, Erna Weeks became Erna Bouillon. Victor was a recent widower, a prominent banker in Ellensburg, Washington, who had been married to one of Erna's classmates in college. When she died, Erna wrote a letter of condolence to Victor, telling him that if he wanted to relieve his mind by talking to someone his own age about his loss and all that he had been through, she would be glad to cook him a dinner and spend the evening visiting. His response was immediate. For a year they kept their romance a secret. "Victor was a conventional man," she explained. Then, to her great delight, they startled their unsuspecting friends with an announcement of their marriage plans.

At this point in her recitation I remembered a wonderful letter one of my favorite aunts wrote me recently. Long ago I had spent a summer in Alaska with Mildred and her husband and discovered, to my eighteen-year-old astonishment, that married adults could be in love – demonstratively, tenderly, even a bit sentimentally. When Jim died I thought life must be over for Mildred. Now in her sixties, she wrote me about her "passionate, head-in-the-clouds affair" with a wonderful man who had been a friend of Jim's. "Don't let anyone tell you," she admonished me, "that young love is better." That is very good news, it seems to me, that not many of us have heard.

Now Erna Bouillon confirmed my aunt's report. "Victor and I were so well suited," she said. "We were crazy about each other. It was the easiest marriage you can imagine: no trouble at all to get adjusted." Their tastes were similar and they shared a passion for ballroom dancing. For the next five years Erna and Victor Bouillon would dress up to go dancing at least two or three times a week.

"Honestly," Erna affirms, "we never had a rift. Now they

say that is impossible and I agree that it is for a first marriage. When you have children you are bound to differ. But we had both raised our families. We were independent people, but we both had a lot to give to each other. And we had so much in common that we liked to do. We liked to travel and took a trip all through the U.S. We went to the opera and to the ballet when it was in town, to lectures, and to good stage and movie shows. Victor always seemed to know what was good in town. He had me join the University Women's Club so we could go there to dance. I never had joined because I didn't have the time and I had no one to go with. So we would go there and to the Washington Athletic Club to dance. We danced and danced."

The happiness of that memory prompted Erna to stand up and two-step around the room. "Sometimes," she confided, "when a good dance number comes over TV I get up and dance alone like this."

Six years after they were married, Victor Bouillon died. "He's been gone nearly ten years now," she sighed. "I can't believe it." We looked at his photograph hanging on the wall – he had a kind face with a forceful expression. From Ellen I knew that Erna's children admired him enormously, too, and had been overjoyed when he and their mother married. To find love again, late in life, must require a generosity of spirit, an openness and caring kind of attitude that contradicts the overplayed image of old age as a time of withdrawal and inward-looking.

All I had heard about Erna Bouillon testified to the delight she takes in being with people, and the concern and loyalty she has for her friends. As a young mother with small children, she suggested to a college chum that they form a group to meet for lunch once a week so they would not feel so housebound and isolated. Ten mothers – they limited the number for practical purposes – toted their babies to each other's houses and pooled a meal. Starved for adult conversation, they talked up such a storm that their husbands dubbed them "the Bolsheviks." Over the years, if one member moved or died, an enthusiastic replacement was found. Eventually they cut their meetings back to once a month. Now, sixty years later, the Bolsheviks are still meeting – with six of the original members plus four newer ones.

I asked Erna about some of the mementos in her apartment and she pointed out a few of her treasures: the solid brass candelabras she carried from Paris; some handpainted plates; an old mahogany secretary. "The red glasses are for my daughter, Pat," she said, explaining that her love of organization impelled her to list everything she owns. With thoughtful consideration for the needs of her children and grandchildren, she has made a folder for each of them, containing a list of what they will inherit from her.

Now she is writing a book about her family. The University of Texas at Austin, in response to her inquiry about some historical information relating to the Meerscheidt family, has requested a copy of her book when it is completed, to place in their library on Texas life. Erna frets because the typist is not bringing her copy back fast enough. Such enterprise reminds me of Imogene Cummingham, the eminent photographer from Seattle, who moved to San Francisco where she was active and productive into her nineties.

"Well, I hope I live long enough to read your book," Erna commented cheerfully as we ended our visit. "You know, at eighty-five you live from day to day." Since her life is such an obvious contradiction of that statement, I started to protest, but she interrupted me by opening a French door to show off her small balcony, which she has just redecorated. I gasped with pleasure at its perfection. Placed in one corner to provide shade for two bamboo chairs was a beautiful corkscrew willow tree, its spiral trunk a slate green, its gracefully drooping leaves long and narrow, like a classical tree in a Chinese painting. In the far corner were two small pots, each containing a slip of a willow tree.

"Yes," Erna admitted when I asked her, "those are starters from the big willow. One day, of course, the large willow tree will get too big for the balcony and I will have to give it away. By that time one of those little starters should be tall enough to give me shade."

We both laughed. Imogene Cummingham would have applauded such foresight. Planning is faith in the future, a means of coping with life instead of being battered down by it. I was grateful to Ellen for introducing me to Erna Bouillon. I cherish the thought of her taking slips from her corkscrew willow tree to make two little starters: willow trees for her future. Such faith and flair and style is the hallmark of Erna Bouillon.

Part Two
Doing What One Loves

"Understanding what you really feel and really want is more breathtaking than climbing to the top of the rimrock in the wind."

MILDRED WALKER
Winter Wheat

A Classic Conflict

When Mark Tobey, the now famous but then obscure artist, was scratching out a living teaching private classes in Seattle, my mother submitted her portfolio to him and was accepted as his student. Her shouts of joy brought my father running from his desk. I yelled with relief. Tobey's classes would keep my mother busy and take the pressure off me. I knew from experience that whenever my mother was not working on her art, she would work on me. I was a teenager with plenty of interests of my own and I wanted time by myself.

My mother's powerful creative urge always needed an outlet. Searching for that outlet kept her off balance most of her life because she was never able to commit herself fully to her talent in a systematic and satisfying way. Her moods swung like the pendulum on a clock. The times when she was taking classes she was happily preoccupied with her art work. The times when she was not, she was touchy and critical of me and my father and my brother. Unlike a ball of clay or an oil painting, we could not be worked into even a partial realization of the idealized versions my mother had created in her mind. This failure made her querulous.

It was one thing to have her snappish when she could not sculpt a line the way she wanted to: we could commiserate and encourage her. But it was quite another feeling, a completely miserable one, to know that we, ourselves, as the material she was working on, were not quite shaping up.

Long after economic necessity compelled her to make all our clothes, Mother sewed for me. Aflame with imagination, she cut dresses without a pattern, smocked the bodices with tiny, perfect stitches, and puffed the sleeves. On me, sway-backed, stomach out, with freckles and straight brown hair, these exquisite dresses were incongruous. Pictures of my brother Watson, dressed in sailor suits she made, with navy grosgrain ribbon edging the white collars, show that she was more successful with him. His cherubic face was suited to sailor hats, but the defiant pout of his lower lip suggests that he did not enjoy being a mannequin any more than I did.

But old habits die hard, and Mother could not shift her creative energies away from doing and making everything herself. She raised us during the Great Depression, when my father's salary often was paid in coupons rather than cash. I bought my first ready-made coat during my second year in college; she thought it was an extravagance. Her function as a faculty wife also shaped her character in a way she could not have imagined when she was an eager student or a fiery teacher: she became a gracious hostess. With her passion for beauty and her eye trained to discern fine craftsmanship, she filled our house with antiques, Oriental rugs, mahogany tables, and Minton china she had ferreted out from thrift shops and auctions. Then she felt compelled to create a setting to match their perfection. When I knew there were infinitely more important things to do, she would corral me to help her scrub the hardwood floors on our hands and knees with steel wool dipped in gasoline.

Had Mother been brought up in a family where women were encouraged to make time in their lives to keep skills other than homemaking alive, she might have developed some self-discipline in her art work. She had the power of concentration and the talent. But when she went back to it, she worked in fits and starts. Driven by a sense of time lost, with all of those years immersed in domestic life to make up for, she worked frantically to regain her sure hand. For weeks she would forget to shop and cook, working late into the night, sculpting and welding in our basement. My father and I would boil potatoes, ham hocks and sauerkraut for dinner after dinner. Then he would announce that he intended to have some visiting professors and their wives over for an evening. Furious with him, and feeling guilty for letting her housework slip, Mother would fly into a frenzy of cleaning, cook a sumptous meal and, looking superb herself, serve it with élan. Then she would collapse, only to revive again as another idea for a piece of sculpture or a painting engulfed and swept her back down into her workshop. It was an exhausting cycle for all of us.

As long as Mother was enrolled in classes, my father would tolerate her neglect of him and the housework. He understood the pressures of assignments, deadlines, and exams. But when classes were over he expected her to catch up on their entertaining, to appear with him at lectures and dinners, and to make arrangements for the caretaking of our house and the disposition of Watson and me so that she could accompany him to whatever distant university he taught at during the summer sessions. Limited by her sense of duty, and without any examples of more imaginative ways to live among the wives around her, Mother never attempted to work out a more fruitful arrangement with him. I think my father might have been amenable to some reasonable plan allowing more time and continuity for her work. But my mother never was confident enough of her worth as an artist to attempt a basic rearrangement around her work.

In the world she knew, money as the only measure of success was an assumption too widespread and unquestioned for her to challenge. "Mark Tobey is a genius," Mother would announce, returning radiant from one of his classes. "Maybe," my father grumbled, "but he is a pretty scruffy fellow who can't pay his rent."

An oil painting of Mother's was accepted for a show of Northwest artists at the Seattle Art Museum and we all were jubilant. She sold a few pictures and my father began to brag about her. But by then Mother was temperamentally unable to move out of her private life into the public world of economic competition. Aside from paying bills, she had no financial experience. She gave away most of her work.

After I left home, my mother's long-established yearning for a life filled with beauty and creative accomplishment was more fully realized than was ever possible for her during the years when Watson's and my needs shaped her existence. Without our schedules to hem her in, she worked with awesome concentration, giving up all pretense of keeping regular hours, whenever an inspiration overcame her. For a time she became a familiar figure on Seattle's waterfront, working at her easel until the shadows of the Olympic Mountains darkened Puget Sound and the straggling spectators who stood watching her drifted away. Once her picture appeared in the newspaper. It showed her with a concentrated frown on her face, squinting, with one eye closed, at her paintbrush that she held at arm's length as a measuring stick to get the perspective right on some fishing boats in the harbor. She was surprised to see herself publicly identified as an artist. Perhaps that picture emboldened her to recreate herself in much the same way she had worked on Watson and me, with the idea for a special character in mind. In any case, whether it was a canny bid for more independence, or a natural drift toward her own predilections, the older Mother became, the more she cultivated her eccentricities like a protective hedge around her real passion for art. As an off-beat personality she could tickle our sense of humor and be indulged. This way she also deflected judgment by our untrained eyes on the merit of her work: we settled our attention on her as an absent-minded character apt to clean her paintbrushes in the saucepan and then make soup. Safe behind her hedge of eccentricity she bloomed. There she was happy.

But even after she and my father sold their big colonial-style home to move into a smaller, one-level house, she could not quite bring herself to make the third bedroom into an inviolable studio for herself. Next to her tools, paints, and easel she crammed in a sofa bed and a chaise lounge for her grandchildren to sleep on. And willy-nilly, we piled in around her, demanding and getting the same attention we always received.

Until recently, I have, quite unconsciously, repeated the pattern of my mother's life. Superficial differences – my traveling to exotic places and living abroad – obscured the similarities. My perception was clouded, too, by my desire to be like my father, a common aim among educated daughters who recognize how much more highly valued by friends and relatives our fathers are. A certainty that I took after him deluded me for decades. My mother was a clear-skinned beauty, after all, and I have my father's freckles and his bumpy nose. I can't draw a straight line or sew a seam, but like him, I love books and academic arguments.

What I should have noticed earlier on is that my mother and

I, and women the world over, are subject to the same sorts of general expectations, quite unlike those for men. As daughters, sisters, wives, or mothers, however diverse our particular circumstances may be, we play out roles that rarely foster our individual talents. My father charged through his life invigorated by his overriding commitment to his work. My mother careened around her domestic compulsions with no one to help her set a straight course for the development of her gifts.

Now times have changed. Many women are working out ways to realize their natural endowments and to do the work they love. But cultural pressures are insidious, cropping up in slick new disguises, like the magazine-manufactured career girls who want it, do it, and have it all: work, love, and family.

All our mothers' lives are cautionary tales. We can learn from them and from each other. On the alert at last, I watch my own progress with great care. And I look to my friends who have been on much the same route as I, who now live lives enriched by work they love – work they either postponed or discovered after the pressure of their child-rearing years was over – women who know from experience that you seldom, if ever, can have it all – and certainly not all at once.

4. The Artist as Her Own Person

ELIZABETH BENSON BOOZ

"I think many people have a sense of shape, of unfolding in their lives."

DORIS LESSING
The Golden Notebook

Elizabeth Benson Booz, in her early fifties, is just now breaking out of her chrysalis – she can practically feel it cracking down her back. For the first time in her life she is conscious of her own distinct configuration. This metaphor of metamorphosis is hers. As an artist compelled to shape her experience into visual forms, she sees herself first as being inside of an egg, gently protected from the world around her. She was nearly twenty before she hatched out on her own. Then she became a caterpillar, roaming about with great mobility, ingesting an incredibly rich diet of every possible kind of plant, until, at the point of her husband's sudden death, she spun a cocoon about herself, remaining for about two years quiescent within it. Then, almost imperceptibly at first, she began to feel fissures on its protective surface.

However apt this analogy of her personality changes to the growth of a grub may seem to her, it does not fit my perception of "Ben" Booz. I first met Ben more than twenty years ago in Lahore, Pakistan, when both of us were young mothers, married to men whose work led us to live overseas and raise our families in a succession of different countries and continents. Then, as now, Ben struck me as a strong woman creating her own life. With her merry laugh and casual, open manner, she projected a confidence I envied. In those days of bouffant hairdos, spike heels, and heavy makeup, Ben scrubbed her face, brushed her red hair back into a short cut, and strode comfortably along over the uneven dirt lanes of Lahore's bazaars in Pakistani-made sandals, a slim, long-legged woman with a winning smile.

At that time the strength of her creative drive which she took so for granted was perfectly apparent to me. True, it was dispersed, scattered in a dozen directions: into the drawings she made for all manner of local causes, into her paintings and book illustrations, into the toys and puppets she concocted out of old socks for the annual church bazaar, into sculptures of wood and stone – but most of all into her family. Ben adored being a mother. She had four boys then, two more than I had; later, her last child, like mine, was a much-desired daughter. The birthday parties she gave were fêtes, enjoyed as much by parents as by children. In a happy throng of various aged Americans and Pakistanis, I caught my first glimpse of Ben – wagging a puppet for a Punch and Judy show in celebration of one of her boy's birthdays. On the expeditions she organized for her family, Ben was always on the lookout for adventures, which never failed to occur.

Ben's and my love of travel and our penchant for telling family stories forged an immediate bond between us so that, through the years, whenever we met, we joyfully exchanged outrageous tales about our exotic lives. Neither of us could resist casting ourselves in the comic role to turn a family incident into a funny story that would, in the telling and the retelling, and the accumulation of tale upon tale, build a family mythology. One aspect of my role-playing was its effectiveness as a ploy to deflect criticism, which I had learned from my mother. Ben also knew the limits and dangers of mythmaking, although she indulged in it as zestfully as I did. Her sense of herself was stronger than she realized, for she seemed to avoid locking herself into a character role. But like many creative women who pour their energies into making a rich family life, Ben was only dimly aware of how central to her survival this creative impulse was. Later, when events forced her to evaluate her fundamental priorities, she realized that her deepest reality was not in her role as wife and mother, but somewhere inside herself. If she were faced with the loss of her husband and children she would endure it somehow. But she could not survive at all if she lost her creative drive.

Nothing Ben can remember in her upbringing seems to have contributed to her ultimate independence and that automatic tiller of creativity that kept her on a steady course, no matter how dim her awareness of it. Born in 1925 to an upstairs life of nannies and governesses in pre-World War II London, of American parents bent on outdoing the British in matters of form, little Betsy–Ben was trained for the passive role of a proper English child. Yet built into this overstructured life was one never-failing formula for good behavior that derived from her mother's own growing-up in a family of Boston artists. Whenever Betsy–Ben grew restless or bored, a pencil was put into her hand and she was admonished to "sit down quietly and draw."

She attended an English boarding school after she turned nine, and was taken to the United States just before the war, where she felt vaguely out of place in her white socks and sandals when American girls were wearing high heels and lipstick. But, after another boarding school, she dutifully followed her cousin to Vassar. Then, as the result of a jolting summer at the end of her junior year, she began to break out of her state of passivity.

The agent who started the process was an independently minded aunt who had gone west as a young woman to work with the Navajo Indians. Aunt Margaret now owned a small newspaper in New Mexico and ran a goat farm on the side. She asked Ben to take over while she went back East for two months, and the adventures of that summer started Ben hatching out of her genteel egg. When Aunt Margaret returned, she marched Ben off to Berkeley to complete her senior year at the University of California. Such an abrupt change of scene had an electrifying effect: eagerly Ben began to learn about life. In reaction to her family background (her father was a banker), she became a Marxist, but, still dependent on her parents, she obtained their consent to go to the Graduate School of International Studies in Geneva, Switzerland. There she joined a group of students called Peace

Through Reconstruction, and went, one summer, with them to Yugoslavia to build a railroad for which she received the ultimate award, a Udarnik medal from Tito, and where, in Bosnia, she met her future husband, Paul Booz.

Paul was eleven years older than Ben, an established economist with the United Nations Relief and Rehabilitation Agency when she met him, the son of strait-laced but liberal-minded and deeply religious pioneer farmers in Kansas. He took life very seriously. While Ben was studying for her M.A. in Geneva, Paul met her every day for lunch, not to whisper endearments in her ear, but to teach her economics. She passed her exams with honors. Paul was a born teacher, Ben the perfect student. In 1949 they were married and Paul began teaching her how to be his wife. By her own admission, he brought her up. As a child, Ben was raised on the upper class side of the green baize door, so it was not her mother, but Paul, who taught her how to cook and to clean, and how to choose her clothes. From the beginning, this worldly, capable husband-father made all the decisions in their lives, and, since their basic values were identical, it never occurred to Ben, this pliant, well-educated young woman, to question them. She was accustomed to authority.

But a small, vital part of Ben's life remained her own. In Geneva, while she was still a student, Ben discovered the world of art. Hours spent in museums and galleries unleashed her artistic impulse. She had continued to draw when it was no longer a strategy for sitting still, and she had acquired considerable notoriety at school and college for her cartoons and caricatures. But now she began to paint in earnest. In her eyes these first efforts were so awful she threw them out. But she kept sketching and painting, and eventually a friend suggested that she have a show at her house, which she did. Some of her work sold and Ben kept on painting. Paul was proud of her talent and encouraged her. Knowing nothing about art himself, he began to learn, and to collect modern art. When something went wrong with one of her almost finished pictures, Ben would take it to Paul for criticism. He could not tell her what the picture needed, but he could tell her exactly which area needed improvement, all that she required to work it through to completion.

Her art work quickly became the one constant in Ben's life and the part of her that Paul found most interesting. At the same time, he tended to be jealous of her work because it excluded him. Being a generous and loving man, he tried valiantly not to mind, but it bothered him that when Ben started painting she didn't want to stop to prepare a meal or to change the babies' diapers. As long as they were living overseas where household help was reasonable and possible to get, Ben and Paul were able to evolve a workable system that allowed her enough free time for her painting at the same time that they were raising their family. The conflict came when Paul decided to return to the United States for further study at Harvard. With two small babies and very little money, life for Ben became a balancing act between her sanity and the needs of her family. Paul had to teach her how to boil an egg and do the laundry. He bought the furniture, chose the crockery, arranged the kitchen, hung the curtains, and taught her how to cook basic meals. Together, before friends came in, they would rush through the apartment, vacuuming and dusting. Surely few husbands ever have been as helpful and supportive to their wives. Without any experience in house-keeping, and no enthusiasm for it, Ben was exasperatingly inefficient. Yet, in a subtle way, she was better off than had she been trained as a girl to be a competent housekeeper. For, even though she feels that she had no image of herself as an artist when she was a harried young mother, she nevertheless knew exactly where the cause of her frustration was; and she had the insight to know that to keep herself from sinking into a state of complete despair, she had to get away from her house and family to replenish her spirit in the art world, on a regular basis. Paul understood, and even though they really did not have the extra money for it, he agreed to her taking two art courses at the Boston Museum of Fine Arts.

Because I too was flung into the same wretched state when I returned with my young family to the United States after the luxury of living in India with ample household help, I understand exactly how Ben felt. But how different our reactions were. From the time I could stand on a stool to reach the kitchen counter and stir the biscuit dough, I had cooked. My mother, whose high standards of cleanliness were set by her Swiss mother, taught me to scrub floors, starch dresses, iron linen, and mend clothes. Only after this womanly work was done was it permissible to read a book or write a story. And money was to be saved, not spent on oneself. Conditioned by this early training, and knowing that, with my dishwasher and clothes drier, I was so much better off than my mother or grandmother, I had no excuse for not doing the household work to perfection. All around me more women were sinking under this sort of guilt load, just as I was, than struggling like Ben to keep afloat.

Ben had her priorities straight. The moment Paul walked out the door to go to work in the morning she plunged into her painting, or later, when she decided to write and illustrate a children's book, she would plunk her typewriter down in the middle of the dirty breakfast dishes on the kitchen table, working while her energy was high, right through to early afternoon. Then she would scoot to make the beds and do the dishes before Paul walked in the door, home from the office. As their life went on, Paul continued to help with the household chores, but his own work increasingly absorbed him. When they lived abroad in Lebanon, Jordan, Pakistan and Bangladesh, no sharp division separated his professional life from his home life as it did in the United States. Overseas, colleagues came to the Booz household with their wives and children for informal meals and long, leisurely conversations. There was time for Ben to keep up on events outside of family life, and with her sound background in economics, she could enter into Paul's shoptalk. In these smaller communities, where people lived ten minutes apart and dropped in without formal invitation, Paul got to know Ben's art friends. And the family-centered way of life in these eastern countries suited the Booz preferred style of living. Home and job flowed together, each enriching the other. As they encountered new cultures, made new friends, and learned new languages together, the Boozes remained a close family unit. But every time Paul returned to the United States to work, his professional life was split from his family life. In the States the children were separated from each other by the structured activities of their peer groups, and Ben was left alone, unconnected except by the services she rendered to the family. The Christmas that each of her five children gave her a gadget for the kitchen she sat down and cried. Here was proof positive that they saw her as an installation in the kitchen which, with a few newfangled devices, could operate more efficiently. What she saw was her creative self shriveling away.

A half hour away, across Washington, D.C., at precisely the same time, in a parallel situation, I was dangerously close to sinking into melancholia. By this time Ben and I each had written and published two children's books, although Ben had illustrated hers as well. I was still trying to write, but only short children's stories, scribbled in the orthodontist's waiting room, or as I sat in the car outside of the grade or the junior high school. Between chauffeuring her brood of five to basketball or Scouts, Ben was still painting. Neither of us had the time or energy for long, sustained writing or art projects. Once or twice we met at Washington dinner parties, those occasions for planned gaiety, but all we did was chat nostalgically about our past adventures in Asia. In the mid-sixties women were not yet *really* talking to each other.

But Paul and Ben were talking to one another, agreeing that their lives were separating them from each other and that the only way they knew how to pull them together again was to go overseas once more. Paul left his job at the World Bank and took a position with the Ford Foundation in Indonesia. I heard that the whole family was wildly enthusiastic to go and from mutual friends who passed through London where we were posted at about the same time, I learned that all the Boozes were thriving in Jakarta and Ben was having an exhibition of sculpture. Three years later an envelope slipped through my mail slot carrying the news of Paul's heart attack and death.

"But it was all right," Ben told me when I looked her up in Washington, D.C., recently. "Paul's death was perfectly all right. It was absolutely out of the blue, but it was the way he would have wanted it. His life ended on a marvelous point. I often think," she said, "if Paul had lived, and we were here in America, with the children gone, living in a little apartment, would we have become cantankerous? Would I have resented having to cook meals for him as he slowed down, and I, eleven years younger, was still raring for adventures? Paul knew best. He really did."

"Oh, Ben, you're idealizing him," I had to say.

"No, I really believe this," she insisted. "He did know. He died during the one week when all five children were in Indonesia. He knew, at some subconscious level, if he had to die anyway, he would do it in the best possible way, at the best possible time, because that is the way Paul did things."

Most women assume their husbands will die before they do, but few make any practical plans for it. I asked Ben if she had made any preparations.

"Yes, we had talked about the possibility of either of our deaths," she answered, "but, in truth, we always assumed that we would die together. Plane crash probably. Both of us hated expensive, traditional funerals, and we agreed that, aesthetically, we wanted to be cremated. So that made one decision easier during that sudden, frantic time of decision making on the evening he died. It was easy and cheap, and Paul would have been delighted."

The day after Paul died, friends urged Ben and the children to go up to a cottage in the mountains. That night, in the mountains of Java, near the equator where the stars are incredibly bright, they all had an overwhelming feeling that the universe was good and that Paul's death was right. "The feeling flooded over each one of us," Ben declared. "We all were sure that even though it was terrible, it was right; that the whole system of the universe is a good system. This conviction just kind of whooshed over me. After that night I am not in the least bit worried about dying, because I know, it's not that I believe, or that I think, it's that I *know* it is all right: the whole system – the living and the dying – is good. We never felt that Paul's death was a dirty trick or that it was a tragedy, or anything like that. It was perfectly all right. That feeling carried us right through."

Such a life-affirming attitude fits Ben. She accepted the inevitable and began putting her priorities in order once more.

"We had a family conference," she continued, "and decided we must all stay together." Their first summer without Paul the family spent in the house that he and Ben had purchased when they were first married, in the village of Yvoire just across the border from Geneva in France, the only home they had kept and the one they repaired to between Paul's assignments.

Like many widows, Ben had no idea of how much Paul earned or what financial arrangements he had. "Not a clue," she said. "And the dear man at the Ford Foundation, who was the head of all these things, said to me, 'Here are your forms for your repatriation. You have so much allowance for that and so much for this.' I couldn't possibly have understood all of those things all at once. Finally he said, 'What you really need is a sugarbowl with your money in it.' So I said to him, 'Will you please just give me a sugarbowl?' He said, 'Well, yes. Here is the total amount and you can come back to the States any way you want, just don't go over that amount.' So," Ben continued, "we left Jakarta to stop over in France for two months, with thirty-two pieces of luggage, two pythons, and a bicycle. The pythons caused some trouble, but back in Yvoire, where they could glide about the house, French friends just loved them. 'So *majestueux*, Madam,' they would say, 'So *majestueux*.'

"In Yvoire," Ben continued, "I told the kids the one thing they could do to help me the most was to be happy because that would take them off of my concern list. They did, and I was able to concentrate."

She spent long hours at her desk trying to understand the tremendous bulk of business she had to sort out. "Paul had done it all," she sighed. "I wrote checks, but he only allowed me to put down the amount on the stub, never to do any adding, because when I took 99 from 100 I came out with 101. So it took me ten times as long as a normal person to do the necessary things. But I began to take the greatest pleasure in it all. I had a little basket and every time a bill came in I would put it in there. Then when I sat down to pay all the bills I would practically say, 'Paul, are you watching me do this?' And I would get a glow of self-congratulation when I finished. I made rules for myself. I keep my stubs very carefully so I know where I am from month to month.

"Immediately after Paul died," Ben asserted, "I went into a kind of overdrive where I worked with great efficiency but not much conscious thought.

"It was a very strange time. In the midst of my busy thoughts, I would hear a voice. My thoughts would all pull back to the edge and leave a space. In this space a wise voice would say, 'Ben, you're doing fine coping with disaster, but watch it. When things get better, don't lose your touch.'"

"Was it Paul's voice?" I asked.

"No," Ben answered. "It was myself, somewhere. I must have been slightly schizoid. It once said, 'You can't move forward until you stop whirling.' And another time, 'Don't bounce. Roll.'"

Roll was what they had to do, because when Ben worked her way down through all the bills and the taxes to be paid, and the children's education was paid for, there was not much money left. The family was also homeless, except for the house in the little French village. The children and Ben collectively made the decision to head back to Sandy Spring, Maryland, a Quaker community whose meeting Paul and Ben had joined in the mid-sixties.

"Sandy Spring is a good country community," Ben declared. "They reached out to us so lovingly. It was the best decision we could have made because there was a good school there for the children, and I fell into a teaching job. The headmaster at Sandy Spring asked me to fill in for a history teacher for two months. That was all. Then I was asked to teach two classes in the high school. So I taught and that forced me to keep learning, which I feel is so important. I worked very hard. It was a great education for me – teaching and making financial decisions."

As other widows often do, Ben too went through what she calls a kind of craziness.

"It was a period when I didn't trust myself," she said. "Fortunately I was anchored to a community. The area where I didn't trust myself at all was in my relationships with men. When you are married," she pointed her finger at me, "you are marked all the way across the board as half of a relationship. And when suddenly you are on your own, you are looked at totally differently, and you are totally different. This was something I was not the least bit prepared for, and I didn't trust myself at all. I didn't have any bearings. In a way, it was very adventurous, but it was *terra incognita*. You know," she reminded me, "I'm a very exuberant person. When Paul was alive, for instance, I would throw my arms around someone's neck and suddenly, when you are single, it doesn't mean the same thing at all. So I had to work out a whole new way to relate to people."

"But don't you sometimes yearn to settle back into a comfortable marriage again?" I ventured.

"I think it would relieve the children if I did." Ben laughed a little. "But at our age I don't think one goes into a relationship the way we did when we were young. I would like to find a man who doesn't have that whole, demanding, possessive orientation toward a wife, but I'm certainly not putting marriage as my top priority. It would just be a nice bonus if it came along. I'm sure that the only place I would find this kind of a relationship would be to work alongside of somebody. I wouldn't meet him at a dinner party. You do something together and you find an alliance, you form a partnership. But when you get right down to it, there are very few men who don't have this residual feeling that if a woman is a wife, she is automatically responsible for certain chores. I have this freedom now to make decisions without consulting anyone, so I would be most reluctant to give it up. I think a good live-in relationship would be what I would like most. I like the bright edge of choice."

"Don't you think," I suggested, "that when you are young you think sex is the central thing in a relationship?"

"Yes," Ben agreed. "That's one of the benefits of getting older. Sex is fine, but it's not central anymore. Ideally, at this point, I would like someone who is a creative person, with whom I could have a good sexual relationship also. Or someone who at least understands the creative, artistic process. Somebody with whom I could share that aspect of my life.

"What was Paul and what was me," Ben said, "was the hardest thing to separate out. Losing him was like the total amputation of an arm and a leg. Everything in my house Paul had chosen, so I didn't know if I was a little crab living in someone else's shell. He had been making all of the decisions. I was standing by, but I wasn't watching very closely."

For about two years after Paul's death, which she considers a normal mourning period, Ben stayed in the safe haven of Sandy Spring, trying to regain her balance. Then, much as she enjoyed teaching, she began to get restive. Ideas for a new life began to nudge her out of her staid slot. Her creative spirit craved change and stimulation.

"Remember," she said, "how I said my mind would pull things to the edge, leaving that little space where a voice could come through? It began saying *Nothing will change until you change!* This was a whole new avenue. To pay attention to myself. To be awake. Not to just drift asleep through the days, but to pay attention as I go."

"But, Ben," I protested. "You have done so much, coped so well."

She shook her head. "What I want to do is to simplify my life. I think of my mother-in-law, a solid, golden person who grew up in a sod hut in Kansas. Those clear eyes that looked across the plains and called a spade a spade. There was no pretense about her. One day she slapped her iron down and said, 'This is the last shirt I am ever going to iron.' No explanation, no fuss. She was finished with that part of her life and never went back to it. What I want to do is pare my life down so it has the aesthetic quality of bare bones."

"Like Georgia O'Keefe?" I suggested.

"Exactly!" Ben replied enthusiastically. "Now there is somebody who is not cluttered down with things. And that's why she is ninety, too. Perhaps our problem is that our energies have been scattered for so long. They were so abundant and limitless, but now is the time to gather them in and focus them. Not let them all dribble away. Take ourselves as the first thing and focus our energies. Women like Georgia O'Keefe, who have an overview of their lives, who can see life as an entity, are on top of it, life is not piled on top of them. In fact," Ben admitted, "since Paul died, in many ways, it has been a very liberating thing – to be fully in charge, to take responsibility for one's own decisions, and not to have to take a partner into consultation. My needs from now on are going to be very limited.

"When I think how we lived, you and I," she exclaimed. "The households we set up! The receptions we gave! The servants," she ticked them off, "the *chowkidors*, the *malis*, the *dhobis*, the *dherzi*, the *hamals*, the *ayahs*, on and on. And all of the extra help to come in whenever necessary."

The very memory of such entourages and their attendant problems exhausted me.

"And do you remember, also," Ben warmed to the subject, "how everyone we knew was successful in some way? They had arrived. They ran something or they were the heads of things or countries. Well, one of the things that I love about being single is knowing people who are not successful in the conventional sense: artists, teachers, filmakers, who are doing what they want to do, not because they can't be successful, but because the whole success bag just isn't worth it to them. Among them we really are all equal. In the success game, reservation is always there – with anything that is organizational and professional, anything that has people jockeying for glory and power. I think that is why I so enjoy being with these people whose names you will never see attached to anything. They are really great people. Their minds are not taken up with money or status. They are not ambitious for things and fame and that is why I feel so comfortable with them."

I could not deny her criticism of life among the powerful. I remembered only too well all those cocktail parties and institutional functions where I tried to make conversation while a diplomat or an editor gazed over my head furtively searching for someone more useful to cultivate.

"Now," I observed to Ben, "I've noticed that when I am away from my home and family I am a very different person from when I'm acting as a wife or mother."

"It probably is a very banal kind of truism," she concurred, "but it has been an important one for me to discover – learning to see myself in a context totally different from that of the family. And the transition I am about to make now is bigger than losing Paul." I asked her to explain.

"I am now going to move away and begin a new life completely on my own. The children have already started on their own lives – the last one has gone off to college – and I'm not going to sit sadly in my empty nest. I'm going to empty it of myself, too! We're still intact as a family, and I trust we always will be, but it's a new mode of operation that suits the new period. When Paul was alive, we functioned in a straight line with Paul at the top. When he was gone, we regrouped into a circle, all dependent on one another. Now we are forming a looser web of mutually supportive adults who all love each other very much.

"Moving on is a kind of organic development. It's not a rational decision at all. I was still thinking of myself as passive, when in fact I was learning to make decisions. But I have to sneak up on them. I can't sit down at my desk and with a swipe of the pen make a move. What I do is prepare myself for them. I say, 'Oh, I couldn't possibly do *that*!' Then I think about it, and when the time comes, I'm ready."

That is the way Ben's creative impulse works: she begins by imagining – letting fantasies about her life flow freely. Then, with her artistic sense of design, she discerns a pattern, faint at first, and fluid so that she can shift the pieces around until she has created a satisfying effect. Then, like testing colors on a canvas, she begins to explore avenues of action.

Also, since 1970, Ben has kept a record of her dreams.

"It's as if my dream life is beginning to have equal weight with my awake life," she said. "I feel it is important for me to be familiar with that world. In your real life, looking back you see a less developed self. But this is not true of my dream life. Old dreams are just as valid as new ones; one dream doesn't develop sequentially out of another. History changes, but dreams are stable.

"And I trust my dreams implicitly," Ben said very earnestly. "There is no trickery in them. No pretending. No false courage. They are in another language and are right. They cultivate the inner light which is absolutely trustworthy. When I put my trust in these inner feelings I am on solid ground."

I asked what school of psychology she favored to interpret her dreams. She replied that she thought dreams spoke fairly directly. She read Freud and Jung and the Gestalt psychologists, appreciates their insights, and used to write comments on her dreams about the probable associations and such. Now she thinks much is lost in translation. "They remind me of developing a film," she said. "In the process of writing them down, as accurately as possible, without interpreting, things come up which you hadn't noticed when you were actually dreaming, the way a picture develops from a negative. The writing down is the developing process. I don't do more than just write it. I don't think about it as I do it, but a whole new significance or meaning comes up.

"Or," continued Ben as metaphors kept occurring to her, "dreaming is like deciphering the Rosetta Stone: it is working in another language. The more examples you have, the more correlations you make. Dreams extend my vocabulary. Sometimes," she grinned, "I can't wait to get back to my dream life. I just know that my dream record is a treasure house I am building up."

And what kinds of signals, I inquired, were surfacing from her dream life?

"A plan," she said, "that I hope will keep me busy and useful and needed. I'm getting into this free-floating situation. The pull of the children isn't the same any more."

So now Ben has moved away from her encapsulated life in

the Quaker community to an apartment near Washington, D.C. She has been doing freelance work – editing, illustrating, writing – while she looked for her "real" work, something that would fuse her artistic talents with her teaching skills. Her plan is to work with nonliterate women, preferably in Asia. When I last saw her, she was packing up to leave for Indonesia on a project for the Ford Foundation – the first big step into her new, really independent life "Those women are the ones I feel such a compassion for, and want to live with," she declared. "Also, there is a selfish component in this, because I hope I will be *needed* until I am a really old woman. There will always be problems to solve, and work to do, and by the time I am seventy I should really know something about them and be truly useful. Age is a very scary thing when you are a woman and single and poverty is a real possibility. But it doesn't matter being poor if you are doing something useful," Ben smiled confidently. "It is important, too," she added, "to form interdependent networks with your friends, and across generations with both younger and older people. Then you just work as long as you possibly can, and when the time comes, find a nice hospice."

She nodded, more to herself than to me. "I used to wonder," she mused, "if, when my chrysalis cracked open, I would come out a grubby little gray-winged fiddle thing that wouldn't live two hours, or if I would come out a bright lunar moth. I was such an unformed, gawky, volatile sort of a girl and such an unquestioning young woman."

"Now I know that growing old is fun," Ben slapped her knee and that old winsome smile lighted her face. "Change is good. That's what keeps you going. I can't *wait* to see what will come next. Life is *so* interesting. The whole process."

5. An Honorable Attorney
MARY COOK HACKMAN

"Work, the object of which is to serve more and more people, in widening range . . . is social service in the fullest sense, and the highest form of service we can reach."

CHARLOTTE PERKINS GILMAN
Women and Economics

Who hasn't longed, in these career-oriented times, to be awakened, not by a kiss to the dubious life of a princess, but to the fact that one has some great, secret talent, which once discovered brings her joy and riches beyond her wildest dreams?

"That is exactly what happened to Mary Cook Hackman," her friend and my neighbor Anne Crutcher told me when we met one day at the market.

"Oh, yes, Mary Cook is one of the world's triumphant people," declared Anne as she picked out a purple eggplant. "She is a successful lawyer, who had never gone to college until she was forty-five." I stopped pinching the tomatoes. "Tell me more," I begged as we made our way to the fish counter. I did a quick mental thumb-through of my own scattered experience for overlooked talents. Maybe there was still time. I can't spell or add, but it occurred to me that maybe lawyers don't have to do either.

"Nobody seemed to think Mary Cook would make it," said Anne as she chose a large sea trout.

"How did she do it?" I wondered.

"Go ask her," said Anne.

"Why, it was hard," Mary Cook Hackman said with a delightful smile when I sought her out in her office in Arlington, Virginia. A petite woman of sixty-six, she has a vibrant air, sparkling blue eyes, and an engaging chuckle. Her blonde hair is curled short. She was wearing a stylish pantsuit the first time I met her, and a simple dress and pearls the next. Her manner is at once gracious and practical.

Her suite of offices is quietly elegant: Oriental rugs on white wall-to-wall carpets, enormous windows with tree-filled views, large warm paintings, and plants burgeoning everywhere. Watching Mary Cook in her tall-backed leather chair behind her huge antique desk. I found it hard to imagine her in any role other than that of an energetic attorney. But this happy, thoroughly attractive woman, was, as Anne said, fully forty-five years old before she was given a clue that she possessed the intellect and the aptitude to become a highly successful lawyer.

Looking back, she thinks her early childhood was, by happenstance, responsible for her eventual involvement in the law. Her mother was a deeply religious person and the family had Bible and other spiritual readings every day. The beautiful language of the King James version fell upon a receptive ear; in law school, the hard law of Moses and the softer, benign words of Jesus were remembered and fitted into the pattern of the law courts and the equity courts. She also read the books in the family library: Dickens, with his concerns for social conditions, Victor Hugo's *Les Misérables*, dealing with the disastrous effect of a harsh law and even harsher law enforcement. By the time she reached law school, these ideas, imbued so long ago, emerged and found their echo in certain of the doctrines of the law.

Marriage to a U.S. Army second lieutenant in 1933, when she was twenty-two, was entirely appropriate to Mary Cook's upbringing. "I enjoyed army life," she said. "We went directly to Panama. There was official entertaining, a lot of it, but at a very low level. We were outdoors quite a bit, fishing and swimming. I'm a good homemaker, but I'm not a good housekeeper, and I'm not a good cook," she declares. "To make up for it, I would at times throw myself into some dumb project like trying to scrub the Panamanian mildew off the wall with lye."

"We lived on an island and could get there only by boat. All the food had to come from town and you had to write up a long list of groceries which would come three days later, or you could order from the PX, but the milk would be spoiled by the time it got there. So it was housekeeping under the most difficult circumstances, made much worse because I didn't know what I was doing anyway."

"So, how did you manage?" I asked.

"Oh, I just did the best I could." Mary Cook grinned. "I should have gone to cooking school, as well as housekeeping school.

"I remember a friend at our post in New Jersey taught me how to use an automatic washing machine. You don't have to know very much to run one," she admitted, "but afterwards I wanted to go home and go to bed. But the phone rang, and my friend said we were invited to play bridge in the afternoon. My mouth dropped; I thought after doing all this laundry one didn't recoup that fast, that it used up your day."

"A lot of women still feel that way," I said.

"Oh, yes," Mary Cook agreed. "It is a set of mind. But," she laughed, "in the end we went and played bridge."

By the end of fifteen years of army life she had moved nineteen times; she summed up the whole problem for women who follow their husbands as they are transferred about in their careers: "You keep breaking off your own life."

By the time she was in her forties, the changing quality of life generally after World War II, the changes in her private life caused by her husband's early retirement, by family illnesses, and a strained budget, resulted in a feeling of loss of identity and frustration. Unable to deal directly with these feelings, she began to strike out into activities outside these family matters. In civics and politics, she found a natural field for her talents and began to take heart that she could be a personage in her own right.

But, hard as it was for me to imagine now, Mary Cook insisted that she still had an inadequate self-image when she was a mature woman in her early forties.

Her first independent political action was to propose a

community swimming pool, an idea she originated that is now widespread in Northern Virginia. A lack of natural outdoor play space for her son sparked her concern. In making a presentation of the project to the Arlington County Board she "almost fainted." But she found she had an instinct and flair for politics that she did not have for housekeeping and cooking. She became president of the Arlington Civic Federation and found that the order and decorum required by Roberts Rules suited her way of dealing with issues.

She found herself involved in an aptitude test, given by Dr. William Morgan and his British wife, Antonia. "Because they were just starting out in their new business venture, the amount I paid them was actually very small, but to me it was an enormous amount. It is now more common for women to expect to invest family funds in their future, but then it almost seemed frivolous," she said. "I had no idea how such tests were conducted, so I earnestly told them everything I knew." She was astonished at the finding that she had an unusual aptitude for law.

"What was your reaction?"

"Well, I was terribly upset. I couldn't think about it without getting hot in the face; I really had an emotional reaction."

For three months Mary Cook was so upset by the discovery that she couldn't think coherently about it. Then in the next three months she slowly began to let her mind play with the notion of doing something about it.

Finally, she had a conference with the dean of the Washington College of Law at American University. Since she had no undergraduate credits, he queried her on a broad range of topics and asked questions, such as if she were cast away on a desert island which single book would she take with her. In the end he said that if she would try college for one year she might be considered for enrollment at the law school – considered only.

That was enough for Mary Cook. Not letting herself look too closely at the odds against her making it all the way to a law degree, she enrolled in American University for her freshman year of college. She took classes which interested her, and found herself energized by all of them. One, on how to edit a small city newspaper, so excited her that she took a semester off to establish a very politically successful, if short-lived, weekly newspaper in Arlington, with Anne Crutcher as editor.

Finally Mary Cook was admitted to the Washington College of Law as a special student with the stipulation she would never receive a law degree because she had no college degree, but if she passed all the courses (which the new dean obviously doubted she would) she would be certified to take the Virginia Bar Exam. Certainly not much encouragement in that arrangement, or from any other quarter. "Except from my mother, of course," smiled Mary Cook, "who believed that all things were possible. She thought if I wanted it so badly I would be able to do it." Her husband, who in the meantime had earned a graduate degree in physics, uncomplainingly paid her tuition.

The first semester Mary Cook did not take a note. "It was like watching television," she said. "All the things I ever wanted to know. Contracts I found fascinating; I loved the intricacies of real estate law; criminal law was horrifying."

The evanescent quality of the law interested her; while fundamental concepts seemed as fixed as the Rock of Gibraltar, when applied to a particular case, the concepts expanded or contracted to fit a myriad of varying fact patterns. The law restlessly moved about, adjusting relationships between people, between governments, and between people and government. The deep moral and ethical overtones of law, proclaiming those acts which are restrained because they are inherently bad, are interlaced with practical considerations, restraining other acts as a mere matter of regulation.

She worked hard, won her case in moot court and won the class award in constitutional law. The dean called Mary Cook in to tell her that she could rent her cap and gown. So, she received her diploma after all, an LL.B. degree, later elevated to a Jurat Doctor degree, from American University. The day she took her last exam some of her friends took her to lunch at a Washington restaurant. "We all got high," Mary Cook said, "right in the middle of the day, and I staggered home triumphant."

Throughout law school, Mary Cook found support through the network of her legal sorority, Kappa Beta Phi. The Kappas held a reception each spring which was attended by every woman judge in the metropolitan area, all of whom were Kappa sisters. "Role models?" I suggested. "Yes," said Mary Cook, "my eyes would just bulge at the sight of these important women who had made it in the law." The decline of sororities, she thinks, is a loss.

Another important influence on Mary Cook was her association with Ira Gabrielson, the retired head of the U.S. Fish and Wildlife Service. They had each been appointed by their respective boards of supervisors to represent the public interest on the Northern Virginia Regional Park Authority; he became the chairman of the Park Authority and she the vice-chairman. "Gabe" was sixty-nine years old when Mary Cook met him, and, she said, "one of the smartest men I ever knew." When he traveled, as he did extensively in his efforts to save wild animals around the world, Mary Cook was the acting chairman of the Park Authority. The purpose of the authority was to create regional parks, an endeavor that entailed enlisting help from both the private and the public sectors. "It filled my capabilities – exactly," Mary Cook declared; she had the great pleasure of succeeding at a job she wanted to do. From "Gabe" she learned lessons about human motivation and political strategy never taught in classrooms. She served as vice-chairman of the Park Authority for eleven years, and is now one of their legal counsel.

Thus Mary Cook's legal and political interests ran in tandem for several years. She was very active politically – in Democratic campaigns and in the local nonpartisan politics.

But her heart was increasingly with the Law. Lois Miller, a sorority sister in private practice in Fairfax County, took her into a courtroom and let her sit at the counsel table for a jury trial, which is the essence of the practice of law. She thought, "I could do that; it would be hard, but I could do it."

"Of course," she noted with a little laugh, "it was a while before I got a chance, because you can't practice law without a client.

"But I had discovered that the courtroom, in which there are rules, is my forum. Virginia courts are very decorous. No shouting, no screaming. Each gets his turn to present evidence and arguments. Brute force gets no advantage."

When Mary Cook passed the bar, she bought her big desk, a fourteen-dollar Bank-of-England chair, some law books, and just sat down. "I never asked anyone for a job; who would give *me* a job?" She was fifty-one. A realtor friend asked if she would handle a zoning case. Mary Cook said, "Yes, of course." "Yes" is the most used word in her vocabulary. With the thousand-dollar retainer fee she rented one room for a law office. The rent was one hundred dollars a month, the phone thirty dollars and her law books cost fifty dollars.

Who were her clients?

"I didn't have many. Oh, friends would send their servants to me, on cases which were non-moneymakers," Mary Cook laughed heartily, without rancor.

"For a long time I practiced people law. Just whatever problems people had, because that was the kind of client I got."

An attorney friend she had worked with in Arlington politics went on vacation shortly after Mary Cook opened her office. He left instructions that the first two cases that came into his office be referred to Mary Cook, and they turned out to be both interesting and profitable. By word of mouth her reputation began to grow. Although in those first few years her gross income ran no more than two thousand to four thousand dollars per year, Mary Cook's commitment to the practice of the law was total. Eagerly, with dazzling speed and clarity, she outlined some of her most interesting cases for me. She sees them as puzzles to be solved. "Land is probably the most intricate of law cases and I like it best because of that," she said. "Taxation is a must in the modern world, and everybody does Wills and Estates. I also handle divorce cases, but the only pleasure I get out of that is helping people to rearrange their lives after a marital breakup."

A few years ago a sorority sister asked Mary Cook to handle her personal injury case, because, as she said, she believed in women lawyers. (Her husband was somewhat skeptical.) She was suing for damages suffered in an automobile accident. Tension was high while the two women waited for the jury verdict; then the foreman came out and read, "We find for the plaintiff in the amount of ninety thousand dollars."

"You must have fainted," I exclaimed.

"Neither of us changed expressions," Mary Cook said, "until we got out of the courthouse. We wanted to appear blasé. Then we went into a state of euphoria."

By this time Mary Cook was firmly established. "The best compliment is when the client on the opposite, losing side of a case recommends me – saying 'I know a good lawyer, but not mine.'" Mary Cook laughed.

"But, to go back," I said. "It never occurred to me that you would have to operate so long at what almost amounted to expenses."

"It's partly our fault as women," she mused. "Our lower expectations. And some people expect to pay a woman less. They think we're in it as a hobby."

"Then fees, attitudes about money, are at the core of a professional woman's problems in getting started?"

"Yes. Definitely." Mary Cook concurred. "It was several years before my income had leveled out so I no longer worried about paying my bills. Eventually my hourly rates rose to the level of other attorneys of similar ability and experience, and my income now is almost as predictable as if I were in the business of selling nuts and bolts."

Because Lois Miller had been so good to her earlier, Mary Cook has let it be known that she will talk to any woman law graduates when they are trying to decide what to do. One of the many who have sought her advice was Amanda Ellis. She watched Mandy in the courts and once in a while they met, as Mary Cook said, "To live it up – tell our 'war stories' and enjoy our successes and admit our errors."

Now Mandy and Mary Cook's son, Emory, Jr., have become partners with her in the firm of Hackman, Ellis &

Hackman, Ltd. Recently Emory began addressing her as "Mary Cook." "I really prefer 'Mother,'" Mary Cook said, "but I swallowed it. You can't remain static."

So, even though she had such a late start, Mary Cook Hackman has arrived. She has been admitted to practice before the United States Supreme Court, the United States District Court of the Eastern District of Virginia, the United States Tax Court, and the Supreme Court of Virginia.

Besides all the hard work, how did she do it?

"I don't know." Mary Cook considered the question carefully. "It would be nice if I were to say to you, 'Yes, I had those aptitude tests and said to myself, "In ten years I'm going to be a successful lawyer."' It's not the way it goes. You struggle and you wait to see how it's going to come out."

"Is it power, too?" I asked.

"Yes. No question."

"The satisfaction of power used well?"

"Yes. But it is also the puzzle fascination. Piecing together the case and winning it. Whether by negotiation or by trial, it is fascinating."

Sometimes Mary Cook and my neighbor Anne Crutcher talk about what they miss by being full-time workers. When they analyze it, they decide that what they are missing are only the things they don't really want to do anyway.

People sometimes remark that it is too bad she did not know of her aptitude when she was young, but she feels that she has had the best of both ends of her life. She had the fun of those happy and carefree prewar years, and she had the excitement of beginning the second half century of her life by becoming a struggling "young" lawyer.

She pushed back her chair and walked me down to her library – three walls lined floor to ceiling with thick, leather-bound law books. I could imagine Mary Cook here, by herself, flipping through those well-known volumes, reading until her "eyes dropped out," searching for precedents like a shrewd detective, piecing her case together like an intricate puzzle, chuckling to herself as she saw it take shape – an honorable woman who has found the work she loves.

6. An Unaffiliated Scholar

CHRIS PROUTY ROSENFELD

"When women are enjoying themselves, the pot scorches."

ETHIOPIAN PROVERB

From a patchwork life of moving (eleven times; five different countries) and of mothering (four children), Chris Rosenfeld has wrested a vocation that gives her the deepest pleasure. She is an independent, unaffiliated scholar. For her, a state of bliss is to be able to perch at a desk all day under the vaulted ceiling of some great library, picking her way through an Italian government report or a French memoir in search of tidbits about the Ethiopian Empress T'aitu – seemingly a strange idea of happiness for a woman as gregarious and vivacious as Chris.

But for the true scholar, research is not a placid occupation; the life of the mind is exceedingly active. "To find something you have been looking for must be as exciting as winning a legal case in court," Chris says. "In the vicinity of a library, my whole psyche charges up. My heart beats faster. My pulse quickens. It's all I can do to wait until my books are delivered to my desk."

Her life has not always centered around libraries. Chris was in her late forties when she took a course on Modern Ethiopian History. In it the professor described a developmental period for Ethiopia and mentioned that the emperor's wife, T'aitu, was a strong empress who, for some time, had actually been a de facto ruler. Intrigued by this passing reference, Chris decided to write her term paper on the empress.

Now, eight years later, Chris Rosenfeld is a recognized scholar in the field of Ethiopian Studies.

She does not have a master's degree or a doctorate attached to her name. But, for making a contribution to the field of African history, she was nominated by a committee of the African Studies Association for the prestigious Herskovits Award. Chris's contribution was her 280-page *Chronology of Menilek II, Emperor of Ethiopia, 1889–1913,* published by the African Studies Center of Michigan State University. It is now used as a textbook at Howard University in Washington, D.C. In 1973 she delivered a paper on Empress T'aitu at the first conference on Ethiopian studies to be convened in the United States. Subsequently she was invited to give a paper at the African Studies Association's annual meeting in Houston. Her topic was *Eight Women of the Zemene Mesafint (1795– 1855),* and in late 1978 she presented another paper to the association titled *Menilek's Medical History: A Case of Medical Diplomacy*, which is to be published as a monograph by the Munger Africana Library at the California Institute of Technology. And she has written two biographical entries for Volume One of *The Dictionary of African Biography.*

This is an impressive list of credits for a woman who, in mid-life, stumbled into the world of scholarship without the required paraphernalia for travel in academic circles. But pure joy propels her, and that is the most reliable fuel there is for success.

When I met Chris it seemed to me that her whole life was organized around her research on Empress T'aitu. "This very often is the case," she told me. "A strong, complex personality grabs you and then you stalk around it. And you find yourself in a garden of other delights. I couldn't have a more recondite subject than an empress of Ethiopia, but the world in which she lived was a fascinating one and worth telling people about."

Early one evening a short time later, I was dashing out of the British Museum Library when I recognized the tall, dark-haired, athletic figure of Chris rushing down the steps ahead of me. Both of us were late getting home to fix dinner for our families, so we decided to share a taxi. I was weary from looking up material for a magazine article. Chris was in contrastingly high spirits from her day's research. As we rode up Oxford Street she regaled me, in her marvelously dramatic voice, with stories of "her" empress and the international intrigues of her times.

Caught up by her enthusiasm, I said that I wished I had a woman of my own to write about.

"Well, get yourself one," Chris replied in her brisk, matter-of-fact manner. "It's not that difficult."

It was not and I did. "What do you think of the subject of Victorian women travelers?" I asked Chris on the telephone.

"Splendid," she said. And before I knew it, she and I were off to Paris in search of documents, two middle-aged women with briefcases and books, traveling on the cheap. We took a bus from Victoria Station in London to a tiny airfield in Kent, then boarded a DC–3 to hop across the English Channel. Both of us were old hands at travel, but we were as excited as kids on their first trip to France because we were on our own in chase of information about women lost in the labyrinth of history.

The next day Chris went to the French Foreign Office Archives on the Quai d'Orsay and I went to the Bibliothèque Nationale. In the evening I sat waiting at our rendezvous-point in an inexpensive cafe on the Rue Saint Jacques. I was sipping a glass of red house wine when Chris rushed in breath-less, her face aglow.

"I found it!" she exclaimed, sinking into the chair opposite me.

"Found what?"

"Well," Chris took a deep breath and composed herself. "For the past four years I have been looking for a pamphlet titled, *Le Docteur Nouvellement Venu*, which Empress T'aitu had ordered written. It was printed in Amharic and French in Ethiopia in 1909. And it is the only document that can be credited in that way to her. I tried everywhere. I've written many libraries, British and American, even the Vatican Library. So there I was today in the French Foreign Office Archives in pursuit of other material and came upon a letter from the French ambassador to Ethiopia which said, "I am enclosing a pamphlet recently issued here." Chris paused dramatically, lit a cigarette, grinned, and said in a hoarse stage whisper, "And there it was!"

We both whooped with delight. People stared at us from other tables. Oblivious to them, Chris went on with her story. "Here I was in this room full of silent heads bent over piles of documents. I wanted to scream out, 'I found it! I found it!' But I couldn't. In tremendous agitation I looked about and saw a man get up and walk out. So I followed him. But he was gone when I reached the elevator. The indicator showed the elevator in the basement, where I knew there was a coffee machine. Down I went, and there he was. I got my coffee then turned to him – I was too excited to speak French – 'Can I tell you that I just found something that I've been looking for for four years?' And he said, 'Bien sur, Madame, I too am drinking coffee because I have just found a jewel long sought.'"

Researchers aid and encourage each other. But Chris still finds not having a graduate degree imposes a tremendous handicap on her. We agreed that it is not an easy task to launch and sustain a profession portable enough to survive the frequent moves made at the dictates of our husbands' professions rather than our own timing.

The waiter brought our first course, Chris stubbed out her cigarette, and I started asking her questions about herself. "One of my problems," she said, "is not being able to keep abreast of what is going on in my field. So I join professional associations to get their bulletins announcing when things are going to happen. Things which ordinarily are talked about in the African Studies Department of a university, I have to learn through newsletters, and I have to make applications to conferences on my own, and pay my own way.

"But," she explained, "I'm too impatient at this point to go back for my degree. I would have to study a lot of things that I'm not interested in. It wouldn't hurt me, but I can't afford the time. I would love to be in a university setup because talking things over with people is marvelous, the exchange of ideas, but I just won't take the time. In some parts of the United States, I could get academic credit for the work I've already done, but I haven't been in the right place at the right time."

Because Chris is married to a foreign service officer, the style of her life has been determined by where she lived. "But absolutely no regrets on that score," she insisted. It is obvious that Chris possesses a saving talent for turning her trials into adventures that become the material for the tales she tells so well. From a one-parent family she emerged a confident woman able to thrive in almost any environment.

"Not really one-parent," she elaborated. "Often eighteen parents." Chris Prouty was born in El Monte, California, in 1921. Her mother died when she was four years old. She and her sister were each taken in by a different aunt; her brother was placed in a home for boys. Their father died six years later.

"I felt no particular concern over being an orphan," Chris declared. "My aunt was a concerned mother and I was the center of her world. She was an unmarried schoolteacher and she thought everything I did was marvelous. So I had a very supportive childhood. Aunt Mabel and her friends played bridge, had their clubs and professional associations, and took trips together. There was always this circle of women. All women. None had children, so I was the one. On Valentine's Day I would get forty valentines. At Easter, eighteen Easter baskets. Whenever I went into a new class at school, the teacher already knew me. In this milieu, of course, I became a quick reader, a good student. They fostered that. My idea of fun in the summer was to play in the backyard with dolls and a math workbook, working problems just for fun. They gave me reading books with questions at the end, not in any self-conscious way, but just because I liked them. They gave me plenty of books. And I responded to all this attention."

The Church of the Disciples of Christ was an integral part of Chris's upbringing. "It espoused a very simple Christianity," she said. "No ritual. No heavy costuming. Not at all fundamentalist. Just very moral. We all went to the Wednesday night prayer meeting. I think my aunts went because it was a cheap supper after a hard working day. We had a nice meal and heard a speech. The Church had a strong missionary movement. People came from Africa or South America or

India and gave us slide shows. It really did make us conscious of economic circumstances in other places in the world.

"I went to church on Sunday mornings and the Christian Endeavor meetings for young people on Sunday evenings almost up to the day I left for College."

Antioch College in Ohio was "back East" for Chris, and there, she said, she "just found better things to do on Sundays. College became too fascinating. Dormitory life was fantastic. All of these people from all those parts of the U.S.! And I certainly appreciated the freedom. Being able to do whatever, whenever, was just too heady for words. I had become quite a deceptive person living at home. I had started to smoke and drink beer and curse. Those were verboten. So I had to conceal my "sins." It takes a lot of time to lie your way out of things. It was a relief not to have to anymore."

Antioch's work/study program gave Chris the opportunity to hold a variety of jobs in different cities. "But the career guidance was not Antioch's thing," she said. "The work/study program was supposed to let you explore whatever field you wanted. However, the trouble and the virtue of that experience was that it was a process of elimination. In my work experience, I eliminated everything that I had wanted to be. I ran through merchandising, advertising, and social work. The orientation at Antioch was to explore feelings about yourself and what kind of a person you wanted to be. Simple. You wanted to be a good person and do things to make the world better. How you would go about it was not very clear. So I took a major in sociology and a minor in drama. I was very active in the theater, and in my last year I was the first woman selected to be the community manager at Antioch, a paid job. I loved every minute of college. But I had no idea of what I would do with that major in sociology."

World War II had begun when Chris graduated from college. She went to Washington, D.C., with seven other Antiochian women, where they set up a household. One of the women helped her get a job on Senator Kilgore's Subcommittee on War Mobilization. For three months, while waiting for the paperwork to clear, she worked as a waitress.

"A household of eight women attracted a lot of men," Chris recalled. "It was obvious to us that Washington was buzzing with every nationality and that they, and the people pouring in from New York, didn't have enough to do for entertainment. So we helped to form the Washington Workshop, on a film, dance, and concert kind of formula. We put on plays for nonsegregated audiences in what was then a tightly segregated city, and we held classes. I taught a drama class and produced a play. I worked for the subcommittee during the day and for the workshop at night. It was a very exciting life."

When Eugene Rosenfeld asked Chris to marry him, she decided she "liked him a lot, liked him *really* a lot," and somehow the proposal was irresistible. "I guess that's love." She was twenty-three years old and remembers, "I knew I wanted to marry and have children someday. But that I would marry so soon after college came as a surprise. I didn't feel compelled to marry by a specific age. It was just that I was not a popular-with-men kind of girl, and was amazed at being asked."

Once Chris was married, the idea of preparing for some definite profession rarely came up. "Though I took a stab at getting a master's degree in psychology – twelve credits of required undergraduate courses – going to India ended that." Her children were her first priority; neither she nor Gene considered having anyone other than her look after them. "That's just the kind of people we were. We assumed that the man went out to work and the woman looked after the children, and produced the rest of the show on the money he earned. I liked it." Necessarily adaptable and fortunately delighted with her pick-up-and-move-on life, Chris followed Gene to London, back to New York, on to India, Tanzania, Ethiopia, and London again, with Washington breaking up these assignments.

"But," Chris said, "I always looked for something to do outside of the ordinary pleasures of diplomatic life. I don't want to kid anyone about that: they were pleasures. I was not restless or impatient about heavy social demands; it just had to be supplemented with something all my own."

Overseas, Chris became deeply involved in amateur theater work. In New Delhi she directed an American play and helped produce several others. When in Washington, "I took classes – that well-known anodyne for housemaid's knee – sculpture, dance, picture framing, or whatever the adult education programs were offering in the community. Nothing intellectual."

Then, on the recommendation of a newspaper friend, Chris was hired for a short-term research job by CBS. She was to read everything on "life at the White House," from John Adams to the present, in search of dramatic incidents. The project was for Jacqueline Kennedy's television program on a tour of the White House. CBS wanted a non-professional with a fresh view and a sense of theater. And it was agreed that she could work flexible hours when her children were in school.

"I'm sure that newspaperman thought of me because of my amateur theater work," Chris surmised. "When the job was over it occurred to me, here I am the possessor of all this material. I'll write a book about it. I saw the fate of the researcher. You've done this work, you get a little credit for it, but someone else creates. But I was a babe in the woods. I knew the material was worth something, but I didn't have the moxie to do something with it. Two other people, who knew what they were doing, did. Anyway, as it worked out, doing anything turned out to be impossible because we moved out again.

"Nevertheless," Chris said with throaty emphasis, "*it was a seed experience!* The whole notion of historical research really grabbed me at that time. I was just ga-ga!" She lit another cigarette. "History *was* more incredible than fiction! Each incident that I read about opened another door. It was thrilling. An ambition began to take hold of me: what I would really like to do is know all there is about a subject and write a book on it. But just how that was to be done, who it would be, and so on . . ." Her voice trailed off. "Anyway, we went to Dar-es-Salaam, Tanzania."

There Chris directed the first play written and performed

by Africans in Dar-es-Salaam, and also worked for a short time as an assistant to the director of a big festival celebrating Tanzania's independence.

"But soon an antiwhite foreigner campaign came down," Chris recounted, "and further work was out the window. So I decided to find out the derivation of all the street names in Dar-es-Salaam. I just had to do something. I got a pack of three- by five-inch cards and made a list of all the streets and started through them. It did offer a bit of interesting history as well as an introduction to Swahili. But mostly, I relaxed and had a good time.

"Then, bang! We were ordered to proceed immediately to Ethiopia. I was heartbroken. We flew from the sea-level blue of Dar to a highland, inland kingdom. A drastically different environment. Addis Ababa is beautifully set beneath some mountains but littered with ugly buildings. As soon as the boys had left for school, I cried and I cried and I cried. Dar-es-Salaam had been so extraordinarily beautiful. You live your life, going and coming, doing everything, in view of the Indian Ocean. You smell jasmine and oleander and magnificent fish are brought to your door and you pick bananas and mangoes from trees. It was a divine life. Aside from the wrench of leaving friends, packing, uprooting the children from school, and having no warm clothes for seven-thousand-feet altitude, we had no wheels for three months because the car was dropped from a very high crane on the dock in Dar-es-Salaam. I rode the occasionally workable public transport and a lot of rickety taxicabs to buy food and procure the needful to establish a home, but it was a hellish adjustment. I would look out of the windows of our house onto the Addis Ababa Police College, which was the color of a donkey, instead of the Indian Ocean, and tears would roll. Finally I stopped." Here Chris mimicked her own no-nonsense voice. "I said to myself, 'It's all right to cry and be miserable. You are not having a big emotional crackup, you're just reacting to something that is true. You are miserable. It's been a rotten shock. O.K., pull yourself together.' So I signed on for a course at the university on Modern Ethiopian History, just to learn where I was.

"That, of course, was where I first heard of Empress T'aitu. All references to her were about what a bad, evil person she was: cruel, greedy, killed people, and poisoned her ex-husband. This type of historical person about whom there are only negative traces fascinates me. There must be something more to her story. The second term I was deeply involved with Empress T'aitu and discovered that the material was very rich. It was also apparent that this material was in French, Italian, German, Arabic, Amharic, English, and Russian. I could do the French myself, but not too well. So I spent my time at diplomatic parties finding someone to help me translate. I found the Italian wife of an American and the German wife of the Chilean ambassador, among others. I thought I would just go on doing this, not realizing that expecting translators to do something for nothing is asking rather a lot. Of course, in Addis Ababa many of the diplomatic women didn't have too much to do anyway. My history professor translated Amharic for me. It didn't really dawn on me what a tiger I had by the tail. But it had dawned on me that a black heroine was a good idea for a book because America had gotten into black history; black studies were just getting started. So I actually wrote two hundred pages of what I thought was a book. Took notes furiously, without any system or viewpoint. But I had written eight chapters," Chris laughed ruefully.

"Other people by this time were beginning to say it was a very good idea. Other people being mainly Richard Pankhurst (who was the director of the Institute of Ethiopian Studies in Addis Ababa and, incidentally, the son of suffragette Sylvia Pankhurst). I was beginning to make contacts with Ethiopian historians. I was still trying to crib information from them in conversations. Thinking, it's not such a big problem to write the story of this woman. 'Do you know the name of her third husband?' You know, stuff like that. I slowly sensed, however, that there was more serious work involved. Getting back to the States, I began going to the Library of Congress and researching systematically, confident that I would have a grip on the source material any minute." Chris shook her head and said flatly, "I didn't know what I was doing! The source material was infinite!"

"But I did know by now that I had to master Italian. I could not fool around with other people's notes. I continued studying Italian when we were posted to London. For one vacation we went to Florence and took a British Institute intensive course and lived with an Italian family for three weeks. Gene studied too. He took beginning, I took intermediate. Within the year Italian was buttoned up for purposes of research, anyway, provided a dictionary was at hand. I still rely on generous friends for German and Russian.

"One of my illusions was that all I had to do was collect all the references to this woman and string them together in chronological order. Of course, when you are writing a biography, the principal problem is to put the individual into her milieu, into her culture, into her political moment. So, after having done three years of research on the life of this empress, I then had to tackle the history of Ethiopia, and that doesn't mean just between her birth date and her death date, but all the sixteen centuries before! You have to know what were the attitudes about women, what were their customs? Were there other women like her or was she unique? So I embarked on this very difficult field – Ethiopian history."

Since that time, scholarly research and writing have become the central passion of Chris's life. She corresponds with Ethiopian scholars all over the world, and is scrupulously accurate about her research. Recently a Soviet diplomat knocked on her front door to deliver to her photostated copies of some hard-to-get diplomatic documents sent by the Academy of Sciences in Moscow.

"I am accepted now as an independent scholar," Chris smiled broadly. "Not just a researcher, but a scholar. The first question you are asked at a conference is, what is your academic connection? I made a joke for awhile and would answer that I was from the Eugene Rosenfeld Foundation. People took it perfectly seriously. Their greedy ears peaked: 'Where are they?' I said, 'It belongs to my husband. He supports my efforts.'" She shook her finger at me. "I can't emphasize often enough that I am only able to do this work because of my financial security. I think of Gene's money as half mine. I participated in the earning of it so I feel fully entitled to half of it. I couldn't do what I'm doing on a limited-time grant even if I could get one – grant givers are degree-obsessed. The nature of my research isn't like that."

After our talk in Paris I thought a lot about Chris's adamant stand on her right to half of Gene's salary. Intellectually I agreed with her position. And certainly the foreign service institutionalized the old-fashioned husband/wife team attitude by expecting us to perform certain social duties and a wide array of other backup services, such as being on permanent standby to meet congressmen's wives or other dignitaries at airports, take them shopping or provide psychological Band-Aids, or just to see the local sights. And certain standards were set for us to lead exemplary lives. Our performance in all of these areas was evaluated in written form in the efficiency reports on our husbands. Two for the price of one was a foreign service shibboleth that is no longer true; the rules have changed. But in our day, maverick wives ran the risk of ruining their husbands' careers.

Never receiving, in one's own name, a paycheck for services rendered subtly undercuts many wives' sense of worth. A few years later, when Chris and I were back in Washington again, I asked her if she still felt like a full partner financially in her marriage. Brave as her words were, Chris did confess to periods of alternate rage and despair whenever Gene, probably egged on by the seductive dream of a second income, suggests that she is throwing herself away on such a non-paying project. And like most wives, she is often stung by the acute embarrass-ment of not having any money of her own. But Chris stead-fastly holds to the terms with which she and Gene embarked on their marriage. Now that Gene has retired and they have settled in Washington, D.C., she feels that she has the right to pursue her own vocation full-time. And it is not as if she were able to walk away from her old working life. Although Gene now lends a hand, it is still Chris who manages the house, doing the cleaning, shopping, and cooking herself. She arranges their active social life, too, though in that area, Chris, from long practice, is adept at informality and a minimum of fuss. Both she and Gene are people-oriented. They play tennis and bridge, go to the theater, concerts, and art shows.

An ideal summer day for Chris begins at six-thirty in the morning, when the house is quiet. She reads magazines such as the *Atlantic* or *American Film*, which she does not allow herself to look at later in the day. Coffee and the morning paper take her until eight o'clock, when the outdoor swimming pool a block away opens. After a quick ten laps in the pool, she is at her typewriter by eight-thirty.

During the day, she may be translating French or Italian sources, typing and arranging notes, or writing and rewriting. About every one and a half hours she takes a ten-to-fifteen-minute break – still thinking about her work, but doing something physical such as mopping the kitchen floor, vacuuming around the dining room, or just shredding cabbage for coleslaw. Almost all her cleaning and cooking chores are accomplished during these short breaks.

At one o'clock she dips into the pool for another ten lengths, comes home to lunch alone, and thinks about what to prepare for dinner. Since Gene's retirement, Chris feels it is doubly important that they minimize their time together during the day, so they stay on separate schedules. Back at her typewriter by about quarter to two, Chris works until four or four-thirty, when she breaks off, refiles her papers, and organizes her next day. Knowing what she is going to do on the following day is the essence of continuity and progress for her. She may write personal letters and do correspondence related to her work, but more often she is too tired even to read. A crossword puzzle, or a game of Scrabble with a friend, or, if it is not too hot, a set of tennis, revives her.

At six or so, she puts either a record of Bill Evans, the jazz pianist, or the music of *A Chorus Line* on the hi-fi, and has a glass of white wine. She and Gene may watch the news on television or go to an early movie. They prefer to eat afterward, about seven-thirty or eight o'clock.

After dinner, Chris reads one of the books from her four

foot stack of pending reading material. Generally it is a biography, usually one about a woman, preferably a royal one, although she is devoted to detective stories and will read them as well as the occasional novel. By ten-thirty or eleven she is asleep. In the winter she does not swim; she hates indoor pools. So she has taken up tap dancing for fun and exercise.

Of course, few days work out that smoothly. Sometimes she wakes up late and feels behind schedule all day. When her typewriter breaks down, she is in a frenzy.

And then there are the inevitable interruptions: even grown-up children have problems, and there are crises, such as Gene's two bouts with cancerous tumors, mercifully treatable and now in remission.

"Even though this book seems to be taking forever, I am not going to give up!" Chris exclaimed. "I find it terrifically stimulating to do something that is hard for me. I adore this work. I have to force myself to get away from it. I know it is good for me; I come back with fresh insights. But I never want to go on a vacation unless it's near one of the world's great libraries. It's too painful to be cut off."

When Chris was asked recently to write a *Historical Dictionary of Ethiopia,* to be published in a series on African countries, she persuaded Gene to sign on with her: she directs the research and he writes up each of the alphabetical entries. "Gene used to be a bit bored with all my talk about Ethiopia," Chris grimaced. "But the last dinner party we went to with some Ethiopians, *he* began arguing with them, citing historical precedents for some of their recent problems. So now he is hooked as well." She laughed with delight over the arrangement she had worked out. Her partnership with Gene abides, but now it is her work that is setting their pace.

7. A Scientist Come Lately

VERONICA KILGOUR

" . . . a life spent in the routine of science need not destroy the attractive human element of a woman's nature."

ANNIE JUMP CANNON
Science, June 20, 1911

"Grandmother Facing a Career Test in New York," headlined a feature in the London *Daily Telegraph*. "Slim, vital, and white-haired, Veronica Kilgour is a grandmother twelve times over," I read before my friend Mary Grant interrupted me.

"Veronica, now, is a genuine late bloomer for you," Mary said. "I've known her for years, long before she began working in tropical medicine. When she was taking her degree, she did her six months' practical work as a dietician at the Middlesex Hospital. I'm nearby, so she would bed down with me the odd night she wanted to stay in for lectures. Hers is a very interesting story, because she did not start her academic work until she was nearly fifty."

A decade later, in 1977, when she was sixty, Veronica Kilgour, Research Fellow at the London School of Hygiene and Tropical Medicine, delivered her first paper as an invited speaker to the International Congress of Photozoology meeting in New York. She had spoken before to scientific assemblies in Britain, and submitted papers at other international conferences, but this was the first time a request had come from a conference committee to her when the meeting was first being planned. As a specialist in research on trypanosomiasis, a form of sleeping sickness prevalent in large parts of the world, her work increasingly brings her into contact with scientists from many other countries.

In 1974 and again in 1975, she made three-month field trips

to Africa with Dr. David Godfrey, head of her group at the London School of Hygiene and Tropical Medicine, to collect and examine blood samples from cattle in order to distinguish between various strains of cattle trypanosomiasis. Cattle production could be as important in Nigeria and throughout central and southern Africa as it is in Texas except for this killing disease. She began working with Dr. Godfrey first at the Lister Institute, where his interest in the inhibitory effect of an antibody to the enzyme ALAT (alanine aminotransferase) led to the discovery that there were many recognizably different forms within a species of this debilitating and often fatal disease. Morphologically, it had not been possible to determine the difference between some kinds of trypanosomiasis that infected humans from those that infected only animals – to isolate the strain that caused a chronic disease from that which produced a very acute disease. Dr. Godfrey asked Veronica Kilgour to work on the problem, and subsequently they were able to show a genuine biochemical marker for the chronic strain.

In 1977 she was invited to teach this technique of identification to scientists in Brazil. It is applicable to other tropical diseases in which protozoa are concerned as well as to trypanosomiasis. Over a period of ten weeks she traveled thousands of miles to universities and research institutes in Brazil.

Not in her wildest imaginings could Veronica Kilgour have projected such a career for herself when she began thinking seriously about applying for admittance to a university when the youngest of her four children was eighteen. She had matriculated in nonscientific subjects from a girl's high school in 1933, but had been unable to go to a university.

"If I'd been free to choose when I was young, I'd have gone into maths," Veronica told me later as we sat drinking tea in Mary's sitting room. "But there was simply no money available for me to go to university, and not many women went, in any case." So she did not take the British qualifying examinations, called A-levels, which are necessary for entrance to university.

As the *Telegraph* reported, Veronica Kilgour is a most

attractive, animated woman, small and well-groomed, with an air of quiet competence. When she was seventeen, her mother decided that Veronica should study domestic science. This decision was based on practical experience: when her parents' marriage broke up, Veronica's mother, for the first time in her life, had to become aquainted with her stove and other mundane matters of household maintenance. Handicapped as she was by lack of training or experience, she wished better for her daughter. So Veronica studied for her teaching certificate in domestic services at Battersea Polytechnic.

"I had to go to a chemistry course there," Veronica said, "and I had never touched chemistry in my life. This was 1935ish, and our teacher was insistent that we should know the atomic theory at that time. Quite extraordinary! The model she gave us was a very good one for a background of the atomic theory that I had to know when I came to do chemistry in 1967 – thirty years on.

"It was the scientific part of the domestic science course that I found really interested me. But I taught for nearly two years and married and that was that. Women had to resign teaching when they married. I had a child the first year and the war began."

Veronica did not mention it, but I remember vividly that at the onset of World War II, the invasion of England by German forces was a daily probability, fighting on beaches and front lawns an imminent specter. With the Battle of Britain there were bombings, deaths, dislocations of families, shortages of food and material goods, rationing. Then came the campaign for North Africa and the invasion of Europe, leaving Britain an exhausted and penniless victor.

Like all Britons, Veronica simply carried on through the war and after, raising her family, doing, as she said, "various mild voluntary work – administrative jobs, secretary of the Workers' Education Association, the Bach Society – and taking courses."

"But you wouldn't have wanted to go on doing that for another twenty to thirty years," Mary interjected.

"No, I wouldn't have. But I do miss not having these

contacts now. And I very much enjoyed my life at the time. But I realized that I wasn't going to be terribly happy once the last of the children had left home.

"My original idea was to go into some sort of social service," she said, "on the grounds that it would be sensible: something would open to me in voluntary work if I had some background, some real knowledge.

"There was to be a new university eighteen miles from where I lived, which would be quite easy for me to get to. This, it seemed to me, was the place I could go to and still manage to keep some semblance of home and house and so on, going. So I wrote to the University of Surrey, to the Department of Social Sciences, explaining what I wanted to do, and asking if they were interested.

"About three months later I'd had no reply, so I thought, if you ask a silly question, you deserve a silly – rather, no answer. But in the meantime I'd seen listed a particular course on nutrition which seemed to me could tie in a little bit with my domestic science background. The children had said to me when they knew that I wanted to be in the social sciences, well, why not get into the university in anything that isn't popular, then once you're in, if you're not happy with the course, the university will usually change to what you want. And I had this in the back of my mind when I went for my place in nutrition. I knew the university accepted some mature students without their doing any A-level examinations at all."

But Veronica did not have the necessary science qualifications. "Now, when I think back," she said as she poured another cup of tea, "I realize that when the University of Surrey told me to come back for consideration for a place when I had A-levels, they never expected to see me again.

"It was in fact rather surprising being given an offer at all, because in my interview they kept asking me things like, had I biology? and I had to say no. Had I A-level physics? and I had to say no – and so on.

"Someone, as I was leaving the interview, said to me, 'Do you know what you are doing?' And I said, 'Oh, yes.' In fact, I had no idea at all."

Had she stopped to assess the practicalities of her situation and measure her probabilities of success, Veronica would, at this point, have gone home to enjoy her small-town life. But she had set change in motion. Without any assurance of where it would lead her, she took an eight-month "crammer" course, passed her A-levels, and was accepted by the University of Surrey. In 1968 she began studying for her degree in nutrition in the biochemistry department.

Beginning with her first two disappointments of not being given a place in the social studies department and having to take an extra academic year to study for A-levels, Veronica was beset by obstacles that most people would have taken as sound reasons for giving up, particularly at her age. When I suggested that she had a lot of British pluck, she gave me an amused smile. "I have just taken great advantage of whatever position I have found myself in," she said.

Rather than waste her energies railing against her setbacks, Veronica turned them to her own ends. She calls her amazing career an accident, but as the French explorer Alexandra David-Neel said, "Luck has a cause, like anything else, and I believe there exists a mental attitude capable of shaping circumstances more or less according to one's wishes."

"In retrospect I may say that A-levels were my biggest hurdle, in fact," Veronica said, "because one had to change one's way of thought, and one's method of studying. And I had several years' work crammed into one year. Even putting pen to paper at public examinations – overcoming the sheer panic of doing this, I think, was the most difficult thing."

But then another difficulty arose. The university which Veronica had planned to attend was to be at Guildford, not far from her home in the small town of Farnham. "But," she explained, "the building was delayed. And by a quirk of fate, my own Battersea Polytechnic was now being given university status and becoming part of the University of Surrey. So, strangely enough, I had to go back to Battersea and commute. It meant going up to London on a train, an hour's journey. Ten minutes to get to the station in Farnham, an hour to Waterloo Station. There I had to take a train back out, which, if it connected properly, would take another twenty to thirty minutes to Battersea. An hour and three quarters was acceptable, if nothing went wrong. I had three years of commuting. But by my last and most demanding year the university had moved nearby."

Usually a university degree requires three years' work, but the nutrition degree included an extra year of practical work divided into two six-month periods of job experience. "I thought originally that this year – which was unusual in English universities – was a frightful nuisance," Veronica smiled. "Because social work wouldn't have me it would mean that I would take four years instead of three to get a degree. But by the first few weeks I was so engrossed in biochemistry and finding it so enjoyable, I didn't want to change anyway."

"And what about your family?" I asked. "How did they feel about this radical shift in your life?"

"My husband was rather reluctant to begin with," she replied. "In fact, he felt that it would be rather exhausting, and my energies would be rather dissipated. But when he found that it was something I really wanted to do, he couldn't have been more helpful."

"And your children?"

"They were all at university or beyond in that stage. I may say that in my first year of the university two of my daughters got married – one kindly saying, 'Well, I know you've got prelims, so we'll get married three weeks before, and that will give you time to study.'"

"Didn't one put off getting married until you had taken your exams?" Mary asked.

"Yes," Veronica laughed. "She very kindly said, 'We're not in a hurry. We'll fit it in during vacation.'"

"What an enormous amount of energy you must have to survive all of that," I observed.

"This may be true," Veronica conceded. "But I just don't know how one measures energy on a scale. You know you have no time to waste, so you get on with it. There was no sort of sitting back and saying I would do it next week.

"Once I got to the university, I was the only mature student in my department – the only one over twenty-five. These boys and girls had recent practice taking notes and memorizing things and reproducing it as the examiners wanted it. My fellow pupils at the crammer course in many ways supported me far more than the teachers. They told me what things to read, and new books and baubles. And we had a very happy relationship. But there was a section at the university who were less than enthusiastic. I later found that because I talked too easily, they felt in some way left out. If I were to do university over again, this is where I would be far more careful – in voicing opinions and making it *quite* clear that I didn't necessarily know the answer, but was putting forward an idea for others to hammer out when there was a general reluctance to talk.

"But I had an advantage in that I was doing things I just couldn't have done when I was twenty or twenty-five years old. I was making decisions and putting forward my point of view calmly, normally, and naturally, without feeling that I had to make a point about it. I was at a more level pace in life. In my generation, at that age, one would have kept very quiet until things got to such a pitch that you couldn't bear it and then you became a bit hysterical. That may have been only a facet of my own personality or of the girls of my generation.

"Now I simply had to pass straight into my work. University was nine to five. The ironing and cooking got done in the evening or late at night because one doesn't have to be one's most mentally alert to do that. In fact, I found what once I thought were ghastly chores like cooking and ironing were so lovely to have as a sort of complete relaxation. They're not demanding. One can do random thinking, listen to the radio."

But for a specially demanding period Veronica pushed herself so hard she could not sleep. Her doctor reminded her that she was no longer seventeen years old, and gave her some sleeping pills to tide her over. Now she sleeps about six hours a night, which she considers sufficient. "I think the great thing is not to resent not sleeping," Veronica declared. "You say to yourself, well, if I can't sleep then I'll just enjoy what there is of this extra time. I revise papers or write letters or read those endless Victorian novels."

Her pattern is to profit from, not fight a problem.

Veronica Kilgour also has a number of other things in her favor. One is that her husband John, a former chief education officer and classics scholar, prefers quiet evenings at home listening to music or visiting with friends to going out. He is very fond of his family. "An absolutely ideal grandfather," Mary testified. "Now that he's retired and teaching classes only part-time, three afternoons a week," Veronica added, "this gives him time to do the things that I should be doing, like going and seeing the children."

Although she misses her social life, Veronica has not lost contact with her friends. As she pointed out, in a small town, "you meet them as you shop or just go around, even if you don't have them to your house or go around to theirs quite so frequently. I would imagine that quite a number of them don't even know precisely what I am doing. They simply knew I was going to university."

Once a friend remarked to Veronica's daughter that she had not seen Mrs. Kilgour for some time, to which her daughter replied, "Oh, Mother is in Africa chasing cows."

No further inquiries were forthcoming. Privacy is respected in Britain. If one wishes to chase cows in Africa, that is quite all right. Criticism not reaching Veronica's ears spares her the time and energy it would take to make explanations and justifications. "The only people who would ever say anything to me would be people who congratulated me – who would say, 'What a good decision you have made.' People supported me. One very kind neighbor, who lived next door, used to provide a meal for me once a week. She would have my husband and me over to her house for dinner. This was terrific. She used to let me choose the day she would do this for me. I used to hate doing laboratory work at the university and there was always one terrible day when I would have two laboratories in one day. But I had this lovely feeling that at the end of the day I could just go home and there would be good company and a meal ready."

By any standard, Veronica kept a grueling schedule when she attended the university. "But going up to London I could work on the train," she said in answer to my question of how she squeezed her studying in. "I had a very nice lot of commuters who made sure that I had a seat and a place to work. They were very good. That was marvelous. That meant I could look at lectures before classes."

And had she not ridden the train she would not have met Dr. David Godfrey, who changed the direction of her career. "He was a fellow commuter from Waterloo. And even in England you can say good morning after six months. He was a fellow compatriot. We walked a little way in the same direction. He was a research scientist working in protozoology and I was very interested in what he did. He was very interested in biochemistry. A large amount of my nutrition course was devoted to biochemistry. It's hard work, but I found it absolutely delightful, a thing I really enjoyed."

So when David Godfrey learned that Veronica was required to take a six-month job for practical experience, he suggested she work with him at the Lister Institute. He needed to know more about a biochemical marker which showed him how much or how well he had broken open the membranes on his trypanosomes. "There was biochemical advice available, very distinguished biochemists working at the Lister Institute," Veronica continued the story. "But they were very much devoted to their own work, their own specialty, and here I was with a six-month period open. If the experiment failed, it was not such a big investment. It was a small step."

At the time, Veronica did not realize what a big step that experience was to become for her. "I said I hadn't any zoology or protozoology," she recalled, "but Dr. Godfrey said I could pick that up quite easily as I went along, and that my biochemistry would be the useful thing."

And so Veronica Kilgour joined Dr. David Godfrey and his team. After her graduation she returned to work full-time at the Lister Institute. When he moved to the London School of Hygiene and Tropical Medicine, she went with him. Now their work has grown so large that a good many other people are involved. Veronica maintains that she has encountered no discrimination as a woman in the largely male world of science. "In fact," she laughed, "the men tend to forget we are women. And right from early on Dr. Godfrey has made sure that I have given papers on what I have been doing to whatever scientific assembly is around. He has made sure that all of his people have done this: that we are recognized, that we are introduced around. I am never introduced as, 'she works for me,' but as 'my colleague,' as we all are."

Mary and I agreed that Veronica was fortunate indeed to have found such stimulating work among such congenial professionals. Did she find that there was any advantage being an older person in her field? I wondered.

"To some extent, yes," she responded with a slight smile. "For instance, when I was at university, a scientist from another laboratory came in and said, 'Look, when you graduate, if you want a job come ask me, and I'll see if I have anything suitable for you.' And he added, 'You realize that you would have to work at a junior level – would this worry you?' When I said, 'No,' he said, 'Well, you realize that what I am hoping to get is maturity on the cheap.'"

We all laughed a bit ruefully and Mary passed the biscuits round.

"Then I do remember an occasion in Nigeria," Veronica brightened, "when I got parted from David Godfrey. I had a Nigerian with me who, I realized, was very unwilling to accept what I had to say, or do. I rather let it go. But I was annoyed. I felt he was just being obstreperous without any real reason. 'Well, all right,' I told him. 'If you don't join in you may miss out on future plans.' It was a situation I couldn't possibly have dealt with when younger. I was told afterward that he was very much nicer to the women technicians working in the university after that."

This time our laughter was genuine.

"And your three daughters," I inquired, "the mothers of your many grandchildren, are they at all career-minded?"

"They are and I hope they will be very much involved with their families," Veronica responded with a warm smile.

"But I am sure that none of them will just stay at home and entertain for their husbands."

"All of the girls have the qualifications and the experience to go back to work if they decide to," Mary added as she collected our empty tea cups. "They should be able to find congenial work."

"But their generation has the advantage of being educated and having some work experience before they have their children. While you," I said to Veronica, "had so much to do just to get qualified, I marvel that you stayed with it."

She looked away, slightly embarrassed by my admiration. "I thought I had missed out on my opportunity," she laughed lightly. "But it just flowed. I say yes to everything unless there is an obvious reason to say no. Because saying yes has been so fruitful."

"And she works very hard indeed," Mary added.

"There is a little pressure on me," Veronica admitted. "Sixty-five is the official retirement age at the school, but if one wishes, one can stay on. It depends very much on what I do in the next few years. But a little pressure isn't a bad thing," she concluded.

Like a greenhouse plant unaffected by the seasons, Veronica Kilgour has blossomed under pressure. A rigorous schedule, a bit of risk-taking, a strong potion of faith, and a lot of yea-saying are her formula for a successful career after fifty in the expanding world of science.

Part Three

When a Woman Holds a Family Together

"Nobility of character manifests itself at loop-holes when it is not provided with large doors."

MARY E. WILKINS FREEMAN
The Revolt of "Mother"

The Ultimate Triumph
of Mary Merhar Miller

In 1900, when she was eighteen, Mary Merhar spent one night in Paris. There she ate a French meal she never forgot. For years she carried the memory of it with her, like a miniature painting of an Old World scene to look at for solace, as she journeyed from her ancient village, Pri Ribnici, in a snug valley of the Slovene Alps, to the copper-mining hills of Montana, and on, deep into the wilderness of Alaska, to the raw, gold-mining town of Fairbanks. Until her children were grown and her husband dead, Mary's life was stark, without comfort, hard beyond my comprehension. But when I met her as my mother-in-law, Mary Merhar Miller carried herself like a queen.

None of us will ever know what it was like in the beginning, when Mary arrived in Anaconda, Montana, to stay with her sister, who had gone to the Far West before her. Our questions of how it all started came too late. No one remembers if Frank Miller, a widower, twenty years her senior, with two children, and a Slovenian immigrant like herself, married her, because he truly loved this smooth-skinned peasant girl with her high cheek-bones. We know that she grieved to leave her sister in Anaconda, but Frank had gold fever and went to Alaska. Mary followed after him with four small children, his two and their own two girls, in a stern-wheeler down the wide Yukon River and up the smaller Tanana to the muddy banks of the Chena Slough.

No one knows if Frank was harsh to Mary from the first, or when his temper began to be violent. Once, he shaved the heads of two of the teenaged girls for being disobedient – girls he did not want and blamed Mary for having. In the little white wooden Church of the Immaculate Conception, Mary knelt to pray for strength and forbearance. Before the statue of the Virgin Mary, she found consolation and a sense of continuity with the world she had left behind. A feeling of quiet joy must have suffused her when she inhaled the sweet fragrance of incense curling from the heavily smoking censers swung, at last, by her own small acolyte sons. In that bleak, gold-rush town near the Arctic Circle, Mary bore seven more children in a small low-roofed log cabin without plumbing. Four of them were the boys Frank wanted.

It might have been the long, cold, dark Alaskan winters, the terrible toil of starting a life from scratch in a harsh land, the always unrealized dream of striking it rich on each new gold mine, which turned her husband into such a tyrant. Thirteen mouths to feed was a heavy burden. He drove the family: fell trees; haul, chop, pile, carry wood; stoke fires; shovel snow; break ice; feed the pigs; herd the goats; dig potatoes; pick wild berries; work the garden; make preserves; bake bread; turn the grindstone; sharpen knives; straighten nails. Never sit down. When the children were driven beyond their limits, Mary interceded: "Leave them go for a little bit."

Work hard, Frank preached. Be honest. Never tell a lie. He whipped the boys and ranted at the girls for infractions they have long forgotten. But for as far back as any of her nine children could remember, they were certain that it was their mother who, for them, stood solid, like the center of gravity.

She did not hint by word or gesture that they should pity her. No complaints from her clouded their lives; her struggle was her own. She exuded courage, patience, and understanding.

The money Frank made from his Miner's Home Hotel and Saloon, one in Fairbanks and one at Iditarod in the Kuskokwim, often went to grubstake a prospector. Mary's objections were fruitless, but Frank had her keep the accounts, so she seized the opportunity to tuck twenty-dollar gold pieces under her clothes in her cedar chest, thereby accumulating enough money to finance her dream – the education of her children.

As a girl, Mary had been eager to know the languages of the travelers who stopped for meals at her father's tiny inn on the road from Trieste to Vienna. With French, Italian, and German dictionaries, she taught herself phrases, until letters from America lured her across the Atlantic. But she never lost her dream of learning and she struggled to pass it along to her daughters. When they were in high school she paid a French woman to give them language lessons and a Mr. Gorbracht to teach them to play the piano. Frank bellowed and raged when he discovered that she had slipped first one, then another, of the five girls out of Alaska to universities in the States. She persuaded the U.S. territorial delegate for Alaska to grant appointments to either West Point or Annapolis for each of her four sons. To enhance the chances of the two boys who opted to take the entrance examinations, Mary sent them, one after the other, to a private preparatory school in San Francisco. In 1935, when he was sixteen years old, my husband, the youngest of the nine, sailed from Alaska to that private school in the States. With him Mary launched the last of her children.

For forty years this indomitable woman concentrated on raising her family and on holding firm against the tyrannical onslaughts of her husband. As he grew older, he did not mellow; Frank's fury with life increased.

Then one day when he was nearing eighty and she still a hardy woman of sixty, Mary sensed a change in Frank. She was alone in the kitchen with him, washing dishes at the sink. He sat at the table, expounding as usual, when suddenly she realized he had threatened her.

Mary hurried to the telephone in the hall and called across town to her oldest, married daughter, her namesake, a woman as strong as she was, on whom she relied more and more.

"Come get me quick," Mary said. "I'm afraid of Pa."

Her daughter came immediately, packed two suitcases and took her mother home with her. For two days they debated what to do. They decided that it would be dangerous for her to return home. All her life she had made arrangements for her children; now she had to take care of herself. Alone, in August, 1939, forty-eight hours after she left home, Mary climbed on a bus leaving for Valdez on the coast of Alaska. There she boarded a boat bound for Seattle, the port she had sailed north from in 1906 when she was a young woman in her twenties. From Seattle she took a train to Los Angeles, where the sister she had not seen since she left Anaconda now lived. Mary never saw her husband again. Six months later Frank died.

Now Mary entered a new era of her life. For the next twenty-five years, like a monarch in the flower of her reign, she made periodic circuit rides to visit her far-flung children who showered her with tribute. For them she had survived. Because of her they held fast.

The first summer Bill and I were married, we returned to Fairbanks hoping to earn enough money to continue college in the fall. It was home for him, a foreign country for me. He was able to start up his trucking business again; the only job I could find was in the bank, drearily counting checks in the basement. Bill was gone many nights, trucking diesel oil to distant gold mines. I, earnest and bookish, was painfully out-of-place in this pioneer society.

When I was alone, my mother-in-law would visit me. She would knock on the screendoor of our one-room apartment, then walk in, a large woman with deliberate movements, whose clear Slavic skin was still tight and smooth across her high forehead. She sat with great dignity in one of our two overstuffed chairs. "Now we listen to the news," she would announce, turning the knobs of the radio with her big-knuckled hands. Until I caught the rhythm of her sentences, her English was difficult for me to understand.

Mostly we just sat – silent. What was I to say to this taciturn woman whose life was so different from mine? Now I understand that she knew, without ever asking me, that I ached with loneliness and wept when I came home from work to an empty apartment. For that reason she came, evening after evening, to mutely comfort me. After awhile, she began to ruffle back through the years, remembering, finally talking as she never could to her husband, as she never had to her children. I began to look forward to her visits. Covering her mouth with the back of her hand, she laughed at the memory of her daring to fling some dirty diaper she did not want to wash out the window of the stern-wheeler as it plied down the Yukon. With a heavy voice, she recalled that first spring in Fairbanks when she discovered that the green logs of their hastily built cabin had exuded dampness through the winter, so that all her hand-embroidered trousseau – the sheets, the pillowcases, the linen, the petticoats, that she had carried so far – was ruined by mildew. And then *she told me how, in the afternoon, when her small children were asleep, she would go behind the house, where she sat on a stump and thought of her family at home in Slovenia. "And every afternoon I cried and cried," she said. She remembered how she lived with apprehension through the long winters, when she sent her small children out in the dark mornings to walk two miles to school, fearing they would let their scarves slip from over their noses, breathe the twenty-to-sixty-degree-below-zero air, and frost their lungs. And finally, how glad she was for little things, such as her thinking to bring mattresses to Alaska to lay across their first birch-pole beds.*

One evening she said, "I'll tell you something I never tell anyone."

It was a tale of defiance. Frank had a Yugoslavian cohort Mary did not like. Bolgsa do ga chasen *("A foolish dolt"), she said. The custom then was for Slavs who emmigrated to send back home for brides. This man asked Frank to help him find a suitable girl. Perhaps he wanted a wife as healthy and hardworking as Frank's. In any case, Frank said to his friend that the woman he should marry was Mary's favorite sister, Rosie, who had come to Montana, but soon returned home to Ribnici. Proud to be the go-between for such a fine match, Frank bought drinks all around. "Write her," he told Mary, "and tell her to come."*

"So," Mary said, "I write Rosie," then her voice dropped conspiratorily, "But I tell her, do not come!*"*

Time passed. Frank was impatient. He badgered Mary. Had she sent the proposal? Why didn't Rosie reply?

At last the letter came. Rosie answered. She preferred to stay in Yugoslavia. Frank flew into a towering rage.

"But I not want this life for Rosie," Mary said firmly. "Frank never know about my letter. If he did, he kill me." Then she looked at me with a sparkle in her eyes and laughed. "But he never found out!" she said triumphantly.

In the last quarter of her life, Mary thrived. Her work was done – honorably and against great odds. She began to enjoy her new life; she knew she had earned it. And her children knew in their bones that she deserved an easier life. As naturally as she had stood up for them, they now helped her.

She returned to Fairbanks. For a long time she stayed on in the big log house, keeping a pot of coffee warm on the old wood stove. All day her kitchen was a meeting place. She dispatched sons, daughters, grandchildren, and their friends in all directions. Her youngest daughter, Emma, stopped in after work with groceries. Son Bob, a successful Alaskan business man, gave her plane tickets and cash to augment her small savings and income from land sales. During World War II she began her cross-country traveling, getting hotel rooms for herself when people of influence were sleeping in the lobbies. After the war, she kept up her regular trips out of Alaska to visit her far flung, ever-increasing family. One son became a rear admiral, another a foreign service officer. She moved with complete composure in the different worlds of her prospering children. Her own confidence was reflected in them. They asked her what she most wanted for her eightieth birthday. A ring, she told them. "All my life I wanted a diamond ring." So, when she was eighty, her children bought her a beautiful big diamond ring.

She went to Disneyland and she watched television with delight. When Mary died at eighty-seven, her children gathered in Seattle for her funeral. "Bolgsa do ga chasen," one of them said in Mary's scolding voice, and they all began to laugh. Astonished at themselves, they found they were not mourning; their memories were too life-giving for them to weep. "Remember how she outwitted Pa in the finances?" "How she used to slip us a five-dollar bill when we were short?" "That delicious potica *she used to make after Lent?" "But how about when she dragged us out of bed to go to Mass in those pitch dark mornings when it was forty degrees below zero?" "Remember when we fought and made too much noise for her, how she crossed her eyes and moaned, 'I go to Tokoyo?'" They clasped each others' arms in laughter.*

If Mary Merhar could have seen how her children honored her memory the day they came together because of her death, she would have covered her mouth with the back of her work-worn hand and laughed until the tears rolled down her smooth cheeks. The heritage she had given them was good.

The immense dignity of my immigrant mother-in-law was rooted in her deep sense of worth as a mother. She knew her children needed her. No amount of defamation from her husband eroded that basic belief that her life was necessary and of value. And never once did she burden her children with a sense of guilt for the situation she was in: she knew it was not of their making; she let them live their own lives. True, they added to her work and to her worry, but they also gave her great joy.

Her children were fortunate. Every child needs a mother and one with a strong sense of herself is the best kind to have. Families, for all of their faults, are, as far as we know, the most beneficial arrangements for children to grow in. A special kind of creativity is required to keep a family viable. Some women have this talent. They are endowed with patience and strength and a long view of life. In a multitude of ingenious ways, they manage to keep a delicate equipoise between their own and their family's needs, so that when their children are grown and their work is done, they are not depleted. Their resilience carries them on to the next phase in their lives.

Motherhood is an honorable profession that has fallen on hard times. These days mothers tend to be much maligned. As the trend toward specialization and professionalization accelerates, they are becoming an endangered species: old-fashioned generalists who make the time and take the trouble to act on humanistic values. While others strive to compete, mothers work to hold the world together.

8. A Pioneer in Paris

CHARLOTTE KESSLER

> "Grow old along with me!
> The best is yet to be,
> The last of life, for which the first was made . . . "

ROBERT BROWNING

The transition made by Charlotte Kessler from the secure status of a doctor's wife to the position of sole breadwinner for their family of five children freed her husband from a profession that no longer interested him. In his peak earning years, when Dr. Alfred Kessler was forty and Charlotte was thirty-eight, he gave up his highly profitable neurosurgical practice in Spokane, Washington, not because he was driven by an overwhelming creative urge to become an artist, as I had romantically assumed when I first met him, but simply because he was bored and irritated by his life in the medical world. "I gave up nothing," was his inevitable answer to the often-asked question of how he could have made such a move – this declaration being delivered with a doctor's tone of finality, in a manner that conveyed it was the distillation of careful consideration.

"I didn't give up anything but money, and money is nothing to give up," Charlotte might add if pressed, but she is not a person to offer her views gratuitously, or one who delights in argument as her husband does. Keeping her own counsel, however, in no way diminishes her strong presence; her low, soft voice has a quality that compels people to listen to her. I think of Charlotte as a physically active person. Yet my sharpest image is of her sitting on a high stool with her long legs crossed, behind the diagonal counter Al built across the corner of one large room of their apartment that serves as the living, dining, bedroom, kitchen, and studio. Her thin shoulders are hunched over a book of Bernard Shaw's letters that lies open next to a cookbook; a strand of blonde hair falls forward over the fine bone structure of her face. Children of all ages, including a couple of mine, meander in and out, looking for food, banging kitchen cupboards behind her. She shouts reminders of schoolwork to be done and appointments to be kept as she turns a page of her book with one hand. With her other hand she dips a long-handled wooden spoon into the enormous pot on the counter stove, reading as she stirs a batch of ketchup she is making.

A pioneer woman in the heart of Paris.

How could she cope? I always wondered. She so obviously relished her life and had what seemed to me the right amount of interest in her children and in Al's painting. Yet life in Paris, in any big city for that matter, is physically hard unless one has a substantial amount of money to buy services. Grocery shopping, for example, has to be done every day, limited by the amount of what you can carry in two shopping bags for several blocks – not very much for a growing family. And the Kesslers live on the second floor of an old building with a dark, curving staircase and no elevator. For a long time Charlotte did not have a washing machine. Now she has one that washes a single sheet at a time. No drier. Sending children on errands and dividing household jobs among them was not "making work"; it was essential, and Charlotte is an adept organizer.

Al built the entire interior of the apartment himself, partitioning three small rooms for the children and building bunk beds and a loft into them. With mingled wonder and admiration, I watched this construction over several years in the early 1970s. Every time I crossed the English Channel and visited the Kesslers, Al actually looked younger and Charlotte more satisfied.

"I admire you tremendously," I told Charlotte the last time I dropped by for a visit. "Apparently you have no trouble understanding or adjusting to Al's needs."

"Knowing each other seems to me the basis of any kind of

marriage," she smiled. "If you don't know your husband's needs and wants, you don't know your husband."

She is right, of course, but how seldom do we really understand someone so close to us and, even if we do, how wise and loving one must be to strike that fine balance between being supportive yet not subordinate. Finding a large share of one's happiness through the joys and satisfactions of a loved partner, and at the same time remaining true to one's own independence and development, requires a rare kind of maturity. Youth generally is too self-absorbed, insecure, idealistic, and argumentative to do the careful building required for mutuality and trust. Shared lives, satisfactory to both partners, take a long time to construct.

I used to think that Charlotte was deprived of a comfortable life and forced to go to work because Al wanted to move to Paris to paint. That was a gross oversimplification. For nearly a decade, all through their forties, Charlotte and Al experimented and struggled to work out a satisfactory living arrangement in terms of work and place. From the beginning, Charlotte was willing to leave behind a conventional life, take a few risks, exchange her material standard of living for greater freedom of movement, and dare to undertake the work of creating a new life with no clear blueprints from the old society and no expectation of approval from the stay-at-homes. In short, she had the requisite pioneer qualities to make a fundamental change in her life.

And she discovered that when Al finally was able to sever his ties with the medical world, she could move on too, often faster than he, to meet new challenges and reap for herself greater rewards than she might have found had she remained a doctor's wife.

Charlotte's Midwestern background bestowed on her a unique toughness of spirit and clearheaded practicality. Her grandparents on both sides were pioneers: her maternal grandfather broke virgin land and was one of the earliest settlers of eastern Alberta; and her paternal grandfather homesteaded in western Canada at the age of sixty. Her father was a circuit-riding minister for the United Church of

Canada, before he became a professor at Illinois Wesleyan. She was born in Urbana, Illinois, in 1924, grew up in Bloomington, Indiana, and went to college there, and graduated during World War II. Her taste for adventure took her overseas to a job as a secretary at the U.S. Embassy in London. There she met Al, a Navy doctor, whom she married in 1946. His desire to specialize in neurosurgery after he was discharged from the Navy meant eight more years of training for him, first at Jersey Medical Center, then at the University of Chicago, before he went into private practice in Spokane. There they moved into a suburban area of professional families and gentleman farmers, living the American dream of security and affluence. "When the children were young, it never occurred to me to do anything else but cart them back and forth," Charlotte conceded. "Took them to parties and so forth. When I look back on it, I think I would have loved to go to school, done something, but I never thought of it."

Al's dissatisfaction, not Charlotte's, spurred them to re-evaluate their lives.

"But one doesn't make a sudden decision," she emphasized. "You just begin moving into it."

Al was precise and analytical about his situation. As a neurosurgeon, he was one of the most highly trained and highly paid doctors in the medical profession. "I didn't approve of the business end of medicine," he said. "Not only did I not like the economics of it, but it got boring to me after a while. It is not really what you were trained for, especially if you are highly trained. You get patients with backaches that are psychological, particularly in the U.S. Most of your patients have psychological problems that you really are not equipped to handle. Every doctor should be trained to treat, shall we say, psychological handicaps. You are sympathetic, but you don't have the time. I was nice to my patients and, if I do say so myself, they loved me. But I would come home mad. I couldn't stand it personally. I think that a doctor who is trained in a specific field, neurosurgery or whatever, is interested in that field for a specific scientific reason. But mainly I didn't like the business end.

"My colleagues used to bore me. Doctors talk about three things: money – stock markets and investments; golf – some talk about bridge, but not too many; and hunting – in the Northwest it is hunting and fishing. I never was interested in any of them."

"Al became more and more disillusioned with the possibility for personal development as his practice became more and more of a business," Charlotte commented. "And he had absolutely no time of his own. We never saw him."

For awhile they cast about for ways for him to cut back on his workload so that he could have some time for his family and for himself; one idea was to practice half-time with another doctor, but that did not work out. Then, just as a respite, they managed to take a year off and go to Europe. England was the obvious choice; school there for the children was no problem. Buckhurst Hill, a suburb just north of London, worked out nicely, except that they kept being drawn to France for every holiday, until, in the fall of 1962, they decided to move there and extend their year by six months to be able to spend a full school year in Grimaud, a small village in the south of France where living was cheap. They rented a very comfortable house for one hundred dollars a month.

"We had put aside a certain amount of money, like vacation money, for our stay in Europe," Charlotte pointed out. "We had savings. A lot of people who have good incomes don't. But it is in both our natures to be savers. Of course we made a tremendous change in our style of life. We knew the big expense for us, like everybody else, would be the college education of our children. But we didn't feel as if we were living off our savings while we were abroad because we had planned ahead for that trip."

It was a pleasant interlude. Neither of them thought of staying on in Europe. They enjoyed village life, learned French cooking and how to bottle their own wine. But Al worried about the children's education: none really took to the local school. It was good for their French but bad for their spelling.

But the experience of living in France subtly changed Al's and Charlotte's attitudes, confirming their belief that time was more precious than money, that a simpler life was preferable to a more luxurious one, and that there were more joys in thrift than in spending.

"By the end I would have stayed in Grimaud another year," Charlotte said pensively. "I felt comfortable in Europe, and felt like staying. It was Al who insisted we should go back because of the children's education."

But not to Spokane. What began as a vacation from medicine altered them both too much and made it impossible for them to return to the old life.

As Charlotte explained, "Al said to himself, just for that year, to have something to do, I'll write a novel and paint. I had given him an easel and some paints one birthday five or six years before. At that time he began painting again after not painting for years. But he didn't have much time for it when he was practicing medicine. It was just on an amateurish basis. But at the end of that time abroad, he was completely engrossed in both writing and painting and no longer interested in medicine.

"In 1964 we went back to Washington, D.C., where Al went to work on a medical research project with the idea that a less demanding job would leave him time to paint – which he found he was more interested in than writing. I think he felt he had a theme and something he wanted to say in his paintings. What he likes are the problems, the technical and creative ones he has to solve in painting. Then, when it is finished, whether it is successful or not, whether you really like it or not, there is a sense of accomplishment.

"So it was at this time that we began to talk about making some changes. It was his decision in terms of what he wanted to do, in terms of what he *needed* to do. But it was a joint decision in terms of logistics and management," Charlotte declared.

For Al to paint seriously, full-time, it was clear that Charlotte would have to earn their living. No creative urge tempted her toward a solitary, self-disciplined life. She liked to be around people. Some small investments and savings could help stretch them through, but those were primarily for the five children's college educations, and would not go far as costs rose.

From the tone in Charlotte's voice, it was clear that she was undaunted by the challenge. When I mumbled something about role reversal, Al staying home all day to paint while Charlotte went out to work, Al chimed in with, "That's a bunch of jargon. I'm against role-model language. The problem is that people like you and me and people in the business world can change their lives *if they want to*. But 95 percent of the world cannot. Everything comes down to economics."

Charlotte took up the theme with conviction. "Beyond certain creature comforts that you can buy, you really can buy only so much to eat. *But you can't buy time*. Time was what Al needed. Nothing he could do would give him that time. So it was not hard to cut back for this. As Virginia Woolf said, you have to have a room of your own."

The economics of the Kessler decision was for Charlotte to find work. She was forty years old, with a college degree in history, and a couple of years' work experience from the period before she was married.

"So I then had to prepare myself for something," she continued in her thoughtful way. "When you stay home with your family, often you are preparing yourself for something else without really thinking about it. When my kids were little, I organized and ran 4-H clubs. The kids were gentlemen farmers' kids, so I didn't have any competition from them knowing more about animals than I did. I had twenty kids or so, and they all had animals of one kind or another. Sheep mostly. One or two had chickens. They entered them in local shows and county fairs. I really enjoyed it. I suppose that was a forerunner to my decision to go into education. When my youngest went to first grade, I went to graduate school. We started off together.

"I got my master's degree in English. I had thought of elementary education, but the more I talked to people, the more scope there seemed to be in English, and I had always loved to read. I think also one of the things that made me choose English was that in Spokane, the last three or four years, I belonged to a ladies' book club." She laughed. "You know, the usual ladies' book club. Not only would I read the books, but I read all of the criticism of them. I found it an interesting approach to reading. Of course it was basically an academic approach. I think that experience was a major influence in my decision to go into English. I found the whole process was fun. I think maybe one shouldn't go to graduate school until one is past thirty anyway. At any rate, I enjoyed it a great deal.

"I did a review course for people from other majors and those who had been away from school. If we did well on that we would not have to do any undergraduate work for our new majors. There were three of us: one from philosophy, one from science, and me from history. We sat around and talked a lot. It was marvelous. Very intensive. Very good help."

Thus what had been Al's need for a new life became Charlotte's impetus to change and grow. She became an English teacher. The flexible hours of a teacher's schedule fit in well with her family life. "You don't work less than a nine to five day," she explained, "because you work nights and weekends. But if you want to go home early to cook dinner because you have company coming, you do, and put your work off. You can make adjustments."

After she had taught a year in Washington, she and Al began to yearn for Europe again. She applied to overseas schools and took a position at the American School in London for one year. Then they moved to Paris, where she taught in an English-language school for six years before she achieved her present position as Assistant to the Dean of the American College in Paris. As I can testify, she loves her work. "It's always changing," she said. "Always interesting."

The day I dropped by her office, students interrupted us constantly to ask her for help, to thank her for some special favor she had done, or just to be reassured by her warm smile and unruffled presence. The scene reminded me of her own house, with children pouring in and out, touching base with her. For several years Charlotte and I exchanged our teenagers across the English Channel as easily as other people might send packages, with little or no preplanning, but always welcoming their arrivals. Children of my friends stayed with her. The young people cut their argumentative eyeteeth with Al in heated political debates, and discussed literature and life with Charlotte. She always cooked enough to feed more than her family, knowing they seldom would sit down to eat without a visitor at the table. As a teacher and an advisor, she has professionalized her mothering talents.

When the door closed on the last of the students, Charlotte said quietly, "That poor girl's mother drinks." She thought a moment, then said with feeling, "There is no doubt but that there is a certain kind of emptiness in the lives of people who do not have to worry about the material aspect of things. If you don't have to struggle in some way, you don't grow. And if you don't grow, the bottle is a solution."

Her observation made me remember Al saying, "I was the one who really convinced Charlotte to go ahead for further studies and get her degree for teaching. When I was in practice I saw all of these women who were reaching middle age, their kids leaving. Most of them were alcoholics. There are more alcoholic women that I know of than men."

There is no doubt in my mind that under any circumstances Charlotte would never have gone that way – she is too purposeful. She and Al believe that freedom demands responsibility. As Al once phrased it, "If you don't have responsibility, you don't have freedom. They are the same thing. It is a paradox. To think you have no limits doesn't work in any society. In order to be free you have to put severe limits on yourself."

Realizing now how completely Charlotte subscribed to this view made me blurt out, "My god, you are a strong, adaptable person!"

She laughed, protesting, "No, I always wondered if we were doing the right thing. Al worried more about the children than I did – about whether they were getting as good an education as they would have had in American schools. I never worried about that quite so much, probably because in my teaching I saw a lot of students in this category, and it didn't seem to do them much harm. The pluses seemed to outweigh the minuses. In the long run I think we did the right thing for them.

"Our decision to live in France, you understand, is quite separate from Al's decision to give up medicine and paint instead. It is a personal preference entirely. In fact, living in the States would make more practical sense. Although Al's work has been in art shows here, it is probably easier to make contacts in the States. And Paris is no longer the art center of the world.

"And I am limited as to where I can work. Financially it probably would have been easier to stay in Washington. The salaries at overseas schools have never been anything great. When the Marymount High School here, where I taught, closed a couple of years ago, it seemed, at the time, a catastrophic event for me. There were not many other schools to apply to.

"But in fact, it turned out to be a very good thing for me," she smiled. "Now I'm on the college level where I feel more at home."

For a moment I had a fantasy of Charlotte standing in a long dress on the Western prairie, cradling a baby in one arm, her other hand ruffling the hair of a toddler tugging at her skirt, while several larger children clustered around her. Behind them their cabin had burned to the ground and she was saying, "Over this way, don't you see? Pa has found some better land."

Without women like Charlotte, children would have a hard time and families would go out of fashion.

She broke into my daydream, saying, "Come on. It's getting late but we still have time to treat ourselves to a Cinzano before dinner."

As she closed the door of her office behind us, Charlotte concluded, "You know I really do believe that in the end things work themselves out, don't you?"

9. A Southern Belle in Business

BILLIE JEAN TYLER

"Happiness is the by-product of an effort to make someone else happy."

GRETTA BROOKER PALMER
Permanent Marriage

In an old bougainvillea-covered house in Austin, Texas, with sea blue carpets and white walls is Billie Jean Tyler's Yarn and Needlecraft Shop. Enter here to a world of dreams. Behold a feast of colors. Tiered niches covering the walls are filled with stacks of yarn in skeins of every hue: luscious yellows, zircon blues, pansy purples, the greens of every shade of summer grasses, wheat beige, peach, and fire red – enough to ignite the greenest imagination into fantasies of quickly made afghans and splendid multicolored sweaters. Festooned on every surface throughout three rooms are needlepoint canvases designed with floribunda roses, Indian geometric patterns, amber-eyed tigers, Victorian houses, ten-gallon hats, and tall-masted sailing ships. There are tapestries for scrapbook covers, purses, trays, picture frames, belts, samplers, tennis racket covers, tote bags, and bell pulls. Elegantly arranged on an antique table is a cornucopia of eyeglasses cases, pincushions, Christmas stockings and Christmas ornaments, jewel cases and tops for wooden shoes. Stacked by the fireplace are huge canvases for needlepoint rugs with Aztec and cactus designs. Around the Victorian sofa are piles of finished cushions, testimony to the rich beauty of completed pieces.

A bell jingled over the door as a customer walked in and sank into a big, puffed cushion. "Billie Jean," she called out, "can I have a glass of water?"

From somewhere within the house a lovely, infectious laugh rang out. "Com-*ing*!" In a moment Billie Jean appeared in the doorway, a merry-looking woman with a rounded figure, her gray hair brushed to one side to accentuate one white strand set in a deep wave. She was dressed in white pants and a yellow silk shirt. "What's the matter, darling," she said with a mischievous twinkle in her eyes. "Are you having a hot flash?"

"Good grief, no," her client retorted. "I was over those three years ago."

Simultaneously the phone rang and the front door was pushed open tentatively by a girl in jeans.

Billie Jean beckoned her in with a big smile, picked up the telephone receiver, lit a cigarette and flicked out the match with a graceful flip of her wrist. "How *are* you?" she said into the phone. "Grandma!" she teased in her soft drawl, then settled into a business-like tone, concluding shortly with a hearty, "Now don't you worry. If you have any more trouble, just bring it in, darling."

The hesitant girl held a needlepoint canvas out to Billie Jean. "I know how to knit," she said, "but I'm not sure I can do this."

"Oh, sure you can," Billie Jean said easily. She told the other woman to go back to the kitchen and help herself to all the water she wanted, then sat down on the red plush sofa, indicating with a pat on the cushion for the girl to join her. "It's fun to try something new," she said in a warm, chatty tone. "Say, aren't you Mrs. Lee's daughter?"

"Why, yes, I am." Her young customer relaxed a bit.

Billie Jean defly wove the needle through the mesh of the canvas. "Just be sure your stitches are always going in the right direction," she cautioned.

The girl did a few stitches. Billie Jean beamed, "That's right," and popped up to answer the phone again, saying over her shoulder, "Never worry about the back of your needle-point. They always look messy like that," Reassured, the girl sat working on her canvas.

Other women came in and asked Billie Jean's advice on

colors of yarns, selections of canvases, sizes of needles. "I never saw anyone with so perfect a stitch still determined to struggle like you do," Billie Jean shook her head in mock despair at one customer, then joked with another, commiserated with a third, and asked about the family of a fourth. A smartly dressed young man hurried in with blueprints of a new shop for Billie Jean. She waved him into a side room, where he spread his drawings out on a large round table. "Isn't she wonderful?" he said to me. Billie Jean rushed back and forth between the architect, the customers coming in and out, and the ever-ringing phone, like an impresario attending to the needs of her theater group on opening night. Here was a world of her own making. Without the brilliant presence of Billie Jean Tyler, the Yarn and Needlecraft Shop would simply be another business. Instead, it is a stunning success.

"There is no doubt about it," Billie Jean conceded as she sat down, at last, to tell me how she got started in business. "You have to show yourself up front." She blew the smoke from her cigarette straight up in the air. "There is no way to make a profit without working six days a week – sometimes more." She laughed. "When I started in, I thought I could work five days and have lots of free time." She rolled her eyes upward. "I was *so* wrong!"

And she was so inexperienced. Not until she was forty-eight years old was Billie Jean faced with either the need or desire to do anything but raise her four children, swim, play bridge and tennis, do some volunteer work, and keep up a full social life with her husband. Then one day she was confronted with the fact that, as she put it, "There was a real financial need in our home."

Billie Jean's husband, Jerry Tyler, had worked for years for a construction firm in Austin. When the firm expanded and moved its headquarters to Houston, Jerry was offered a more responsible position there on the management level.

"But I refused to move." Billie Jean grimaced. "I knew Houston and didn't want to live there. I said," and she wagged her shoulders in self-mockery, saying in a singsong voice,

" 'I don't want to raise a family in Houston. It's too humid, too crowded' and 'What am I going to do without my friends?' That," she continued firmly, "was the most horrible thing I could have done to Jerry personally. My husband should have come first. He would have had a high position there now. The children would have done perfectly fine in Houston, just the same as here. But I was very, very spoiled."

So Jerry bowed to Billie Jean's wishes, stayed on in Austin, and attempted to establish his own building firm. After a few small jobs he had to declare bankruptcy.

"We were going through our savings like you wouldn't believe," Billie Jean said. "It was really devastating, simply terrible on Jerry. And I felt I was to blame. That is the reason I went into business."

Under the pressure of financial losses and inevitable recriminations from Jerry, Billie Jean took it upon herself to hold the family together. In a turnabout prompted by feelings of guilt, she assumed, for the first time in their married life, a share of the financial responsibility. And, like my mother-in-law, Mary Merhar, Billie Jean sought comfort in the Catholic church of her childhood.

"Oh, I'm very devout," Billie Jean said in her cheerful way. "I don't know what I would do without my religion. I rely on it every day. I love to go to church. I need my religion. I just feel that everything that I have done and accomplished is because of my religion. It gives me strength and guidance. I go to church and I get my questions answered. Things will happen, and I will say to myself, there is no way they could have happened without guidance from upstairs."

Billie Jean feels blessed in her business career. She started out on a very small scale and now owns two prospering stores, one in Austin and one in San Antonio. Her business acumen is further validated by the fact that she has just been elected to the board of directors of a corporation.

What is particularly noteworthy about her success is that she built it on a very common feminine skill – knowing how to knit and do needlework. From a cottage craft she created, in a very short time, a thriving commerce. And the experience awakened all her latent business and managerial talents. If an immediate personal need had not prompted Billie Jean to try her wings in the realms of trade, she might never have known the deep satisfactions she now enjoys as an independent entrepreneur – being her own boss and the employer of thirteen other women, all of them friends. "I really love it," she said.

The last thing Billie Jean ever imagined she would become was a successful businesswoman. She was christened Barbara Jean Mueller, but called Billie Jean from the day she was born in San Antonio in 1922.

Her mother was a great beauty and a former folk dancer for Austria – a woman of immense determination whom her daughter admired greatly. Billie Jean told the story of how her mother, one of a large family of modest means, decided that she wanted to go around the world. So she obtained work in a candy factory, where she learned to hand-dip chocolates. For several years she saved her money. Then she set out, via the United States where she had cousins in Texas. "In San Antonio she went to the summer beer festival," Billie Jean giggled, "saw Father and turned to a cousin and said, 'I'm going to marry that man.' She had never even met him. She was something!" Billie Jean threw back her head and laughed heartily. "She always said to me, 'Billie Jean, you can do anything that you want to!'"

Her father agreed and encouraged his daughter's dancing abilities. With great tenderness in her voice, Billie Jean recounted how her father would take her, when she was a child, to ballet classes and wait while she practiced for two hours after her class. "I had a fantastic childhood," she bubbled. "Couldn't have anything better."

Her father was a baker who came to San Antonio from Germany to work for an uncle in a dry goods store. During the depression years of the 1930s, when Billie Jean was in grade and high school, her family moved from their house to small living quarters behind a small bakery he opened. "My mother served the customers," Billie Jean said. "Dad worked his fanny off and it turned into a successful business. My mother was a warm and loving person, and I can't even count the number of people we took care of. Someone would come, like Hans Schwartz, a cook from Munich, who now has a very successful restaurant in Galveston. He had injured his arm. It abscessed and he had no money to go to the hospital to have it taken care of. So Mama said, 'No question, Hans is going to come and stay with us.' For six weeks she kept great big pots with Epsom salts boiling on the stove. She would put towels in them and I can remember her taking wooden spoons to dip the towels out and twist them because they were boiling hot. Then she would put them as compresses on his arm to get the infection out.

"But at the same time that we were eating tripe," Billie Jean made a wry face, "Mama made sure we had help in the house."

After grammar school, Billie Jean was sent to a convent boarding school in San Antonio. "My Dad believed in it," she said. "Besides, he said I was too much for him.

"But," Billie Jean giggled, "I wanted to go to the local high school more than anything else in the world. I could only come home from the convent every six weeks. So finally Dad said, 'All right, darling.' I came home and I had the most handsome boyfriend. In September San Antonio is just cooling off after the sweltering summer," she sighed romantically. "So one day he said, 'Do you want to go to school this afternoon?' and I said, 'Oh, heavens, no!' So he said, 'Well, let's walk home and get our rackets out and go play tennis.' So I said, 'Great! Marvelous!' On the way home we stopped at the drugstore and got triple-decker ice cream cones. School was a good half hour's walk from my house. We went walking down the street . . ." She stuck out her tongue, licking three imaginary scoops of ice cream. "When I got home that night, Dad said, 'How was school?' I said, 'Fine! Just great!' He said, 'Pack up your bags. You're going back to the convent.' I had told him a lie. I was back there the next day. The nuns looked at me," Billie Jean pursed her lips, and in a goody-sweet voice said, " 'We knew you would be back.' "

Yet Billie Jean maintained that she enjoyed her years at

the convent. "I had an awful lot of fun," she said breezily. "The Mother of the convent taught me to play bridge and I loved it. Those nuns play a lot of bridge. Well, when I graduated, the nuns said, 'Of course you will be coming back here to college,' and Dad said, 'Of course she is.' I said, 'No! I'm going to the University of Texas.' After all those years I was so boy crazy you cannot believe it. I went absolutely wild at Texas and didn't make my grades. I played bridge and played with the boys, and played with the boys and played bridge. I just went completely out of my mind. Dad, being a very strict man, said, 'Super. You don't have to study?' He didn't give me a chance. I was too young. I went to Texas when I was just seventeen. I was so immature. He didn't give me a chance. That was one thing. I could never make a boo-boo. Never be a failure, because he didn't expect me to. So I said, 'How am I going to go to school? I don't have any money.' He said, 'I don't know.' So I started working at the Internal Revenue Service in Austin. Then Dad said, 'It is time you went back to convent to college.' I said, 'I'm not going.' That was my only choice, so I never finished college. And I really have regretted it. When I was selected to serve on a board of directors, they sent me a form to fill out, and on it was a space for your college degree."

After starting as a file clerk at the IRS, Billie Jean was promoted fairly rapidly. Like many women, she did not discover her flair for mathematics until she was in a work situation. "I just loved it," Billie Jean said happily. "I went to night school and took some accounting courses. Then I worked up to being an income tax examiner, responsible for auditing individual tax returns."

Then, one fateful weekend in September, 1945, she went dancing with Jerry Tyler, whom she had known since she was sixteen. He was on leave from military service. "I looked at him and he looked at me," Billie Jean batted her eyes, "and he said, 'You know, I adore you.' And we were married the next June.

"I always thought that when I got married I would go back to school. Then I had one baby after another. I had a lot of fun," she winked. "Probably too much fun."

"But, in fact, I don't know why I ever got married." She swung back to a serious mood. "That's the truth. I stayed at home until I was twenty-three. I never had any desire to leave. I adored my father and loved my mother very much."

Now Billie Jean has transferred her great capacity for love and affection to her own family. "You just look at my children and know they have been hugged and kissed to death," she said. "I don't think it hurts them. I spoil Carl, the little boy, because I absolutely adore him." She beamed. "I think men should be waited on.

"But Jerry learned to cook and now he likes it – sometimes." Billie Jean lit another cigarette and fidgeted from sitting so long. "He will help when we have a big barbecue. It's really nice to have that kind of support from a husband. It makes *all* of the difference."

But there were periods when Jerry would become sullen and resentful of all the time that Billie Jean put into her business. He felt neglected and complained. "When he said the house was getting to be a mess and that we never saw anybody anymore (neither of which was true), I knew he was hoisting danger signals," Billie Jean said. "So I would get a girl friend to take over for me, and just take Jerry on a little trip – to New Orleans, or Key West, or Mexico City. And we would play and play for a week or so, and then everything would be O.K. again. I tell you, no business is worth losing a husband for. I've seen that happen too often. And those high-powered businesswomen end up very lonely little old ladies, you can be sure of that.

"But all play can get boring too. For years I enjoyed being free to do what I wanted to, go where I wanted, do a bit of volunteer work. I wouldn't have missed it for the world. But one day it was just too much. I had it up to here." She drew her hand under her chin.

Circumstances have a way of suiting one's needs. Billie Jean's disenchantment with her way of life coincided with the advent of her family's financial need. And all the threads of her earlier life began to come together.

Since the day she was ten years old, when an aunt plunked her down in a chair and told her to sit quietly and work on a piece of needlepoint, Billie Jean has loved any kind of needlework. Everywhere she ever went, she was always working on a piece. People would notice and comment on her projects, and she responded in her open, easy way; in that manner she made many friends. Talking to strangers, she shared ideas and gained useful tips.

But until a woman gave her the idea for classes and told her what to charge, Billie Jean had not thought of turning her pleasure into business. At a large family gathering of aunts, uncles, and distant cousins in San Antonio, a cousin showed her the basketweave stitch. All the way home in the car to Austin, Billie Jean worked to perfect it. Up to that time, she had done only the simpler continental stitch. Her friends clamored for her to teach them the basketweave, and she began to give classes around her dining room table. At first she could not bring herself to charge them. Finally they were the ones who insisted on paying her. "I have fantastic friends," Billie Jean emphasized. With their help she gained the confidence to say, "All right, I'll set class fees." At that crucial moment she knew she had found the way to help shoulder some of the family's financial burdens. Her children (the youngest was fifteen) helped her fix up the recreation room for classes and she was in business with a two-hundred-dollar investment in yarn and the commitment of her own time to teaching. Her clientele was built from women's clubs all over the area. "I learned by doing," she said. "The women in my classes wanted me to choose the patterns and the yarn for them. Luckily I had a little stock my mother had given me and, with that as collateral, I was able to borrow four thousand dollars to rent a little house I converted into my first shop. Imagine," she laughed, "starting with that teeny little bit of money."

Now, ten years later, at fifty-eight, she has a paid inventory of nearly one hundred thousand dollars in her two flourishing shops in Austin and San Antonio.

In those early, heady days, when Billie Jean's business

prospered beyond her expectations, she was tempted to open more new shops at every invitation from a large store or shopping mall. And for awhile she thought of establishing herself in Houston and Galveston; prospects were excellent. "It was pretty exciting to be successful," Billie Jean admitted. "I would come home and say *I* did this, and *I* did that, and Jerry would say, 'Now look here, gal, you're getting too big for your britches.'" Her eyes widened with affected surprise. "He is a very easy person," said Billie Jean slowly. "Very, very cool. And I'm hyperactive. Always have been." She took a long drag on her cigarette and blew out a cloud of smoke. "I know I would not have been able to do what I have without him, and now he is very proud of me. Almost all of the women I know in business are divorced," she sighed. "Business takes up all of your time. Expand and I would be working eight days a week. Jerry is doing well selling building materials. We have a very, very full social life. Jerry likes to go out and I never say no to him. I am a very strong girl. But you know, I have reached my limits physically. And my family is really important to me, far more than my business, so that is what will have to give."

Family-centered, church-oriented, stylish and sophisticated, Billie Jean is a mixture of tradition and modernity. She has not had the time or occasion to think much about the women's movement. "I went into a woman's business, so I am not interfering with men or competing with them," she said. But when she takes her place as a director on a corporate board, she will be one businesswoman as an equal among several businessmen, and that, she acknowledged, is going to be a tricky new experience.

A customer poked her head in the door. "Billie Jean, you're not moving into a shopping mall, are you?" she moaned. "I saw an architect with a lot of blueprints he said were for your new shop."

"Oh, heavens no!" Billie Jean jumped up. "Don't you worry. This property has been sold for development, so we have to move. But I'll find something warm and cozy again. It will be all right."

Billie Jean will keep her show open, no question. Her customers are her enlarged family for whom she provides instruction and encouragement. Like most mothers, Billie Jean is a purveyor of dreams, whose enthusiasm and belief in one's ability may exceed reality. But it is irresistible.

I know. I left her shop with a Peter Rabbit needlepoint pillow and several skeins of the most gorgeous brown, white, and peach yarns. I can scarcely sew a button on, but Billie Jean is sure I'll have no difficulty with the continental stitch. "Come back if you need any help," she called out gaily. "But starting with something small like that, I'm sure that you won't have any trouble." An example such as Billie Jean's makes anything seem possible.

She gave me a big wink and a gorgeous smile. I could easily imagine Jerry putting his arm around her and saying, "Now who ever would have guessed that one of the smartest business gals in Austin would turn out to be my own little Billie Jean – one mighty fine woman, any way you look at her."

Part Four
Brave Women Alone

"I am not afraid of storms, for I am learning how to sail my ship."

LOUISA MAE ALCOTT
Little Women

Travelers Seeing the World with Their Own Eyes

My mother awakened me in the middle of a bright moonlit night, when I was eleven, to look out the train window at my first palm tree. Then she left me alone. Snug in my berth, leaning back on my pillow, I stared at the fantastic shapes flashing by in the California desert. Alone, my concentration was so intense that I can still remember, forty years later, the sound of the train wheels clicking along the rails, the gentle sway of my berth bed, the smooth texture and clean smell of the white sheets, and most of all, the delicious sense of being a solitary traveler streaking through the night.

A year later, when I was twelve, I really did travel alone. One evening in Seattle, my parents put me on a Greyhound bus for an overnight journey to Idaho. I had to change buses in Portland at about 2 a.m. "Don't take yourself seriously at that hour of the night," my mother had cautioned me. "It is a low point. What you think of in the middle of the night when you are by yourself won't hold up in the light of day. Don't worry if you get a little frightened or depressed. Dawn comes early."

Anticipating my fear, she described and thereby dissipated it.

Women in the West have a long tradition of traveling by themselves. Now that my mother is in her late eighties, with her memory failing, the sharpest images her mind retains, and the ones which bring a joyous light to her eyes, are those she summons up from her solitary rides on horseback through the forests and mountains of Idaho, between her family's ranch and the small towns where she taught school. Riding alone, she was alert to every sight and sound and smell. Her cry of "Look!" rings through my childhood. To this day her eyes dart about, picking up sights that delight her, things I never notice and strain to see: a raccoon by the roadside, a bird's nest under the eaves, a black butterfly on a dark tree trunk. Old habits keep her on the watch.

Her younger sister, my Aunt Luree, is a watcher too – soft-

spoken and quiet from being so much alone. In the summers of my childhood when I visited her on her Idaho ranch, she taught me to ride a horse. Ambling along at a comfortable walk, Aunt Luree on her favorite chestnut mare and I on the piebald, Patches, a pony she had found lost in the hills, Aunt Luree would point out a gopher hole to avoid or a patch of pretty yellow mustard to look at. She told me that the cattle sometimes ate the prickly red blooms of the cheet grass and got them lodged in their mouths. Most of the time she was silent, but I could feel her thinking about the countryside.

Her son, Dwain, my age, challenged me: boy versus girl, country versus city. He slapped Patches' rump so he shot forward with me clutching the saddle horn, barely keeping my seat. Dwain led me through fields where bulls lowered their heads and glowered at us, up creeks where hornets nested in hollow logs and stung me, not him, and down rocky trails where our horses stumbled and shied. With Aunt Luree as my ideal, I would not cry or give up. I saw her as a woman as much at home in the world as any man around her. Only once that I know of did she accede to any special consideration. That was in 1925, when she was pregnant with Dwain. She wanted him born on their ranch on the high Joseph Plains, but Carl, her husband, said no. Since there was no doctor for miles around, he was fearful of what might happen at the birth of their first and, as it turned out, their only baby.

So, in the eighth month of her pregnancy, Carl borrowed a saddle big enough for Luree to sit in, and rode with her down the twenty-eight miles of switchback trail to a landing on the Snake River, where a small steamer stopped to drop off mail and supplies for homesteaders. There she boarded the steamer, while Carl returned home to look after the animals. Sixty-five miles up the Snake River, Luree got off the boat at Lewiston and took a train to Pendleton, Oregon, where her married sister lived. Six weeks after Dwain was born, Luree made the return journey. With her small baby boy in a box tied in front of her saddle horn, she rode back up the switchback trail to her isolated home.

Horseback always was her preferred way of travel. In 1935

the family moved to town for Dwain's schooling. Carl and Dwain went ahead in the car. Luree chose to ride herd on fourteen head of horses that they took with them. Crossing country she had never been in before, she drove the horses over one hundred miles from New Meadows, Idaho, to Vale, Oregon.

Later, back in Idaho, whenever I visited her, we would ride together up into the hills surrounding the Payette Valley. There she had a favorite spot where she came by herself every evening to watch the sunset. From a lifetime of looking, every hill and valley and the Blue Mountains beyond were as dear and familiar to her as the faces of her loved ones.

There is a special quality in the way one looks at things when one is alone – an intensity of observation, an originality of response, not diluted or even enlarged by the reactions of another person. Being alone, one gets to know oneself. My mother and my aunt passed on to me the belief that it was a luxury being able to travel alone – not always, but often enough to gain a sense of being one's own person.

My mother-in-law, Mary Merhar, always sat up straighter when she recounted how she crossed the continent in 1900, from New York to Anaconda, Montana, on her own. She was eighteen and could not speak English. On the train she met another Slav, an older man who said he would help her change trains in Chicago. They went into the big depot bar and restaurant together. The man ordered beer for himself and a glass of wine for Mary, saying smoothly that she had several hours to relax before her train left the station. At this point in her story, Mary narrowed her eyes shrewdly. "Then I get suspicious," she said. "Something about this man does not satisfy me. I do not trust him." In a classic female maneuver, she excused herself to go to the ladies' room. Instead she ran down the long bar, asking if anyone spoke Slovene. A bartender did. "Run!" he told her. "Your train is leaving in five minutes!"

"I just catch it," Mary smiled, "and get to Montana O.K." The satisfaction of her escape still cheered her decades later. To have traveled so far without the protection of a reliable man, and to have outwitted an unreliable one, gave her confidence. All through the years when she was raising her family, Mary

never left the small town of Fairbanks, Alaska. But when she
was sixty, her self-reliance reasserted itself: by bus, boat, and
train, she traveled thousands of miles, once again alone, to
start a new life.

To be sheltered is also to be shackled. Only by stepping out
to move freely through the world can women see life and judge
it from their own perspective instead of secondhand.

One does not have to be an explorer or traveler to voyage
outward. The independent journey is a state of mind as well as
physical movement. If a woman has gone directly from her
father's command to her husband's protection, as so many
women of my generation did, with no solo trips in between, then
the first step out of the house on her own seems fraught with
danger. It is reassuring to remember that, although historians
have seldom remarked on the fact, there always have been, and
always will be, many brave women traveling alone.

10. An M.D. with Empathy

KATHARINE BUTLER

"Medicine is a profession which naturally appeals deeply to women, as they are instinctively concerned with conserving life."

VIRGINIA GILDERSLEEVE
Many a Good Crusade

Why would a woman want to become a doctor after she was well along in another career, and how did she do it? I asked my friend Hope Meyers these questions when she told me that her favorite late bloomer was Dr. Katharine Butler. "One of the most marvelous people I have ever known," Hope said. As to her being late blooming, Hope ticked off the fact that Dr. Butler was thirty-seven years old when she was granted her medical degree and forty when she began her practice. When she retired in 1965, Dr. Butler was an associate professor of clinical medicine at Cornell University, consultant in medicine at The New York Hospital (founded in 1771 by King George III, and associated with Cornell University Medical College), and had her own private practice.

"I think of her with joy and devotion," Hope declared. "At crucial times in my life, when I was quite young, and later, too, she was very helpful to me. She is highly skilled in dealing with people; a woman who is much more than just a medical practitioner."

Two doctors I have known gave me the kind of friendship Hope referred to, so I was eager to meet another member of this dwindling band of old-fashioned doctors who administer to the whole person, paying attention to one's general problems as well as to the condition of one's esophagus or metatarsus. I called the number in Pennsylvania, which Hope had given me, of the retirement center Dr. Butler recently had moved into. On the telephone her clear, firm voice and her vigorous laugh put me at ease immediately, and prepared me for the person I met, when, a few weeks later, I drove through the countryside of snow-covered hills to visit her in her new home near Philadelphia.

Katharine Butler was a New Englander through and through. She took me in with one glance, her long face breaking into a wide smile. I noted her fine, straight nose and felt the steady grip of her handshake. She is of medium height, but so erect that she at first seems taller. The cold February day that we met, she was wearing a tweed skirt and a bright blue sweater that set off her neatly waved white hair. At eighty, quick-moving and obviously fit, Katharine Butler has that air of invincibility that develops from a lifetime of looking after oneself and others with singular competence.

I would have guessed that she came from a long line of independent New England women which included some workers for women's suffrage, some scholars and some schoolteachers. Katharine was amused by my speculation and picked up on it with a responsiveness that animated all our conversation that day and when we met again later. She is a superb conversationalist who listens so well that she catches what one wants to say before all the words are out.

We settled down comfortably in the warm living room of her new townhouse, she sitting in a bright yellow chair and I in a soft-rose wingback. It is a glowing room, tastefully decorated, full of polished mahogany tables and lovely old keepsakes: gilt-framed family portraits, glass paperweights and small brass boxes. The rosy tones in her Oriental carpets are accentuated by red pillows on her Federal love seat. A tall amaryllis with tangerine blossoms stood in front of the glass sliding doors leading directly outside, where the sun glistened on huge piles of white snow.

"An interesting point," Katharine speculated as she handed me a cup of coffee. "When I think about my mother and all of her family, there are no role models there. They all had protected lives. Mother was afraid even to have me go alone, when I was sixteen, the short distance from Providence to Boston – even with someone meeting me at the other end." She laughed. "When I lived in Boston, on Boylston Street near Copley Square, Mother had a fit. She didn't know as much about New York, so she couldn't be too specific about her worries when I was there. There I lived at the YWCA between trips I made as the Y director of the Southern Student Division. I would be away fourteen days – thirteen of those in a sleeper. Sometimes she didn't know where I was in the South. I don't think I appreciated at all how hard this was for my mother. I think the whole concept of my being off on my own was far beyond what anybody in her family thought was wise or prudent. I'm sure that she got quite a lot of flack I didn't know anything about."

One can only guess what strength it took on Katharine's part to fashion her own life out of this protected environment. Born in South Weymouth, Massachusetts, in 1898, she had a strict upbringing. Her father was a clergyman. "If I didn't go to prayer meeting, I couldn't go to a dance," she recalled. "My father used to call for me at nine o'clock, practically until I was in college."

He was a graduate of Amherst. His concern for people and his deep commitment to social action made a lasting impression on his daughter. "Interesting that he thought I should go to college," Katharine continued. "No question in his mind. It was just assumed that I would go to Mount Holyoke. I didn't care where I went, as long as I got away from home," she said with conviction. "My mother took a dim view of this because she went to Miss Porter's. All of her family did. So she just learned to do a bit of this and that, and be a lady.

"I was rather quick and not thorough – that kind of student. Not very profound. I was no great brain – no honor roll or Phi Beta Kappa. *Thought* I was a great athlete – basketball, skiing, and tennis in the early days. Girls had to earn the money to pay their basketball coach in high school then. Boys had their own."

It was in seventh grade that Katharine had as a teacher a

woman she later realized had a great influence on her, one who kindled her interest in science – Miss Helen Gay Pratt, herself fresh out of Mount Holyoke, teaching her first year. "She taught me a course of physiology, had just taken it herself, and taught it beautifully," Katharine told me. "Both seventh and eighth grades were in one room, with half of us studying and half of us reciting. I was fascinated by everything about *digesting* and *breathing*," she rolled the two words out lovingly. "So at Mount Holyoke, I chose zoology, because of Helen Gay Pratt. I thought about taking medicine during my second year."

But at this pivotal time of her college life, no one encouraged Katharine to follow her natural bent for medicine. Career guidance for girls was unheard of. World War I was raging, and she ventured the idea of becoming a nurse to her uncle, one of the first anesthetists in Boston, who quickly squelched it. "It's a dog's life," he said. "You can't do that." She was "kind of downed" by his reaction, and by no support from her parents. "They never gave it any serious thought." Then, in her senior year of college, Katharine was interviewed and selected for a special program on community service that all the New England colleges participated in. Representatives from each college lived for six weeks in New York, visiting settlement houses and learning how social workers function in a large city. "A big deal, really!" Katharine emphasized. "And I had to turn it down because my mother made such a fuss. She said she wasn't well, and in a way, she wasn't. She wasn't that ill, though. She just wanted me at home. She was beginning to think I was getting away. I talked it over with my father and there wasn't much we could do about it but give it up. A great disappointment.

"The expectation then," Katharine explained, "was that a woman would be married and have a family, all in capital letters. Or live at home and have a job."

Because Katharine did neither, her mother fretted at her through the years. Like so many mother-daughter relationships, theirs jolted along in the old ruts of opposing attitudes, until Katharine finally took stock of their situation and set it straight, with an inspirational burst of honesty – but not until she was over fifty, a mature woman with a medical practice, and her mother a widow. So set are old family conflicts that it takes great insight and creativity to rearrange them into happier patterns.

Katharine told me how she did it: "I used to go back to Providence from New York to see Mother very often. I had many things to do, but I made a great effort to get up and see her. She really was lonely. She would call and I would go. I would leave people in the hospital and people sick and someone else on call. Every time I went, she held before me as a model a girl who was so wonderful to her widowed mother, who had a job downtown, and worked at the church, and sang in the choir, and who was very nice to her mother's friends. I got tired of hearing about her. It was not pleasant.

"So, one night as I was riding on the train, I got to thinking how I dreaded going. And I thought, 'Now really! Take yourself in hand! You spend hours in your office talking to people about their family problems. Why can't you do something about your own? So I thought for awhile and decided 'I'm just going to have to explain a few things to Mother.' So, sure enough, I hadn't been there more than a half hour when she said, 'Oh, I suppose you have to take the three o'clock train back tomorrow and isn't it too bad? It seems dreadful that you can't be here.'

"I said, 'You know, I thought about that all the way coming up on the train, and I finally decided, Mother, that it isn't my fault. If you wanted me to be like this girl who is held before me all of the time, you and father did everything wrong. I don't know how I got this way.'

"At first she was noncommittal about it. Then I got to elaborating on it – about what they might have done – like not letting me go away to college." Katharine gave a short laugh. "The saving grace of my mother was her marvelous sense of humor," she continued. "She was a gay little woman and I think she spent a great many years having a hard time being the wife of a clergyman. So the end of this conversation was that she thought it was pretty funny too. We laughed over things she and father should have done to raise me differently. And you know she never said any more about my coming home and about this other dutiful daughter of her friend.

"It's true. She had a nice quirky humor and was a good sport. I used to smoke. She thought it was awful and chided me about it, saying no lady would ever smoke. And I said, 'Mother, if you were living in my era, you would be the first to smoke. You know it perfectly well.'"

Katharine knew her mother worried over her. Once she overheard a friend remark to her mother, "Has she ever thought of library work? It's such a dignified occupation."

However, despite surface frictions, Katharine was true to her parents' values. As she pointed out, "I had no choice from my background but to do something worthwhile."

In college she was active in the Young Women's Christian Association. As the representative from Mount Holyoke at a national convention, she made her maiden speech advocating a change in the 'Y' statement of purpose, and, as a result, was offered a job in Boston as the 'Y' assistant executive secretary for ten colleges in the area. All hopes of a career in medicine or any related area of science were put aside. "My thought was to get off the family's back and become independent." She took the job. "I lived frugally, saved my money, and eventually went to graduate school at Columbia University and Union Theological Seminary and got my M.A. in religious education."

After she had taken time off for her M.A., Katharine became the director of the Southern Division of the Student YWCA and traveled through all of the states south of the Mason–Dixon line and east of the Mississippi. It was here that Katharine's trenchant manner and plain speech landed her in more than one prickly situation. Issues such as race relations, labor-management problems, and international cooperation, as well as religion, were among the Y's major concerns. These topics often inflamed feelings in the South. "I should never have been sent down there," she maintained. "I was too direct. I didn't know what I was doing." After innocently reporting on the highlights of a Midwestern 'Y' conference, where these issues were discussed, to the assembled student body of a girl's normal school in Athens, Georgia, (no longer in existence), the president of the school got up to close the meeting. Katharine's eyes flashed at the memory. "He prayed for me, and asked all the girls to pray, that I should be forgiven for saying the things that I had said to them."

Variations of that experience plagued her throughout the South. She was deeply moved by the inequalities evident at that time, and it was her nature, when she saw injustices, to step forward and speak up. "When I got back to New York, I was on the carpet. I was very shaken." But she went back to the South, made some solid friendships with both black and white men and women, and at the end of two years fought being transferred back to the Northeast division. "I wanted to stay. The South was very vibrant, very vital. There was change. The girls were responding. You could feel it. Whereas in the Northeast I felt that other secular organizations were coming in on the 'Y' and it was retreating into a much more deeply religious, spiritual and inspirational movement, and I just felt this was not what I preferred to do. I wasn't comfortable arranging retreats – all that inner looking for students. I don't think of myself as a spiritual sort of person. I think I was running out of sympathy with the trend in the 'Y'. Everyday I was in the Northeast, I was working myself right out of it. Sometimes I think that if I had stayed in the South I never would have changed careers."

Looking back, the closing of this option to do what she considered social action work in the South with the 'Y' was a fortunate one for Katharine, because it motivated her to take a risk she might not have had the courage to try had she been able to stay in a secure, satisfying job. It was a low point, but also a time of great ferment. With a friend, she went that summer to Europe for an international student conference. "The most exciting thing I had ever done," she recalled. It was 1928. The next year, she worked at a 'Y' summer camp for adults, using the project method of teaching that she had learned at Columbia. "Here I was, getting very valuable material that would have been accepted for a dissertation, but I didn't want it. Ph.D.'s in education were selling apples on the streets of New York." It was the year of the Great Crash: 1929.

"Besides," she elaborated, "I thought there were a lot of Ph.D. dissertations written that were not exactly vital to life and death. A lot of minutiae that took up time and were not very practical. I was annoyed with some of the kinds of research that were going on. This was true in science as well as in the humanities. Still is. Writing a whole book on the antennae of a cockroach or something."

After such flat statements, Katharine always paused and looked straight at me, at once giving me time to absorb what she said and watching to see how I reacted. This time I urged her to think of all the factors that had led her to embark on the long study for a medical career.

"When I was getting my M.A.," she responded, "a psychiatrist (he later became my patient) led a discussion group on the psychoanalytical problems of teenagers. This appealed to my sense of actively helping people. I was absolutely fascinated. I would have liked to go into psychiatry – here I draw a distinction between psychiatry and psychology; between those who have medical training and those who do not – but studying psychiatry would have taken too long, been impractical.

"Remember, in the meantime, here I am thirty, and I'm not married. This was a great disappointment to my mother. Good grief! How could I get like this?

"Another thing, it was getting hard to keep up with my friends. I enjoyed seeing them. I would visit them, but they were all tied up with little family problems and the children. It got to the point where it wasn't much fun. I couldn't share in the sense that they could share with each other because I didn't have any children. And so you find yourself withdrawing.

"Also, I think there is something about traveling around, doing an administrative job, always working with groups, spreading out all over the Southern region or the North-eastern – you don't really belong. You're not in the community. You're nothing. And especially when you're not married. I realize now, in retrospect, that going to the hospital every day, *this* becomes family – being a part of the hospital staff. I always worked at a clinic. I was making rounds. I was going to conferences, was in my office. I spent, I suppose, half of my time in the hospital without pay."

So Katharine sought advice about applying to medical schools. She still remembers clearly what a professor told her: "I don't know," the professor said. "It takes an awful grind. There is an awful lot you won't enjoy."

But the idea had seized Katharine. "At least if you are a doctor you can work," she told herself. A lot of people in the 1930s were not working. "And medicine really was my natural bent," she repeated. "In my family we never went off the handle about medical things. We took them on a very even keel. My mother was a very practical person. She took care of all kinds of friends and neighbors and family. Nothing threw her. We could talk about and understand medical problems. There was no hush-hush."

And she could do some good, could be of service. This was the *sine qua non* of anything Katharine did: her strong moral sense had to be satisfied.

But it took courage, particularly for a woman entirely dependent on herself, to make such a radical career change. While many factors entered into it, Katharine confided that there was one extremely personal circumstance that helped her make her decision. At the age of thirty, she had lost thirty pounds. It was a difficult thing to do and the fact that she was able to do it contributed enormously to her self-confidence.

"About this time I was wavering," she said. "I was not sure what to do. I had a pain in my hip, so I went to the Cornell Clinic and the doctor said, 'You ought to have your tonsils out and lose thirty pounds.' I was not flabby fat – just a sturdy girl, five feet three inches tall and weighed one hundred fifty-five pounds. Why nobody ever put me on a diet, I don't know. I just plain overate good wholesome food. I ate a lot of home-made bread. To this day I would rather have a piece of good bread, almost, than cake. The doctor told me I needed nothing but a thousand-calorie well-balanced diet. It was June. I went to work at a 'Y' camp. It was very hard, because at camp I had a little house with a fireplace, so everybody came for staff meetings in the evening and brought their coffee, cake and cookies. And I would sit there and pour out the skim milk. But I lost thirty pounds and stuck to my diet from then on. At one hundred twenty-five pounds, I had self-esteem. And I never had any more pain in my hip. The weight loss gave me a great feeling of competence – just when I was changing my life, when I was beginning to see an opening." Heavy women often have no idea how morale-boosting a weight loss can be.

Another fortuitous development was that, at the camp, Katharine met and worked with a psychiatrist only a few years older than herself. This woman had borrowed money for education and Katharine saw that it could be done. Determined now to apply for admission to medical school, and encouraged by her new self-image, she worked another year and saved enough money to enroll at Barnard University to study physics and chemistry for a year in preparation for the entrance examinations. "That first semester at Barnard was touch and go," she remembered. "I had a heavy load. Physics then was not premed oriented. I knew that if I failed I could go back to the 'Y' and get a job. I would be disappointed, but I wouldn't starve."

One of Katharine's problems was that she had been out of school so long that she was critical of some of the courses and unwilling to cram for what she saw as inapplicable information. "The head of my department scolded me roundly," she said, tapping her fingers on the arm of the chair like a teacher calling a class to attention.

Earlier, before she had enrolled at Barnard, Katharine had called on the dean of the Cornell Medical School to inquire if she might apply there. While he had not been truly encouraging, he did not turn her down. Columbia University told her they never took anyone as old as she. When her grades in physics began slipping, "I was upset and scared," she remembered. "I went to Cornell to see Dean Edwards. I thought it was a good idea to let him know that I still intended to apply. He said, 'Well, how do you like your chemistry and physics?' And I said, 'Well, of course, it is not correctly oriented. Will you tell me what a man standing on a ladder that is at a forty-five-degree angle against a wall, who has a paint pail weighing two and a half pounds on his shoulder – and I have to figure out the friction of the ladder against the wall – what has that got to do with medicine?'

" 'I'll tell *you* something, Miss Butler,' he said to me. 'You have to forget what you know about education. Maybe you don't think that has anything to do with medicine, but once you get started on it, there will be a lot of things you'll have to learn, *whether you like it or not!*' "

Katharine looked me in the eye and laughed heartily. She obviously appreciates people who speak as honestly as herself. We agreed that it was difficult to return to school after one had experience in the world. You question more, are impatient, and want all the subject matter you have to study to be pertinent to your own interests.

"I remember at one of my initial interviews for Cornell, Dean Edwards said to me that he thought my age would be against me. He took a chance on me. One of the other interviewers asked if I had enough money to last for two or three years and I said, 'Oh, yes,' when I didn't know where my next meal was coming from."

In the fall of 1931, when she was thirty-three, Katharine was accepted at the Cornell University School of Medicine. No more traveling and speech-making, arranging conferences and leading discussion groups. No more time for long philosophical talks. No more extra money in her pocket. From the status and independence of a professional woman with a responsible job, she had to scale down to a limited, disciplined and penniless student life.

"I lived on less than most," Katharine said, "bought fewer books, borrowed them or used the library. Got a secondhand microscope. Did everything the hard way. My personal loans hung over me and worried me. But my background helped.

I had been taught to think twice before spending. I never spent money with abandon. All through med school I wore somebody else's clothes. Never bought a thing. The styles were changing; beginning about 1929 or 1930 dresses were getting longer. A couple of friends who were taller handed their things down to me."

Ten to twelve years older than her fellow students, Katharine worked hard to keep up. She had little social life. "Too busy. I had horrible nerves before exams. Felt I would fail every one."

As an older woman experienced in working with people, Katharine knew that she was different from her younger fellow students. "They used to call me the social worker, because I think I had more compassion than a lot of them. It was a combination of just me and experience. For instance, when a patient died, we were supposed to request a postmortem from the family. It was very hard for me to beat a family down to get that postmortem when they were upset and opposed to it. But it was very, very important. We were graded on how many we failed to get. The idea was that you were going to learn something that would just revolutionize medicine," she said with an edge of sarcasm in her voice.

"My second year I worked at Bellevue Hospital as assistant resident. A lot of people assumed I would be a pediatrician because I was a woman. I said, 'I'm sorry. I've never worked with children.' I thought I would be better with young adults because I had worked with them. I asked a woman friend, 'What do you say to people when they *assume* you should be a pediatrician?' My friend answered, 'Oh, I tell them that sick children scare me to death.' I said, 'Well, you and me both. You can't talk with them, can't reason. I'm not about to take care of a sick child.'

"I didn't want to do anything in surgery. In the first place, doors are practically closed to women surgeons. This was true in so many places. The excuse was that there is no place to put them. Standard thing. On the whole, surgeons still are reluctant to take women.

"So it sort of fell down to general or internal medicine. You begin applying for an internship in your senior year. It's just like getting into college now. You had to go for interviews. It is very disruptive. It's like fraternity rushing – just ghastly. You don't know where you are going to be."

When Katharine was offered an internship at The New York Hospital, the person most pleased, after herself, was Dean Edwards. "When I came back from the hospital he was standing in his door with a grin from ear to ear. I said, 'I guess you know.' He said, 'Yes, I know.' He took a chance on me. I was an older student and a woman. Luckily he didn't know that I didn't have any money," she said in a delighted voice.

After her internship, Katharine worked for a year at the Bellevue Chest Service, where Dr. Helen Gavin was one of her attending physicians. When Katharine was ready to set up her own practice, Dr. Gavin gave her office space to start her off, let her take some of her own extra calls, and do lab work in lieu of rent. Within six months, she could pay her way. At forty, Katharine Butler was launched on the career she had contemplated when she was nineteen. Her early instincts were correct: medicine suited both her talents and her temperament.

In describing the rewards of being a physician, Katharine's face lit with enthusiasm. "I maintain an interest in knowing more about the structure of the body," she said. "The cellular life – the physiology – the chemistry – the thing that is just beyond belief. We are fearfully and wonderfully made. This is a constant challenge: to know more about the body, to understand it.

"Also, medicine is a natural for women. Taking care of people is an extension of being a good mother. For me I suppose it was a substitute. I still think women are different from men. That doesn't put either one of them down. Different biologically. I don't think that you can say that kinds of thinking are different for men or women. We tend to put bad labels on differences like that, so I don't want to make that differentiation. It is an individual thing. But I think that a nurturing role is inherent in women, a caring is in their genes. Of course a lot of women don't have it to the degree I'm making out. A lot of women stay in research, but for the person who likes to take care of people, medicine is a natural thing to choose."

And as an internist or general practitioner, Katharine was able to treat the whole person, as many young medical students today are electing to do.

Clearly, Katharine Butler found great joy and fulfillment in taking care of people. As her friends and patients testify, she cured by example as well as by medical treatment; her own sterling character infused them with the confidence that they could get better. "I wasn't very good at giving drugs," she admitted. "Hadn't taken anything stronger than an aspirin myself."

Katharine kept up her interest in psychiatry while she was practicing medicine. From her second year in medical school, she lived with the psychiatrist she met at the 'Y' camp the year she decided to change her life, and they shared a lifetime of professional comradeship and mutual support until her friend died in 1973. And for ten years, Katharine had a standing Saturday lunch date with another psychiatrist who had practiced general medicine until World War I. "He used to like to talk to me about what was going on in medicine and I would get a lot of information from him about general psychiatric problems." She led a full and satisfying life, spending mornings in her office seeing patients and afternoons in the hospital or clinic.

Then, at sixty-seven, Katharine faced another big decision. "Life was getting very thick at this point," she said. Her friend, four years older, with whom she had shared an apartment for many years, wanted to move from New York to Florida, which they did. "After being indoors all of those years," Katharine said, "it was very nice. Before I decided to go, my patients said to me, 'Why don't you just keep a few of us?' But it was impossible to cut down on the number of patients and still maintain an office. Couldn't pay the rent and all the other expenses." Contrary to the popular image of all doctors making enormous profits, Katharine's income never was large. She gave a great deal of her time, free, to clinics.

"I can't remember when I got out of debt," she replied to my question with an air of surprise. "You would think I could, but I can't. Medical expenses were always going up and I had huge carrying charges."

This was said without a tinge of complaint. But on the subject of how the public now feels about doctors, Katharine became exercised. "I can't be unemotional about it. The image of doctors is spoiled, maybe justifiably, by a few. People don't appreciate how hard the rest of them work. When people criticize doctors, they probably are correct about some. Then I have to say, 'I'm sorry, but all of the doctors I worked with were honorable and honest – full of integrity.' "

Without realizing it, Katharine described herself: a woman who chose medicine, not to make money, but to serve humanity in a direct, practical way. Finding the right profession to do this was a long struggle. But as a doctor, Katharine Butler fulfilled her own high standards of service. She made a genuine difference in the lives of hundreds of people who remember her as a vital, insightful and inspiring doctor who cared.

Just meeting Katharine Butler, now in her eightieth year, is an invigorating experience. Was she happy with her new life? I asked. "Retirement is just like taking a new job," she stated. "It's what you bring to it. You have to have something going on in your head. As a friend wrote me, old age is not for sissies."

"What a good way to put it," I said as I stood to leave. "All the long-lived women in my family made me realize that I was not going to be young forever. And I saw that life was a series of upheavals."

"You don't know how valuable your family experience is to you," Katharine said feelingly as we went into her bedroom, where she helped me into my coat. "In our present way of living a lot of family experience is lost. I think that we've missed out on a lot, removing ourselves to a retirement place like this. This way the young have no experience or idea of the older period of life. In the 1960s we were in a jam because of the idea that if you were over thirty and opened your head you were an old crone. I think we're over this now. But one of the things that is hard about being retired is the lack of a wide circle of stimulating relationships. Every once in a while, I feel very isolated."

From the pile of letters and papers on the walnut secretary opposite her bed, I could see that Katharine kept up with her friends through an extensive correspondence. Books and magazines were stacked beside a comfortable chair and ottoman. It was a sunny, inviting, lived-in room.

"Yes," Katharine agreed, "I spend a lot of time here. I enjoy the housewifely things I never had time for before, like needlepoint. And I have a great time cooking. I even like to iron, I really do. I'm very busy keeping house. It doesn't bore me. I used to think, when I was practicing medicine, that when I retired I would sit down at two in the afternoon, with my feet on a chaise lounge, and read a book. I have never done that. I think it is almost immoral to sit down in the afternoon. I'm more of an activist than a contemplative," she laughed. "I've got a garden started out there under those piles of snow."

"What a winter we've had," I shuddered.

"Yes, but soon I'm off on a short trip to Greece with a doctor friend and his family. I look forward to seeing those sunny Greek isles, but most of all, I hope to get in a little shoptalk.

"I think that happiness isn't quite the right question," she concluded as we walked down the hall to the front door. "Happiness, I think, is not a permanent thing."

"You catch it on the wing?"

"Right. So I have some very happy moments."

A brave and excellent woman alone.

11. The Long Journey of a Photojournalist

MARILYN SILVERSTONE

"It was as if she had an appointment to meet the rest of herself sometime, somewhere."

WILLA CATHER
The Song of the Lark

Read a good book at the right time in your life and it will haunt you forever. When I was a young woman with three children under five years of age, a status other than motherhood was inconceivable to me. Then a friend gave me a copy of *Kristin Lavernsdatter* by Sigrid Undset to read. This trilogy about a Norwegian woman extended my view of life as few other books had done. The fact that Kristin lived in medieval Norway presented no barrier to my identification with her. Her temperament was closer to mine than many of Tolstoy's or Flaubert's heroines. Because I felt exactly as she had when she was a young woman, I had no difficulty growing older with her. When she came to a point in her life where those she loved had moved beyond her help, and the world she knew had changed so she no longer felt at home in it, I was as devastated as she was. The thought that I might reach that same juncture occurred to me for the first time. I understood how Kristin threw herself into life, working with high energy and total concentration through each day until she dropped exhausted into bed each night.

What, then, does a mature woman do when she awakens one morning to find those crowded years of intense living are over before she had time to consider her future? In the Middle Ages there was an honorable solution. After a brief period of anguish and reappraisal, Kristin threw on her warm cloak, put on her stout shoes, and set off on a long journey to a convent by the sea. There the nuns accepted her into their ordered life. Her spirit remained vigorous; she was active and honored to the end of her life.

No strong sense of vocation set Kristin on this path to a religious life, although she eventually did become a nun. Without much conscious planning, she accepted the alternative open to her: the religious community offered tranquility after a stormy life, security after the erosion of her position in the secular world, and a sufficient challenge in the task of learning humility to satisfy her robust spirit. A fitting culmination, it seemed to me, of a vivid life.

So when I received word that my old friend and colleague Marilyn Silverstone had gone to Nepal to become a nun, I thought of the parallel between her and Kristin Lavernsdatter: as surely as Kristin chose her path to the convent by the sea, Marilyn had been journeying all her life toward that monastery in Nepal. Both settings are exotic and medieval, but the impulses that directed these women to a religious life are timeless and universal: a yearning of the human heart for release from temporal concern and a desire for spiritual joy and peace. In March, 1977, one week before she became forty-eight years old, Marilyn took the vows of a Tibetan Buddhist nun.

Since she was fifteen years old, in Scarsdale, New York, Marilyn, too, was haunted by a book she had read – *Secret Tibet*, by Fosco Maraini, a lyrical account of a mysterious world she vowed one day to see. A passionate resolve made in adolescence by someone with a strong will can alter that person's life in subtle and long-reaching ways. Marilyn's resolve became a touchstone against which she rubbed every choice of action to determine which one promised to take her one step closer to Central Asia. Her taste also was formed by Maraini's book. From the moment she first saw a desert landscape, when she was sent west to a summer camp in Arizona, she loved it. The wide, open space, the deep blue vaulting sky, the subtle earth colors all fit Maraini's description of the great Tibetan plateau. After graduation from Wellesley College, Marilyn worked in New York on *Art News*,

Industrial Design, and *Interiors*, and then on documentary art films in Italy, but these jobs were only steppingstones on her way east. She became a photojournalist, covering assignments first in Europe, then in the Middle East, and finally in Asia. When she saw the Negev Desert in Israel, and covered the war in India's Rann of Kutch, and visited Indian Army outposts in Ladakh, she dreamed of the great, high, silent desert of Tibet. On an assignment in Japan for the London *Daily Telegraph Magazine*, she photographed Fosco Maraini. "You changed my life," she told him. "It's true," she repeated many times to me. "His book started it. Some little spark led me on. And I've never looked back. I was always wondering where it was going to lead."

This spark led her most satisfactorily to India. In 1959 she bested a horde of journalists and photographers from all over the world, who had been waiting more than a month on India's border hoping to catch the arrival of the Dalai Lama, who was making his escape from Tibet after it was invaded by the Chinese. Marilyn took the photograph of him that *Life* magazine chose as its lead picture. Not quite thirty years old, Marilyn, with that success, broke through to the upper echelons of a new, glamorous, and highly competitive profession. The entire Indian subcontinent up to Iran and east to Japan became her beat.

She met Frank Moraes, the preeminent Indian editor and journalist. Soon they were as necessary to one another as two could be. It was the beginning of an enduring, tumultuous, but mutually supportive and dependent relationship. Although Marilyn and Frank never married, they established a home in New Delhi and were to all intents and purposes husband and wife. American ambassadors, Indian officials and the whole diplomatic corps extended invitations to them as a couple.

Before long Marilyn was elected to the prestigious international cooperative of "concerned photographers" called Magnum, founded by Henri Cartier-Bresson, Robert Capa, David Seymour, and George Rodger for freelancers who wanted to work in their own manner as opposed to being staff photographers. Her photographs appeared regularly in

Newsweek, *Time*, *Life*, and *National Geographic*, as well as in newspapers and magazines all over Europe. In 1963 she covered the wedding of American Hope Cooke to the crown prince of Sikkim and felt as if fate had arranged for her to be in this Himalayan state once protected by Tibet. Two years later the prince became the ruler or Chogyal of Sikkim and Marilyn was there to record the colorful coronation. The Shah of Iran's coronation in 1967 was a spectacular event drawing hundreds of reporters and photographers from every major magazine and newspaper in the world, each jockeying furiously for an advantageous position. The French picture magazine *Paris Match* flew its own plane, specially equipped with a darkroom, into Teheran.

"I asked myself," Marilyn told me later, "what, in all this pageantry, will really be the most personal, the most touching. And it seemed to me that it would be when the Shah crowned his queen, Farah." Marilyn's picture of that moment was so moving that *Paris Match* and *National Geographic* both used it, even though they had hundreds of shots from their own well-serviced and well-equipped staff photographers.

The life of a photojournalist is one of tremendous pressure, particularly for a freelancer. Getting assignments is just the beginning. Arrangements for shipping film overseas are tricky, waiting for its arrival in time to cover an event, nerve-racking. The freelancer works out her own transportation problems, slogs through official labyrinths on her own to obtain passes and permits, fights through crowds or negotiates for a favorable spot among a limited number of positions at a formal occasion, from which, after long waits, she finally takes her photographs. Then, getting the exposed rolls of film out of the country to meet a deadline continents away is ulcer-producing. Hours too late and the whole enormous effort counts for nothing.

Marilyn covered floods, famines, funerals and wars, working at a feverish pitch. One week she might be living in an Indian village, the next staying in a maharajah's palace. The sixties was an exhilarating time to be in India and she was there at the center of all major events. While Jawaharlal

Nehru was prime minister his nation enjoyed great prestige; he imbued his countrymen with a sense of purpose and a desire for progress that helped sweep his daughter, Indira Gandhi, into power toward the end of that decade. Several times Marilyn's pictures of Prime Minister Gandhi made *Newsweek*'s covers.

"O.K., now tell me what you think of these," she would say to my children, aged seven, nine, and eleven, as she spread a batch of her photographs out on our dining room table in Bombay. She was as single-minded and original as a child herself. The four of them looked at the photographs as equals. Her observations and anecdotes were not censored for their sake. They trusted her and gave her their honest opinions.

Because of my children, Marilyn asked me to work with her on an assignment to do a book for a "Children Everywhere" series. I had fiddled around with little articles for local groups and had published a couple of stories in small magazines. With Marilyn I learned how to work. Her concentration was formidable. For that small children's book we spent unbroken hours, from the time my children left for school at 8:00 A.M. until I picked them up at 3:15 P.M., in her small, hot hotel room, day after day after day, poring over pictures, struggling to create matching lines of dialogue, arranging, rearranging, starting all over again. We didn't break for lunch. Marilyn sent for food. Greasy samosas or soggy doughnuts arrived and she devoured what came without noticing its taste or consistency. Happily our *Bala: Child of India* earned us another contract and we became colleagues. We collaborated on four children's books, two of which took us on treks in Nepal and Sikkim.

Women traveling alone in Asia sounds very adventurous. Actually, Western women can go anywhere on the Indian subcontinent in complete safety, without any of the apprehension they would feel being alone in any large American or European city. As a legacy of the days of the British raj, white women are a class apart, not to be hassled in any way. So Marilyn and I traveled with impunity. Her empathy for the people enabled her to blend into any crowd in a magical manner. Tall and blonde as she is, she never attracted more than momentary curiosity; she was never mobbed or plagued by people staring at her cameras. Her concentration on the event at hand was like a force emanating from her, turning people back to their own affairs. On a festival day I lugged her extra cameras and lenses, wading behind her, knee-deep into the Arabian Sea, surrounded by thousands of dancing, chanting Indians carrying clay images of the elephant-headed god, Ganesh, which, when they reached deep enough water, they dashed beneath the waves. As Marilyn photographed them, the people looked not at her, but at me.

She was curious to experience everything in a newly accessible but very ancient land. Before it became a fashion for the youth of the West to travel light through Asia, Marilyn, with sixty pounds of cameras and one change of clothes, scoured the subcontinent for stories. She recorded a vanishing way of life among the princes and nabobs and maharajahs. With Frank she toured Africa. She was restless, constantly on the move, nervous, strung taut with apprehension; it was often difficult to sustain a conversation with her. When she stayed with us she sometimes slept half-dressed so that she could make an early morning pickup at the airport. I've heard her retching in the bathroom before an assignment. She lived in a subjective world, intent on her purposes. In her rare states of repose, she appeared indolent; actually she was carrying on furious, raging, interior dialogues. More and more, her gaze was turning inward.

Originally fired by a sense of the importance of taking photographs to show the world that what was happening in India demanded attention, she began, in the late sixties, to wonder if it were truly worthwhile. Nothing seemed to change. She began to see photography as a predatory art. The glamor of her life began to pale. She rushed from Delhi to Dacca to cover a terrible flood in Bangladesh. The stench of the corpses nauseated her. A week later back in Delhi at a party she was passed a plate of hors d'oeuvre. They seemed to have the same odor of rot as the corpses in Bangladesh.

This is how she explained her disenchantment to me:

"When you've been in photography long enough you see the impermanence of everything. You see enormous disasters like the floods in Bangladesh and Bihar, and then you see another, and you realize how repetitive they are. Also, somebody who is up one day is down the next, or in jail.

"You go out and you photograph and you get – not inured, that's not the right word. You get cynical. Not inside, because you know how awful it is, but you know just how to take the picture to please them back home. And then you realize you could have taken that picture someplace else. You are choosing – constantly choosing how to do it. Your very act of taking a photograph is choosing. In big catastrophe-type photography you think of the market at home. You can't help it. You go down a line of kids and find the one who is most grabbing and terrible and sad. It's sort of awful.

"You find you are getting glib with your hands. You can do it.

"You have to keep telling yourself, 'I'm doing some good because if I take a picture here and show it there, they are going to get some help.'

"You get to taking pictures of people like pieces of meat. All people are raw material . . . to grind up and send off no matter who they are. Not that every poor person is good and every rich one bad. Photography is a good leveling influence too.

"But you are always an intruder in somebody else's life. I had never taken a picture if somebody didn't want me to. But I got to this point where I couldn't invade anybody's privacy anymore, pointing a camera at them. I really couldn't hold a camera to anybody anymore. I just couldn't do it.

"Another thing was happening: people were beginning to equate me with a camera. If I am not a photographer, Marilyn Silverstone, then what am I? Am I anything? Look in there. Where are you?

"You can't take part in anything and photograph it. You can't participate and photograph. In a way you get jaded.

"And living in India is . . . well, there is such a tremendous difference between the way the upper crust and the mass of people live. Our house was a showcase. It's an embarrassment. Living like that bothered me. More and more I thought some day there's got to be a rising up.

"I thought about Mother Theresa [a nun who works with the destitute and dying in Calcutta]. If I could just join her it would be something worthwhile – but it just isn't me. I'm not a social worker. I have too many blocks. I just couldn't do it."

Marilyn felt at this time as if she were in some dark corridor with no way out. For Frank, too, it was a period of turmoil. Always a fiercely independent political observer and highly respected critic, he now was under severe pressure from Prime Minister Indira Gandhi to write only favorable notices of her regime. He refused. She threatened his publisher. Frank found himself in an untenable position. A habitual drinker, he now seemed bent on oblivion. Finally, under considerable harrassment, he decided to move to England. Marilyn stood by him. Though she cried on leaving India, she loyally set up a household centered around Frank in London. Their golden interlude was over and anguish filled their days.

Looking back later, Marilyn remembered that period as miserable beyond description. She knew that Frank had lost all heart to live and was destroying himself. Her own efforts to find work came to nothing; certainly her lack of enthusiasm must have shown. So she set herself the task of learning the Tibetan language in six months – studying grammar to block out everything around her. It was as if something interior were driving her to study the language to keep a lifeline with one of the five Tibetan Buddhist lamas she had done a story on the year before in Sikkim. He was called Khanpo Rinpoche and he had agreed to teach her the beginning elements of Buddhism. She had said then, to another lama, that a cog was out of place in her life, and he had replied, "Yes, I know." That stayed with her, like an omen. She felt as if she were moving into a new phase of her life without really knowing what it would be.

In this way Marilyn more or less slid into the study of Buddhism. She maintains that there was no great moment of decision, no agonized should she or shouldn't she. No adding up the pros and cons. Those of us who knew her in India understand.

After another year of agony, for himself and for those around him, Frank died. By disciplining herself to become a Buddhist, Marilyn found her center point and prevented herself from drifting into a breakdown of total despair. She saved her own life.

This year (1978) Marilyn and the lama, Khanpo Rinpoche, came to visit us in Washington, D.C. They stayed about a week and we had a fine time. My mother was very impressed with Khanpo. She approved of his dignity and manners. He was amazed at her great age (eighty-six) and paid her due respect. She invited him back. He said he would come.

To all outward appearances Marilyn has not changed much. She wears the long maroon skirt of a Buddhist nun, and a red blouse, but she was always partial to long skirts and Indian-style shirts. When she took her vows her head was shaven. By the time I saw her, her hair had grown out to two inches all over, a style that suits her stunning features better than any of her old hairstyles. I reminded her that in a letter she wrote announcing her new status she had said that at last she had solved those two terrible problems: what to do with her hair and how to have something decent to wear.

She laughed and said, "Sometimes I think, what am I doing in these clothes? I've got myself into some sort of uniform. But it's made it easier for me to live with other people. When I was wearing civilian clothes everyone thought of me as a photographer and were waiting for me to take pictures again. Now people don't expect me to rush around being a photographer anymore. It was so difficult and now it's no problem."

But wasn't she, I suggested, going against the contemporary emphasis on individuality – on everybody "doing their own thing?"

"Yes, I think about it a lot," Marilyn answered. "Here I've gotten myself into a uniform and, while not into a rigid society, into a form. Into a discipline that seems to be so totally against today's trend. Yet, maybe because I have been ahead of the trend for so many years, because I had such an unstructured life, and my emotions were so free-form, maybe this is a necessary stage. Because I am so freewheeling and formless, maybe it is a good thing to have a form.

"I never thought of becoming a nun," she continued, "because I thought I would look too funny with my head shaven. I was much too vain. It's true. Then one day I began to think about it and wondered whether it would be an appropriate thing to do. I had already taken my vows as a Buddhist. The idea began to grow on me. It was a stupendous kind of step, but it came to my mind and wouldn't go away. And I couldn't think of anything else. I was moving into it. Getting deeper into it – getting enfolded."

So she wrote a letter to Khanpo. He replied, "It is easy to take vows, but difficult to keep them." She asked another lama and he said, no, it would be good for her not to become a nun, that she should wait three years at least. And Marilyn for the moment felt relieved. But, she discovered, the lama had been testing her resolve, so that when she felt moved to ask him again he replied that he had wanted to see if her mind was firm. Now that he was sure it was, he thought it was a very suitable step for her to take. She was at a good age and had no husband and no children to worry about.

To become a nun she had to change her name, her clothes, and her point of view. She is not attached to one spot. She may travel, but she feels as if she has a family in the Buddhist religious community. A great sense of warmth and joy enfolds her.

Now that she is renamed Ngawang Chödron, it is easier to change her feelings about herself, she told me. Through all the trials that assailed her before, she was preoccupied with how she would meet each new test. It was her Jewish heritage to worry about trials and survival. Fleeing from the pogroms, her grandparents left Poland and arrived in America with nothing. Marilyn's adolescence was haunted by the holocaust of World War II, by the news of concentration camps and the genocide of the Jews.

"I went through this period of gathering things for security.

I was so insecure. You know, thinking about goods and chattels.

"But once I started studying Buddhism, my other interests and concerns just dropped away. It was a very difficult challenge because it was so foreign. But once started there was no way to turn back. What would I turn back to? Get married? Go into a career again? There was no other person. And no point. I can't go on and on about the perfection of a picture. I can't work myself up over it.

"Even now, though," she continued, "I have so much residue of activity it is difficult to stay in one place. The whole day should be spent in study and meditation. I find it a gradual process to get myself down from that habit of physical activity – I'm so used to dashing about."

Was she unequivocally happy with this new life? I asked her.

"Oh, yes." Her face lit with a radiant smile. "It's so joyous. And I feel good about this way because I worked for twenty-five years first. I worked my ass off. I can say that. I earned it. Because I did it all. That world of photography – I don't miss it, I don't feel pulled back. This way was hard at first, because with the scattered kind of mind that I have, I find I'm a bad practitioner. Changing your interior is hard work. You can only do it yourself and in fact, you know that by going somewhere else you are only copping out. This is very important. You are never bored. You may get a little restless and get up and go out for a bit, but you know you have to get back to work on yourself. You have to be alone, which I never could be before. It is very difficult to unattach yourself. To meditate. I'm still not very good, but at least I'm beginning to be on a more even keel."

What, I asked her, were her plans? She smiled as if she expected just that sort of question, and said, "I don't think of them in the heavy way I used to. I'm much more relaxed. I'll go back to Nepal, but I'll come back here, too, every so often. Nuns who live at monasteries have certain rules, but they are free to come and go. Sometimes I feel a great yearning to go and stay at a retreat. I look forward to it. The secret, though, is just to keep walking through life without analyzing it too much, or clinging to it too much. Just walk on. It is hard to do sometimes, but if you keep remembering, you can."

When Marilyn and I were together before, I always used to find myself running at least ten paces behind her. Now I knew that she would wait for me to catch up. The razzle-dazzle hassle is over. She has started up a long, difficult path struggling to be humble and enduring enough to find peace in that ancient paradox: freedom through discipline. After such a vivid life there is sweetness in solitude.

12. A Travel Agent on Her Own

BETTY PAGE STARK

"Travelers are always discoverers."

ANNE MORROW LINDBERGH
North to the Orient

"I was tired of being a lady jock."

Betty Page Stark, delivered her one-liner with a humorous sparkle in her very large hazel eyes, then turned and walked ahead of me to the inner office of her travel agency in Bellevue, Washington. Lean, wiry, five feet four and one-half inches tall, she carried herself with that light, taut air of an athlete in peak condition. Behind her big desk piled with papers and timetables, she perched in her black leather chair, a compact watchspring of a person. Sunlight from floor-to-ceiling windows reflected off the white brick walls so I could clearly see that Betty Page's healthy glow was naturally hers. A woman in her late fifties, with three grown children, she still has a trace of youthful boyishness in the way she holds her body. Her short gray hair curls over her forehead. When her face breaks into a wide smile, as it often does, she looks like a pixie ready for high jinks.

With three other women, she formed the Galaxy Travel Agency when she was fifty-three.

"There had to be more than just being a lady jock," she grinned. "I thought my brain was going to go plop, like a dead tennis ball. But I loved to ski, play golf, tennis, and, you know, do anything outside."

Betty Page taught my friend Irene's five children how to ski on the same mountain slopes near Seattle where I tried to learn how to do a snowplow turn on my own when I was in high school. Betty Page did not learn to ski until she was married and had children, when she and her husband moved from the East Coast to the Northwest. But she came from an athletically accomplished family; her father was a tennis champion. She played golf and tennis with her husband, Bob, when he was home, but since he traveled a great deal, first as a salesman for Armstrong Cork, then as division manager for Owens Corning, Betty Page found most of her partners among like-minded women with free time. Also, she was an explorer at heart. "When Bob traveled, I did the same with the kids. We explored everything and it was fun. I learned how to drive in snow conditions. Bob fixed the station wagon with chains and off I went. I think I really invented the seat belt. I used to tie those kids down with diapers so they wouldn't flop around, while I was learning to drive in snow.

"But all of a sudden – I can't attribute it to anything in particular – I just had this feeling that if I don't use my brain, I'm going to explode. I really think that it was God's way of preparing me for what was ahead." Betty Page took her glasses off and rubbed the narrow bridge of her nose before she went on.

"So I talked to Bob about it: the fact that I wanted to do something more stimulating. Sure, I told him, we could still play golf and tennis on weekends or after his work. But Bob had this idea that he didn't want his wife to work. I could have skiied all day and all night, and he wouldn't care. He was so unselfish. His idea was that he had traveled so much while I stayed home with the kids, that now it's your turn, you go and do your thing. Every Christmas Bob gave me a ski vacation. I've done all the ski areas in Europe. I would go whenever it was convenient for him.

"'You know you're going to be talked about,' he said. Which I was. You know," her voice quavered with mock concern, "'Mother goes off on ski trips and leaves the kids.' I used to chaperone schoolbuses on Saturdays. You got your lift ticket free if you chaperoned. I was skiing with guys who were chaperoning on the buses too. So I got talked about then. I used to go up and take lessons when the kids were in school, but I was always back when they got home. After taking lessons for three years, the people I was taking from thought I should be an instructor. And that's how I became involved in teaching.

"Now I've got a daughter jock. The other night my son-in-law Ron called. (I adore Ron – take my daughter, but give me my son-in-law.) And he said, 'It is six o'clock. Do you know where your daughter is now? She's playing tennis and after that she's got a soccer match.' He said, 'You know, like mother, like daughter.'

"I said, 'You know, Ron, that I don't play soccer.'

"He and Page have four little girls. Bob felt, and I felt, that I should be home when the little ones were growing up. Page does too. It's an old-fashioned feeling. She's at home all day. Her latest is seven months old. She feels she has to have an outlet. Something that is active. Right now her only outlet is sports. Ron does the same thing. They take turns. They are really great.

"Bob never skiied. After I taught all day Saturday, we would go out Saturday night. And boy, I never said no.

"Bob really believed one should be oneself. He said, 'It's nobody's business but yours and mine, what we do.' We were able to talk, and this is so vital – communication. I think one reason was that he traveled so much he really wanted to catch up when he was home. Of course, that way not much goes under the table; everything comes straight out. It can have its hard part, but it forces you to look at it. We all can talk – our whole family. I just feel you can talk about anything if you are honest with yourself." Under Betty Page's direct gaze, it would be hard not to be truthful.

"I always felt as if I were my own person," she said, "but I don't take any credit for it. It was bred in me when I was growing up. My grandmother always told me to believe in myself as a person – that if I thought whatever I was doing was right within myself and with my God, then not to worry about what other people think. Now if that isn't liberation, what is?"

Betty Page's grandmother was English. She not only passed her moral precepts on to her granddaughter, she also bequeathed her an accent, so that even now, after all the years that she has lived in the West, Betty Page's *r*'s are soft and her enunciation faintly British. "I loved her. To me home was not home without my grandmother," she said softly. "I was primarily raised by her. I am very proud of being a Virginian, born in Richmond in 1920. My grandmother lived with my parents. She was really very liberated for her day. She had relatives in Boston and that's where she was presented to society. She said she felt like a filly paraded around in the paddock. 'I would not endure your mother coming out like that,' she said.

"In those days everybody in the South had a cook and a maid, so my mother didn't have anything to do. She was very talented. She painted. The amount of volunteer work she did was astronomical. But she also was an alcoholic. I did not notice because I was not allowed to notice. We never used the word 'alcohol'! My mother took to her room. They said, 'Your mother is not well today.' None of her friends knew she drank.

"After I was married, I used to go back every weekend when she was drinking. I couldn't understand why my father didn't do anything about it. He could afford it. One of my father's closest friends was a psychiatrist."

This unhappy experience of a family trying to hide or gloss over a personal tragedy, plus the influence of her grandmother's independent outlook, must have increased Betty Page's determination to face the world squarely and set the facts straight. At her mother's funeral, she had it out with her father and family friends: "I think what triggered me was that her friends said I had broken her heart by moving west and taking her grandchildren away, pulling her heart strings and all that jazz. I thought my father was going to smack me in the face. If he had, I probably would have smacked him back and said, 'Well, basically it's your fault.' But the word alcoholism has always been a hangup in my family, when it's really like a heart disease."

When Betty first moved to Bellevue, in the early 1950s, it already was well along in its rapid growth from a small town across Lake Washington from Seattle to one of the largest cities in the state. Not one to enjoy morning coffees ("That to me is a waste of time."), she did not find it easy to make new friends. "I used to have Bob call me up every afternoon at four o'clock to see if I were still alive."

Since she had been involved in various volunteer activities with her mother, she eventually gravitated to the same sort of work in Bellevue, where she found like-minded friends. "When the kids were little, we used to dump them all in one playpen while we were doing a volunteer project." Her most intensive efforts were directed toward getting a hospital built for Bellevue, so it would not have to depend on the medical facilities in Seattle. "We decided we needed a hospital on this side of Lake Washington," she said. "Three or four auxiliaries formed. There had been several close calls. And we had two personal tragedies." One of Betty Page's children ran through a plate glass window and nearly died during the drive into Seattle. Another lost a kidney in an accident. "We were nine years just working to get the property for a hospital," she sighed. "It took money. We fought for a public hospital rather than one owned by doctors. And we won."

So Bob must not have been too surprised, after the hospital effort was over, when Betty Page told him she had to do something more, or she would "go bananas." She recalled his reaction: " 'Fine,' he said, 'Why don't you?' – which sounded to me like, 'Why haven't you?' I'm sure that if I had said, ten years ago, or even fifteen, I'm going to do this or that, he would have said, 'O.K. Do what you want.' " Many of us, looking back at our own lives, have the same feeling. We wonder now why we did not stop and look at ourselves earlier, to see where we were and where we were going. Most barriers to change were self-imposed, growing out of old attitudes about ourselves more than any restrictions imposed by others. Betty Page's own answer was, "I guess I was just having too much fun as a lady jock. I didn't really want to commit myself to anything because of the ski season. Had to stay loose to get to the slopes. If you commit yourself to a job. . . ." Her voice trailed off.

"I had been a medical technician. A friend kept trying to get me to go back. Said there was a desperate need for med techs. Bob said, 'What are you going to do?' I said, 'I don't know. I really will have to go back to school.' Then somebody would call to play tennis."

After high school, Betty Page had attended the College of Westhampton, which was the women's side of the University of Richmond. "There was an imaginary line that went down the middle of the lake," she said. "We used to swim under that line. Then I went to Johns Hopkins, which is very competitive. I was in the allergy clinic there. I meant to go to premed, but the banks closed. My father had money and lost money and started over again. He thought the next best thing to being a doctor was to be a medical technician. At Hopkins I spent half my time disguised as a resident, in the theater, watching operations. Medicine is still very close to my heart."

But instead of joining the Johns Hopkins medical unit that was sent to the war zone in Africa in 1942, she married Bob. "The biggest major decision of my life," she said with finality as she stood up to stretch.

Having to sit very long does not appeal to Betty Page. "The only thing I hate about the travel business is sitting down at that desk. I stand as much as I can. They all tease me. I can't type standing up, though." She made a wry face. "I had to learn to type from scratch. I signed up for the beginner's class. It was terrible, because everyone else had taken typing in high school. When the teacher said, 'O.K. Start,' all I could do was take the cover off the typewriter."

Leaning back in her chair again, with one leg drawn up across the other knee, she continued, "A lot of people asked me, why don't you sell real estate? I thought, well, that sounds like fun – maybe. I got books and was studying like mad – getting up at six o'clock to study for the real estate exams. I was really out of the habit of concentrating. It was awful. Then I caught wind of the travel bit. This was a whole new ballgame. It sounded exciting."

The idea came from a close friend of twenty-five years, who was casting about like Betty Page. They began to consider possible business ventures. "It was a matter of should we or shouldn't we. At the time the CAB (Civil Aeronautics Board) required that a new travel business had to have two owners who had had at least two years' experience. Neither of us did." But, happily, two of their friends did, and were interested in changing from employee to owner status.

"We all knew each other," Betty Page said. "I was the oldest (at fifty-three) of the group. We were talking on the phone and had about three or four meetings. I called the United Airlines representative. He didn't know me from a hole in the wall. But I said, 'I'm Betty Page Stark, and I'd like to know how to open a travel agency.' He was very nice. He said, 'Well, what you do is write to the CAB in Washington, D.C., tell them you are Betty Page Stark and you would like to open a travel agency, and how do you go about it.' So I did. And I got a very nice letter back and it said, 'This is the way you do it. You send us five dollars and we will send you more information.' And so I did that. Had all the information and regulations on what you had to do to be approved. And I thought, 'Oh, what the hell. Let's do it!'

"All of the husbands thought we would never make it. They said, 'There is no way,'" she shook her head deliberately from side to side, "'that four women will ever make it. They can't make a decision and they can't get along.'

"But we're equal partners. We started very small. We were very undercapitalized. At first we couldn't take all the business that came to us, because we didn't have enough cash flow. But everything just went bing, bing, bing!" She snapped her fingers.

"After the first year all four husbands bowed down and said, 'So sorry. We were very wrong.'

"Another friend, who is a bookkeeper, said, 'If you want another partner. . . .' We said we did and took her in as a fifth partner. Books had never been my forte, but I thought, what I don't know isn't really going to upset me. We all took turns doing the books and doing the ticket reports."

Galaxy Travel quickly became a million-dollar business. They moved from the crowded two-room office where I first met Betty Page to a large three-room suite in a new building, where I visited her again a year later. Now the five women owners employ three other women and are still expanding. And they have bought, as an investment with two other travel agents in different agencies, a condominium in Hawaii.

But, after that first year of grindingly hard work, when Betty Page felt as if she finally were getting the world by the tail, a terrible blow fell: "We discovered Bob had cancer.

"When I found that out I just wanted to stop and be with him. But he would not let me. Because he worked every day. He would get chemotherapy and he would be so sick he couldn't stand up. But he would manage somehow to pull himself up and go to work. Until two weeks before he died – then he said, 'Let's go to the hospital.'

"His spirit was marvelous; he gave us strength. He was very elated over the fact that I was in the business and he was not concerned about me. He said, 'I know you, and I know everything is going to be all right for you.' He kept saying, 'This is harder on you than it is on me.' Our doctor said the same thing: 'It is much harder on the family than on the patient.'"

She and Bob were planning to go on a golf tour to Scotland. After he died she could not face going without him. Instead, she kept long hours – pouring her energies into her work, forgetting herself. "This business can involve you completely. It was my salvation," she said. "I would be lost without it. Three years before Bob died, God tapped me on the shoulder and said, 'Get moving.' I've tried to tell Page that she can learn from my experience – that when her children get older, she better prepare herself. I really feel that every woman should be prepared to look after herself. Men are.

"I don't feel it's a woman's world by a long shot. I think men are in a world that not many women will enter. It's not that I don't think they are capable, don't get me wrong. There are brilliant women. But not enough women have had enough experience.

"The hardest part for me is not having someone to talk things over with. Many women are dependent on men's advice. Maybe I just haven't been in business long enough to know all the answers. But I hope that I never reach the point where I feel that I can do without a man, because I am not anti-men. I know a lot of women who are anti-men. I don't feel that self-assured. We were married for thirty-three years. I depended on Bob."

Fortunately, though, Betty Page is gregarious, what she calls a people-lover. "You have to be, in the travel business," she said. "You have to have patience. If you don't, it's not your bag, that's for sure. You're planning the whole itinerary of a small group, say three couples, for a two month's trip through Europe, which takes lots and lots of time – reading, studying, digging. You write fifty-two letters. Then they call and say, 'Sorry, we've changed our minds – we're not going.' If things like this bother you, it's not for you.

"One of the reasons we have done well in our business is because we have made a client feel a trip to Portland [Oregon] is as important as a trip to Europe. There are a lot of people for whom a trip to Portland *is* as important as is a trip to Europe," she declared.

Another reason for Galaxy Travel's success is the careful planning, the checking out of arrangements – accomodations, meals, travel connections – by the women themselves before they send their clients off. To prepare for a forthcoming golf tour she is going to head, Betty Page recently drove eleven hundred miles through Spain and Portugal. Before she left, she said, "A friend called and asked me to speak to her church singles group. I have a hangup on singles groups. But I said O.K., because I was doing this driving trip, and I was going by myself. And they wanted a talk on singles travel."

Without knowing a word of Spanish or Portuguese, Betty Page, now single herself, set out. In Malaga, she rented a Spanish Seat (which rhymes with Fiat), and discovered that the first turn marked on her road map was wrong. "There was a detour," she said, "and I was on one of those round-abouts going round and round. Then, all of a sudden, the car stopped. I thought, 'Holy cow, what now?' It was like four o'clock, and the rush hour. Just horrible. Horns bleeting. A policeman came over and put his head in the car window and smiled. And I smiled and said, 'English?' And he shook his head, 'No.' So I said, with my hands, 'The car won't go. I get out. You get in the car. See if you can start it.' He got the picture. I got out and was charading with my hands, telling the policeman that the car wasn't starting. And all of a sudden I realized that the traffic had stopped. It dawned on me that I had on white pants and a blue jacket. And I thought, 'I've always wanted to be a traffic cop.' So I directed people, and the policeman started laughing, and I thought, 'This is great.'

"I love the Spanish people. There is no language barrier. I do charades very well. I went everywhere. Every corner I turned was an experience. I saw so many beautiful things. I talked to myself to keep awake, because I had miles and miles to drive. I was stuck to my Seat by the time I got through, I can tell you. I got lost many times but no problems."

Then Betty Page looked down at her hands and was silent for several minutes. Deep in thought, she absently twisted the large diamond ring she wears on the third finger of her left hand. It is a diamond that has been in her family for eight generations.

Looking up again, she said quietly, "I had to think twice about whether I wanted to share what happened. It was such a beautiful, such a personal experience. I was in Portugal, trying to find the Pousada Des Braz, the inn, which is the same as the Parador in Spain. I could see it on the top of the hill, but I couldn't find the road up. Nothing anywhere there is built for the car. I had been up and down and back and forth and backtracked and circled, recognizing the same stone wall, for at least an hour and a half. Been over the maps, and stopped and chatted, in nothing you know, with people. No luck. Finally, I saw three elderly women, and I mean elderly, standing in the street. Snag teeth – black shawls. So I thought, 'I know damned well they don't speak English, but who knows? They might be able to tell me something.' So I stopped and pointed to the Pousada. They could see it too. First I said, 'English?' They shook their heads, 'No.' Then one woman came over. I turned the window down and she smiled, and she had one tooth, just one. She started rattling directions in Portuguese. And the other two just stood there, shaking their heads. Marvelous! So this went on for about three minutes. Finally the two other women came around to my side of the car, opened the door and beckoned me to come with them. And I thought, 'Whee, what am I getting myself into?' Nothing but stone walls along the street and this big wooden door. This village was like a dungeon, really.

"So I thought, well, three women, you know. And they're as old as Methuselah. Nothing's going to happen.

"They gestured that I pull the car over closer to the wall, lock it, and bring my purse, which I did. And then they opened the door and I walked into the most gorgeous patio I have ever seen in my life. All tiled. Magnificent flowers – the colors you cannot believe. Just gorgeous. And it looked like hundreds of people. There weren't that many, but a huge family in a sort of semicircle, just sitting around. Some women were knitting. There were babies, children, and men, too – the fathers and the grandfathers of the families. Beautiful, just beautiful. I don't know if they all lived there, or just called in everybody to see this crazy lady.

"This was about five o'clock. And I wanted to get up to the Pousada before dark. So, I took one of the women's black scarves and put it over my head and I got across to them that I was a widow and that I was by myself and traveling alone. I could tell by their expressions that widows don't travel by themselves. I think they thought, 'This is a crazy American.' I'm sure that's what ran through their heads. They gave me a glass of wine. I don't drink wine, let's say that I'm not a connoisseur, but I thought I would insult them if I didn't take it. There was a beautifully laid table – the linen was exquisite.

"And so in this semicircle," a tinge of amazement crept into Betty Page's voice, "I just started talking – with this black scarf still over my head. I talked my problems out to me:

what was in my life and what I was going to do. I had several things coming up, decisions that I'm going to have to make soon. I thought, 'You know, you're really talking to God.' And then I started to cry. Only I didn't know it until I saw that some of the women had tears. And then I knew I was crying. We had no verbal communication at all. But we had communion.

"I don't know how long it was. I really don't. Then one of the younger fellows brought his child out, just a precious, beautiful little child. It sort of broke the spell. And they invited me to eat with them. And I had sardines that I had heard about, but not been able to find. They were delicious. We all ate bread, excellent bread, a salad. I thought, when I saw the salad, 'I shouldn't eat it, how do I tell them?' But I just couldn't not take it.

"It was getting dark. I kept telling them I had to get up to the Pousada. So one of the men came out and drew me a map. I followed that and it led to a village I don't think they have discovered yet in Portugal, I took another turn and there I was on a dirt road. Ahead of me was a big sign that said, Pousada Des Braz. I had been like two minutes away."

And deep into an experience now hallowed in Betty Page's memory. Back home she told the church singles group she spoke to, "Go *anywhere.*"

The world beyond her doorstep does not frighten her. With her frank smile and guileless eyes, she expects the best of people and that is what she finds. As any good traveler knows, expectation is the best assurance of a good journey. Add to that the advantage of age. In almost every country but ours, there is a deep residue of tradition that honors parents and grandparents. Lithe and energetic as she is, Betty Page does not try to look like a glamor girl of the forties or hide the fact that she is the grandmother of seven.

In that Portuguese village, Betty Page was her uninhibited self – as ingenious and curious and confident as any of that stalwart band of Victorian lady travelers. Her English grandmother would have been proud of her. She is a brave and sympathetic lady who has discovered, like generations of women travelers before her, that to travel alone does not always mean to be alone. The world is full of helpful men and sympathetic women.

Part Five
Women Defining Themselves

"To struggle for strength. It sounds so dramatic. One does the best one can, and then one goes to bed. And that's how suddenly one day, it becomes evident that one has achieved something."

PAULA MODERSOHN-BECKER
Letters and Diaries, 1876–1907

Crisis, Change, Action

Before I could read, I knew that women lived through many complicated changes in their lives; by comparison, men's lives seemed linear and one-dimensional. This awareness came to me early in childhood, because I was moved from my crib straight into the double bed in our guest room, and thereby began sharing the most intimate hours of the night with a wide variety of relatives, friends, and a good many "overnighters" I had never met before. As I grew older, this bedsharing seemed to me an imposition and invasion of my privacy. Now, looking back from the vantage point of fifty years of experience, I realize that it provided me with a rare education.

My father was a gregarious man, the eldest of ten brothers and sisters. He felt that houses should be full of people. Ours, with only my mother, brother, and me, seemed to him empty. So, to my mother's despair, he invited friends and near-strangers to "put up" with us, cavalierly ignoring details such as the planning of meals, entertainment, arrival and departure dates. ("Remember us? When we met you folks a couple of years ago at Jim's place in Missouri, you said, 'Be sure to stay with us if you ever get out West.'") A surprising number of visitors from all parts of the States, as well as Europe and Asia, found their way to Seattle and our big colonial house. I remember the look of surprised delight on my mother's face when she came into the kitchen one morning and told us that the Japanese man spending a week with us had made his own bed – and as neatly as any woman could. He slept in my brother's single bed. Where Watson went when he vacated his bedroom, I don't know. Older than I, he was moving into the male world of baseball, basketball, and golf. I stayed home and shared my bedroom with the women guests.

For all her objections to my father's excessive hospitality, my mother invited a good many guests of her own. People tended to confide their troubles to her. Her visitors (not counting family) usually were hardship cases: young men or women without jobs, particularly during the 1930s. They tended to stay for months.

By the end of the thirties, when I was in high school, I called the guest room mine. I had put up on the walls and taken down, with each new wave of interest, pictures of dogs, horses, baseball players, ice skaters, movie stars, and finally my own boy and girl friends. Still, at a moment's notice, Mother would say, "Just clear a space on one side of your dresser, will you, and empty a drawer or two, Mabel (or whoever) is coming for a little visit." So, while I was preoccupied with growing up, these women moved through my life.

Vaguely I became aware that their passage through my bedroom usually came at a time of change in their lives. They were graduating from college and looking for work, or had come to Seattle to start a new job, or they were having a crisis with their husbands (few divorces in those days), or were agonizing over an important decision about their careers. These women were facing themselves in front of my dressing table mirror, and trying to decide who they were and what they should do. Since they came in all ages, from young to old (old by my definition being anyone with gray or white hair), I saw that the natural state of women's lives was crisis, change, and action.

Mother was a great advocate of action, even when she couldn't take it herself. "It's not so much what *happens to you, as* how *you let it affect you," I can still hear her saying. As an artist, she looked at life as she looked at a canvas. It was up to you to choose the colors for it. If you tried one and didn't like it, take turpentine or any solvent, and wipe it out. The intent was to keep the colors harmonious and achieve a picture with depth and balance.*

Many of the women who stayed with us were schoolteachers and single. In the years of the Great Depression, most public school systems required women to resign when they married, so their jobs could be made available to men, the traditional heads of households. I remember Janet, who sat at my desk, doodling on my scratch pad and mumbling to herself, while I lay in bed, back turned against the light. When I gathered up my school books in the morning, I saw neat rows of checks and minuses marching across my lined paper. "Janet is trying to decide whether or not to marry Don," Mother explained. "She soon might be the head of her department, you see, and, well, he's a nice man, but perhaps not too steady. Janet will be taking quite a chance if she marries him." She took the chance and, a few years later, was back with us, sobbing night after night into the pillow next to me. While I washed the dinner dishes, I listened to Mother and Janet, sitting in the breakfast nook, planning how she could make a new start in life.

"Know your own mind! Speak up! Look men straight in the eye!" my great-aunt Martha would admonish me, taking off her pince-nez glasses before she climbed into bed. I admired Aunt Martha. She was married and she had money, but she had problems too. Her husband traveled a lot.

My little Swiss grandmother, in contrast, was the gentlest person I have ever known. Looking at her gold signet ring that I now wear, with the engraved letters "LT" for Louisa Tuescher, evokes for me a picture of her kneeling to say her nightly prayers, her right hand, with this ring on her second finger, cradling her left hand, her forehead resting on her crossed thumbs. Summer or winter, she wore a long white nightgown. Her hair, which during the day was swept up in a soft swirl on the top of her head, hung in a gray-black braid down her back, to below her waist, at night. In a firm and quite audible voice, she quickly said the Lord's Prayer, then settled in to count her blessings. These took a long time. I lay on the far side of the bed, mesmerized by her set of teeth that she put in a jelly jar, filled with water, on the bedside table. Her list of blessings always began with her thankfulness that Tom, her husband, had not lingered, suffering, from the accidental gunshot that killed him. Then she thanked God for her son, Clarence, even though he lived only twenty-nine years and died in the great flu epidemic of 1919. Her five living children, for all the worry they still caused her, she listed, one by one, emphasizing their good features and her fervent hope that their lives would work out all right. I kept a sharp ear out when she came to her grand-

children; sometimes she slipped in a worry about me that I was not aware of. It is a responsibility to be a blessing. Last, she considered herself, and, after her general gratefulness to be alive and in relatively good health, she took the time to mention the small pleasures of her day: seeing an old friend, finding some full-blossomed dandelions to make dandelion wine, and discovering in the mail a letter from a distant daughter. Then she gave herself a short sermon on meeting the next day with an open heart to receive the joys she was sure were waiting for her. With her inner world thus tidied up for the day, she slid into bed next to me, and slipped immediately into sleep. So did I.

Only now am I appreciating the strength of these women who passed through my childhood. These fortifying memories of them came into focus for me not long ago when a friend was encouraging me to write a book that I had talked about for so long. "But I never seem able to find the time to do it," I argued. Her smile was as gentle as my grandmother's when she replied, "Most of the obstacles in our lives are those we impose on ourselves."

What she meant was that we impose unfair judgments on ourselves because we give more value to the opinion of others than to our own. When what we really are is different from what people want us to be, the tension becomes unbearable. Many women are cruelly caught in situations so alien to their natures that breaking out is necessary for their very survival. Others see ahead of them the end of a period when they are needed, and a desperate urgency to keep their lives meaningful overcomes them.

Then they are fortunate if they can trust to their own inner voices, or to the wise counsel of someone such as my mother who sat in our breakfast nook so long ago saying to Janet, "Of course you can go back to your teaching. It's what you think about yourself that counts."

13. Old Values, Endless Needs

IRENE THORSON

"The most practical thing in the world is common sense and common humanity."

NANCY ASTOR
My Two Countries

"Here you are at fifty, and you have all sorts of problems besetting you," said my old friend Irene, as we sat sipping iced tea on her sunlit patio overlooking Lake Washington. It was a summer afternoon in Seattle. Behind us the sliding glass doors to her spacious house stood open. Surrounded by cerise and sapphire-blue rhododendrons, we looked across a wide, immaculate lawn that sloped down into a natural wooded area dense with madrona and evergreen trees, which formed a jade-green base to the sparkling blue water and snow-capped mountains beyond. People who live in settings of such breathtaking beauty somehow should be exempt from ordinary human problems, it seemed to me. But Irene shook her head and thrust her hands deep into her pants pockets. With her naturally curly brown hair, finely threaded with gray, and her wide-eyed candid expression, she looks as genuine as she is. Slouching in her chair, she continued in that wryly humorous tone so characteristic of her.

"You have menopause and you're sort of creaky," she said. "And on top of that you don't know who you are. It's almost too much. You are frustrated and you are panic-stricken when you discover that you don't know who you are, or what you like, or what you can do. The problem is that women of our generation have been total, total mothers.

"But," she shrugged her shoulders, "I made up my mind that once the children were gone, I was not going to sit up here in this big house on a hill and decay."

"So one fine morning you just decided that being the mother of a bunch of kids like yours was not much different from being a bailiff, so you would hie yourself off to court and get sworn in as one?"

"Well, not exactly," she laughed. "I really didn't have anything like that in mind at all."

What Irene and her friend were looking for the day they went to the Clearing House for Volunteers was something different and more significant to do. As doctors' wives, they had served on all the standard committees; now that their children were nearly grown, they wanted to branch out, away from school and hospital-centered activities, to find some work with more challenge and interest. "No stuffing envelopes, please," they said. "We want to fill a genuine need." At the time, there was an acute shortage of bailiffs in Seattle courts, and a three-month training program for volunteer assistants had been instituted. To qualify, a candidate first had to be interviewed.

"So off we went," Irene said, "all dressed up in our best suburban style dresses – nervous as anything. I hadn't had an interview since I went to work for Puget Power twenty-five years ago." Her large brown eyes shone with amusement. "Suddenly we found ourselves ushered into an office to be questioned by a young black man dressed in jeans and a sports shirt. I've never felt so out of place in my life. Everytime he asked us a question, we felt that our minds were like sieves: nothing there. And we had to pull out our glasses to read the application forms – a dead giveaway as to where we were in life. I was sure he was laughing his head off at us."

But they were accepted into the program, and, after her training period, Irene Thorson was assigned as an assistant bailiff in Seattle's Seventh Municipal Court, in the heart of the city at Fourth and James Street – catapulted into a world she had never known.

She was fifty-two years old, a college graduate who majored in education and English but never taught, the wife of a practicing pathologist, and the mother of five children. She had not worked at a paying job since her first child was born.

"By the time that I got my children through high school, I knew teaching was not what I wanted to do. Then here you are," she nodded to include me, "and you don't know in what direction to go. You have the time and you have the energy – which you probably never expected you would have – to do something of your own."

It was true. In the thirty years or so that Irene and I have known each other, we always have been too busy to ever imagine that a time would come when we would sit down to talk about ourselves. When we saw each other over the years, we caught up on the news of our children, bustled about getting meals for our combined families, and kibitzed while our husbands reminisced about their days together in Alaska before they knew us. Now, looking back, we saw with regretful clarity our own shortsightedness.

"I think both you and I would be very different if we had something in our lives that was just ours," Irene said thought- fully as she stirred her tea. "But we accepted everything. Never had a doubt about what to do but stay home and take care of kids. Never questioned anything. Now I wonder how we could have been so dumb.

"Just think," Irene straightened up in her chair, "if we had something that was ours – not necessarily a job, certainly not a full-time one when you have little kids, but an interest or a part-time job – if we had had something like this all along, we would be much better people in all sorts of ways. We would be more decisive, more flexible. We would have been making choices on our own and they would not be any big deal. Decision-making is difficult for women. Your husband has been the one who decided on all the important things. So you get all hung up if you try to make a big decision. In fact, you can't decide what to do at all. All of my friends have this problem. They feel it is necessary to make a decision about themselves, but they can't come to one. They just panic when they put their foot out the door. They can't see themselves without their families, because all decisions previously made have been in terms of family. They have been organized to make decisions all of the time, of course, but those have been for the children, for the husband, for the whole family. But never one that just affects them primarily. Never have any of us said, yes, I want this, and then gone for it. We don't know what risks are involved. We are afraid of failure. If we had some experience outside of the family, then we would know what was involved and it would be no big deal – just one more decision. It would be a success or a failure and that would be it."

But Irene and I were raised with the expectation to be good and loving wives and mothers. Albeit we were better educated than our own mothers, careers were not what our parents wanted for us. In their view, women who worked did so out of necessity and were to be pitied, or they worked for personal gain and so selfishly put themselves before their families. When Irene and I were married in the immediate post World War II period, life was poignantly precious. Boys we had grown up with, gone to school with, dated and danced with, had been killed in Europe or Africa or the Pacific theater of war. Some of our girl friends lost their fiancés. Women we knew were young widows. To be able to marry good, vigorous men was an exhilarating affirmation of life. Our husbands were eager for families. The times bred a sweet urgency to have children.

"Irene, I don't know anyone who has worked harder than you have, raising this family," I said. "And now here you are in this demiparadise with a devoted husband and your kids all headed in the right direction. You should be sitting back, smoking your pipe, and taking your kudos."

"I'm just not a hedonist," she retorted.

"I'll bet that's your Scotch kirk background making you tally up the worth of everything you do."

"Could be," she grinned.

Both Irene's parents immigrated from Scotland, first to Victoria, British Columbia, where she was born in 1923, then to Bothell, a small town near Seattle, where she grew up. The parents of her husband, Ted, were immigrants also, from Norway. She and Ted were married when he was a second-year medical student at the University of Washington. Irene worked, they had no money, and his training took seven more years. By their tenth wedding anniversary they had five children. The last one, Mark was handicapped – why they never knew; how much never could be accurately measured. With his birth, Irene's life changed fundamentally.

Mothers of children whose lives are in some ways limited suddenly are weighed down with a crushing anxiety. Doctors can tell them very little. Specialists disagree. Husbands help out – after work. They are young men working long hours to establish themselves. Essentially alone, the mother must summon all her creative energies to understand this special child, and with infinite patience guide his fitful growth. Each of Irene's days was determined, first and foremost, by Mark's needs. Without making them feel slighted, she tried to fit the needs of her husband and other children around Mark. "I felt as if I were on a rack," Irene said.

It struck me as a measure of our times that, after Irene had poured her heart and energies into her family and raised Mark to heights beyond anyone's expectations, she was not content to rest on her well-deserved laurels. Without the spur of economic necessity, and not driven by a passion for any particular endeavor, she still felt a push to be something more than a wife and mother. Looking around her, she saw that women in her position were not happy.

"I am convinced that many suburban women live lives of quiet desperation, isolated in big houses and gardens," she explained. "They are beginning to get pressure from their husbands, now, to work. It's the thing to do. But they are caught in a bind, because at the same time that their husbands want them to work, they also want them to be available to take trips, to be at home when they are, and to keep running a good household. Money is not the motive, because whatever jobs these women could get would be bad paying. They have no work experience. And what little they made would throw them into another income bracket anyway."

Seeing these women caused Irene to take stock of herself. She was on the shady side of fifty and feeling fine. For the first time in her life, she had some freedom of choice in how to use her time – if she could just figure out what to do and then make that difficult decision to follow through on it. In her case, nobody was pushing her. She had to define her unrest; it baffled Ted. He was looking forward to retirement, leading a quieter life and spending more time with his family than he had been able to do when the children were growing up. Irene's position was one of the most difficult to be in – free-floating in a sea of vague possibilities, none of them irresistibly attractive.

Like most mothers who did not hold a paying job, Irene had performed a variety of volunteer services, from being the president of the PTA to working with the Seattle Art Museum and with the Guild of Children's Orthopedic Hospital. For years, she included foreign students in her family. Sponsored by the Rotary Club, some stayed for as long as a year. Three were Japanese; the others came from Argentina, New Zealand, and Australia. Her house was always full of family and friends. She counseled troubled teenagers, comforted bereaved neighbors, and cared for her terminally ill mother-in-law. For longer than I could have managed, she looked after my outrageously demanding but irresistible, lovable brother-in-law, who stayed at her home when he was in the last stages of emphysema. How many more took shelter in that loving household I can only guess. In 1968 the Thorsons were chosen by the YMCA as the Family of the Year. All of them are imbued with the idea of service.

"If you are educated and able, you should put something back into the community," Irene declared.

This conviction determined the route she took – no dramatic plunge into something entirely new, but back into community service, only this time with the idea that she would try working in a field she had not explored before.

In her self-evaluation, when she was thinking about what to do with her newfound free time, Irene did not credit herself with any special skills. Friends, myself included, told her she would be a superb counselor. She was not interested. "I've had enough of that with my kids," she said. It was just a happy accident that placed her in a situation she never would have chosen or felt herself especially qualified for. But a bailiff needs to be a calm, confident person who moves with great assurance, exudes both sympathy and firmness, does not get rattled, is sensitive to the mercurial emotions of people under stress and is never threatening to them – like Irene, a rock of reliability and realistic compassion.

She has survived a more rigorous training ground than a Ph.D. candidate: it is easier to deal in abstract concepts than with the random behavior of unpredictable children, especially one like Mark. Scientific problems are tidy and manageable by comparison, their solutions measurable and reliable. But the problems of raising a child such as Mark can never be clearly predicted and defined. Her own good sense and intuition are about all a mother has to go on. Each day is fraught with emotional ups and downs. The mother lives with the ever-present anxiety of whether or not she is dealing with the child in the most positive and least damaging way – and she can never quiet a guilt-tinged wondering as to why he was born with a deficiency. For her there is no eight-to ten-hour escape into an entirely different world of work.

We discussed the days when Mark was growing up. "There is just no way to explain the physical and emotional exhaustion, the fear and the daily apprehension," Irene stated. "I don't think men ever understand it.

"I just didn't have enough strength to do what had to be done with all those little kids. I was exhausted all of the time. Mark was such a difficult baby. I remember how unhappy I was and how I thought, I just can't make it.'There was always someone needing something. I could never get enough sleep. Ted was a tremendous help. If he had not been, I would not have made it."

And Ted has always maintained that without a mother like Irene, Mark might have been a very disturbed person instead of the lovable, responsible, and increasingly self-sufficient adult he has grown to be.

No one knew if he could cope in the regular public school system.

"I didn't tell my folks anything about Mark's problems,"

Irene said. "I just pretty much kept them to myself. They knew he had a hearing problem. Fortunately, they didn't live long enough that they had to face anything more. But I think it was hard for our kids, his brothers and sisters. I'm sure there were times when they had to stand up and be counted. And I was the one who was explaining: 'Your brother is a little difficult, but he is your brother. This is something you will have to live with.'"

A streak of stoicism and granite perserverance kept Irene from floundering in any mires of self-pity. Seeing that Mark was stretched to the limit of his capabilities became the central concern of her life.

"He went to a private nursery school and did well," she recalled. "That teacher felt he should go on in a private, special education school. I really didn't know what to do. So I talked to the principal of our public elementary school and he said, 'Well, Irene, I wish you would give us a chance. Let's put Mark in kindergarten and watch him and see how it works out.'

"So," Irene continued, "he got through the second grade, then through the third, but it was getting harder and harder for him. I knew all of the teachers because they had had my previous kids, so that made it easier. They could talk to me very frankly. But by the fourth grade, Mark had to go into special education. He had a hard time with it. He rejected special ed because there were so many kids so much worse off than he was. But it was good for him. He had a great teacher and he learned a good deal about tolerance of other people. He learned a relationship with other people that he would never have learned any other way. Later the high school kids would come to him with their problems that they couldn't talk over with any other kids. He listened seriously and he was sympathetic."

For years Mark teetered between the everyday world and the restricted protective life slow learners are relegated to. "I wanted to keep him in as normal a situation as possible," Irene explained, "able to function in ordinary affairs.

"He had to go through fourth and fifth grades in special ed.

Then his teacher told me that he wasn't going to progress any further there, he was at the top of his class, and that if we were going to make a move to get him back in regular classes, we should do it before he left grade school. So I went to an older, very structured, old-fashioned teacher and put it to her, and she said, 'Well, I've had all the other Thorson kids, why not try Mark.' There was no nonsense about her. She and Mark had a very good rapport because he knew where he stood with her."

Looking back, Irene can see how and why Mark succeeded in the sixth grade. But she also remembers how she felt then. "I used to wake up every morning and think, can Mark make it through today? That low-level strain. Will it be a good day or a bad day? Will they call me from school and say, 'This is it!'

"At the end of the sixth grade, the teacher said, 'Mark may have real trouble in junior high.' So I went up to the school. By that time I knew everybody in junior high too – all the counselors and the principal. I told them Mark was coming and we planned a course for the seventh grade. In the eighth, he started falling behind again."

From then on, Irene fought to keep Mark going. He had special training for two hours a day, then returned to the regular classroom. "So he had the social contacts with his friends," she said, "but there were times when it was particularly difficult for him in school, especially in big classes in high school. He would get bored and become disruptive. Children like Mark have a short attention span and a high degree of frustration. They have very immature reactions – a very short fuse. The constant, twenty-four-hour-a-day worry that you are never without is that he may turn off and begin using drugs and alcohol and become a delinquent. To keep him on the straight and narrow so that he would become a good citizen was a constant concern." Irene let out a long sigh.

"I would talk to the teachers and say, 'I understand your problems with Mark, but he has problems too.' I would work with the teachers I knew well, the ones I had a rapport with because of the other kids. By then I could say to the principal,

'No, I don't want him to have that teacher, but this one.' He needed teachers who felt they were not only teaching their subject, but a lot of other important things too. More and more it became a concern just to get him through."

But at last, one day in June, Mark proudly took his place with his class on the platform for the graduation exercises from Bellevue High School. The little freckle-faced boy I remember running to catch fireflies in a glass jar, whose jumbled words I often could not catch, had grown to a man: six feet four inches tall, a solid two hundred twenty pounds. And there he sat in his cap and gown. Parents and students fidgeted and whispered as the principal intoned the seniors' names and they came forward to receive their diplomas. Finally he came to the T's. "Mark Thorson!" he called out. Mark stood up. Instantly the entire graduating class arose and broke into cheers and applause. The audience joined the clapping. Mark, red-faced to the roots of his sandy-colored hair, stepped forward. Beaming with joy, he shook hands with the principal. He had made it. And his many faithful friends shared his triumph.

Irene's eyes filled, and Ted was mystified, as he had been before, by Mark's immense popularity. Whatever elusive quality it is that accounts for his social success, Mark's achievement is a vindication of Irene's faith. With unstinting love and immense effort, she safeguarded him from infancy to responsible manhood.

And then, at this point, Irene began to phase herself out of her full-time job with Mark. But from long habit, she continued to appraise herself in terms of her family. Her reasoning was, "If a woman over fifty finds something she enjoys doing, her kids will know that the life of their mother is not over. This example is better than anything she can tell them. Besides, we have all seen our own mothers, who did not develop interests outside of the home, and we have felt the burden of guilt they thrust on us for not spending more time with them. Communication was difficult, because we had less and less in common with them as we grew in experience. We moved into a world of increasing complexity which they had not dealt with. We don't want to be like them. We don't want to burden our kids with guilt for our own emptiness. Having a mother who is herself independent and self-sufficient in the most important ways – that is, emotionally and intellectually – fosters independence in kids," Irene concluded.

So, more to set an example than to serve her own interests, Irene summoned up her courage and went to work at Seattle's Seventh Municipal Court. Shortly after her training period, Irene's supervisor, Theresa, had to take some time off and asked Irene to fill in for her. Theresa was a young black woman, energetic, humorous, and efficient. She and Irene took to each other immediately. "Before I go, I'm going to get you on the payroll," Theresa said. Irene objected, protesting that she would be willing to do the work without pay, because, after all, she was a volunteer. "Oh, no, you won't," Theresa told her. Her bailiff job was her living; it was important to her. If Irene were to fill in for her on a volunteer basis, she would be undercutting her. Irene saw the point, agreed, and she and Theresa became fast friends.

At first, Irene was reluctant to tell Theresa anything about herself. When she started working at the court, she was fifty-two years old and felt overwhelmed by the amount there was to know. She was afraid that she was too old to learn it all, and worried about her accuracy on the job. A bailiff is concerned with documents of the people in custody, the court dockets. These are records of ordinances violated, pleas of guilty or not guilty – a record of what happened in court with each person. Accuracy is, of course, essential, because someone could be released wrongly or incarcerated inadvertently unless the record was clear and accurate.

But she stayed with it, trying to master the paperwork and keep her other duties straight. Before the court opens, the woman bailiff goes down in an elevator to the women's jail and unlocks four sets of steel-barred doors, beyond which she meets the matron, who hands over to her the women prisoners who are scheduled to appear in court. Sometimes there are as many as ten. The bailiff then escorts them back through the four doors, up in the elevator, and down the hall to the holding room which opens into the court. If any prisoner got out of hand in the hall, Irene was told to shout, "The bailiff needs help!" and was assured that it would come. She locks the holding room door and is responsible for the prisoners until she delivers them back to the matron.

When the judge instructed Irene on how to handle the prisoners, he pointed out that they generally were very frightened people. If she appeared calm and unhurried, and never reacted quickly, it inspired confidence in them. He cautioned her to move slowly, even though she might feel very pressed and busy, and to take time to explain very carefully to the prisoners exactly what would happen to them. Above all, she should never reveal any sense of her own agitation, as such a feeling is very contagious. It was like telling a fish how to swim. Irene had schooled herself in calmness and patience for twenty-five years.

"Weren't you ever worried?" I asked her after I had seen the corridors of the court building, crowded with some menacing and a few really startling looking people.

"Well, about all they could do is hit you over the head," she laughed, "and that's not so bad. Usually a prisoner has a sense of her own agitation. Once one said, 'Don't walk behind me. I'm going to blow.' Another got pretty upset and accused me of taking her shoes, but I sensed her irrationality and didn't argue."

Once both the men and women prisoners are in the holding rooms, the bailiff opens court by banging the gavel three times and saying, "Seattle Municipal Court, District Number One, is in session and the Honorable – is presiding. You may be seated." If anyone does not stand when she bangs the gavel, the bailiff motions them up. The day I went to court to watch Irene, all she had to do was fix her level gaze on someone to make him or her comply.

One day, after Theresa had been gone and Irene had filled in for her, she came back and greeted Irene with a kiss right in court. It was an open affirmation of their friendship, which came to mean a great deal to Irene. She admired, trusted, and learned a great deal from Theresa. Theresa was very gentle with most of the women offenders, Irene told me. She was compassionate and understanding, but she hated pimps with a vengeance and was capable of chewing them out in a language they could not mistake.

As soon as she mastered the whole procedure, Irene began to enjoy the professional sociability that goes with a job outside the home. Another dividend she had not anticipated was her husband's interest in what she was doing.

"When I came home and started talking about my day in court, Ted was really fascinated. I didn't realize how much so at first. It made a more stimulating relationship for us. A marriage is much better if both partners are bringing something to it. I found out that he didn't know much about the court and I didn't know much about medicine. We talked about problems of the court's relationship to the underprivileged, the handicapped, the minorities and that sort of thing.

"I think our involvement in separate occupations was better than if we were both doing the same thing. Professional people tend to get narrower and narrower. They get tunnel vision and their profession is sometimes all they can talk about. They are not at all well-rounded. If the wife only serves as hostess at social gatherings in the home, she isn't bringing much to the marriage intellectually. She can talk about the kids or an interesting article she has read, but that's not terribly stimulating. The husband is limited in his talk to the wife about his profession because she doesn't know the technicalities. So what do you have? Not much, if you ask me.

"A woman doesn't have to have a professional job, just something that brings in a whole new perspective that neither husband or wife would have thought about if she hadn't gone outside of the home."

To her great amusement, Irene enlarged another man's perspective also. After working two years in the municipal court, one of the policemen said to her, "I must admit you've changed my idea of doctors' wives. I thought of them as a bunch of women who spent all morning drinking coffee and talking on the telephone and all afternoon playing bridge or golf at the country club."

That is the last way Irene would spend her time. She has moved on from the bailiff job, now, to a pilot program helping older people define problems with social security, wills, estates, funerals, and such, before they see a lawyer or go to the small claims court. "I had gone as far as I cared to go in the bailiff job," she said, "had learned all I could. I got to the point where I realized I was sitting in court and not hearing the people as individuals. I really thought I should get out. It becomes an automatic thing that you have to do. You become more interested in your paper work than in the people involved."

In community service, Irene continues to grow.

Having been too often on the receiving end of unfeeling reactions to Mark's problems has made Irene particularly sensitive in a way that a professional person often is not. She is a serious defender of humanitarian values – not in the abstract, but on a one-to-one, face-to-face level, where few people take the time and trouble to help another person out. There is not much glory on that grass-roots level. But there are special rewards: the warmth that flows between two people who understand each other, even for an instant, and in so doing perceive the wonderfully delicate interdependence of all living things. Reaching out for experiences like that has a cumulative effect: it creates a perceptive, responsive person like Irene. Family and friends have always counted on her. Her special talent is to hear a call for help and to respond. Raising Mark, she enriched a human life and spared the community a problem. With her old skills, she is now moving in circles beyond her family, into the community. She has discovered that the community needs her as much as she needs the stimulation of new challenges. The only changes she is making in her life are changes of setting. She knows that she is not immune to the pressures to be a "working woman," a "somebody," but, clear-eyed and honest with herself, she also knows that she will continue to answer those calls for help that touch her most deeply. Irene's humanity defines her.

14. Crossing Over to the Lesbian Community

BETTY SMITH

"Love between women is seen as a paradigm of love between equals, and that is perhaps its greatest attraction."

ELIZABETH JANEWAY
Between Myth and Morning

When my brother told me that Dorothy and Harriet, school-teachers and two of my parents' best friends, loved each other, I could not imagine why he thought it worth mentioning. I knew they did. They lived together in their own house and they took all their vacations together.

"Dorothy and Harriet are coming for dinner tonight," my mother would say, or "Do you want to go with Dorothy and Harriet to their cabin for the weekend?"

My father was a public school administrator in the 1930s and many of our closest family friends were teachers – unmarried women. Married women were not hired until World War II.

Nothing was more natural for me as a child than to go off with Dorothy and Harriet to their little summer cabin on Puget Sound, to swim and lie in the sun, and to sleep and read, and maybe to search along the beach with them for agates and glass fishnet floats. Another woman couple had a summer house built over the water. I loved to stay overnight there, snug in bed, listening to the water slap against the pilings.

With other women I learned how to plant primulas, gather oysters, chop wood, watch for deer, and make fudge. These women brought me dolls from China and Japan, Czechoslovakia, Austria, and France, to start my doll collection. They remembered me in Italy: I have leather bookcovers tooled with gilt. And books beyond counting. And memories of dinners in restaurants, and hikes in the woods, and, as I grew older, searching discussions and fierce debates. These single schoolteachers were the mentors of my childhood and youth, and dear family friends.

Those who lived together were certainly lesbians in the sense that their devotion was to each other and not to a man. They did not close the door to their shared bedrooms with twin beds. But sex, either heterosexual or homosexual, was not a topic for open discussion in the thirties. And so, un-labeled as lesbians (but not unrecognized), these women were able to make unself-conscious friendships with whomever shared their values and interests; they were not perceived as primarily sexual beings, but as full human beings.

This very civil circle of school people was not, I later learned, a microcosm of the world. At college, Radycliffe Hall's book, *The Well of Loneliness,* documenting the anguish of lesbianism, was passed around with prurient interest. But it was long and boring, and the women I knew, who I now recognized my brother was telling me were lesbians, were not like those in *The Well.* My friends' lives were neither sad nor bad – and certainly not frightening. The people who fright-ened me (then and now) were vividly described in the marked passages of Henry Miller's *Tropic of Cancer,* a banned book owned by a returned G.I. which we circulated in a college bookstore paper cover. In Miller's world, sex was conquest: men violating women, violence exciting and enhancing sex.

How far it was from the civilized milieu of the lesbians that I knew. By now I recognized that I was heterosexual, or straight, but that did not make me feel that these women could no longer be my friends. What I did not realize was how difficult life was becoming for them, as sex edged economics out as the main topic of conversation. They were, of course, closet lesbians. "Coming out," declaring themselves after a lifetime of acceptance as simply teachers, was too traumatic. It would be like suddenly painting their noses blue, noses that everybody was accustomed to and never noticed anymore. Once blue, they would be all people would look at from then on. Declaring they were lesbians would overemphasize a most private aspect of their lives and painfully change their status in the community.

So I should not have been as surprised as I was to find that the women my age who were lesbians were unwilling to be identified as such in interviews. "We have no problem being open with all of our family and friends," one said. "Except Aunt Mary," her friend reminded her. "Although she's a dear, sophisticated lady who has seen a lot of the world, we're afraid she would be shocked."

That these two busy, professional women, whom I had not met before, were willing to let me come to their lovely surburban home to talk about their lives, and then decide that I should not use the interview, puzzled me at first. So I dropped by Lammas, the women's bookstore near my house, and asked my friend Mary Farmer, who owns the store, what she thought. Mary is a lesbian feminist by her own description, and twenty years younger than me. She told me that there is tremendous pressure now on all lesbians to declare themselves. They need support for each other, and the younger ones have a desperate yearning for older woman role models.

Mary acknowledged, with a touch of impatience, that for women in their forties or fifties, the late bloomers I was looking for, to step forward to be counted with their sisters was not easy. The complicating factor I had not anticipated was that many of the lesbians in this age group had been wives and mothers. For twenty or thirty years, they had built a sizable network of professional and family ties. It is a terrible irony that now, in the 1970s, it is in some ways harder to be a lesbian than when that word was not spoken. Once identified, they and those they love may be exposed to insult and derision. And their professional work, rather than being judged on its merits, may be exploited for the sensationalism of their newly discovered or newly declared sexual preference.

Nevertheless, Mary was able to introduce me to someone else who was willing to be interviewed: a delightful woman in her late forties, who had been married for seventeen years and had two children before her affection for, and sexual attraction to, women led her into the lesbian world. She was candid, funny, and perceptive. Over lunch, we became friends. And then, a few days later, she called to say that she had second thoughts. Would I consider making up a composite person instead of using her interview? "I wouldn't want to be in anything that ended up as a best seller in Grand Junction," she said.

But I cannot see people as composites: the political views of one, the aesthetic views of another, the tragic/comic experiences of another add up to a nonhuman figure. Lesbians are as diverse as any other group of human beings. And I was interested in individual lives, different from mine, because I see a bit of me in all of them, and thereby inch a little closer to understanding the mystery of myself.

In the end we agreed that with her name changed, and a few identifying details altered, I could record some of the things she told me, using her, not as an exemplar of lesbian life, but as an example of one late-blooming lesbian: one who did not know or act upon her homosexual feeling until she was well into maturity. "There are a lot of us," Betty (as I will call her) assured me. And she agreed that each one was interestingly different.

Betty is now forty-seven. Eight years ago, she left her marriage of seventeen years and, within a few months, "drifted," as she said, into the lesbian community. A small woman, with a straight sharp nose and thin mouth, she projects a very professional attitude, suitable to her work as a financial analyst in a high government position.

"I come from a family of very strong women," she said. "Esther, my partner, comes from the whole Jewish family thing. So we're both strong." She pushed her bifocals back up the bridge of her nose, so that I noticed a sly twinkle in her gray-blue eyes. "In spite of that, we've been together more than five years. I would say it is a total relationship, even though we live apart. We are as close as any married couple. She is very traditional – very much the Jewish mother. Many strong Jewish women become lesbians. She had been in the center of things, in the Sisterhood at the synagogue for many years when we met. Tremendous energy. But I guess," Betty laughed lightly, "that nobody else was as right for her as I was."

Like the other women I talked to, Betty had not thought about finding a lesbian relationship when she made the break from her husband. "I just had a very hard time with marriage," she said. "I think it was this lack of control over my life. I always felt like a kept woman. I couldn't adjust to it. Yet I never went out and got a job then. I majored in economics. Later on, I was so glad I had that degree. I think even then I had a pride in competing with the guys. But I never thought beyond that. Only later did I think about boards [for her graduate degree] and the job interviews. Most women don't think that far ahead. Maybe it's different now, but in the houses we lived in, the dorms and the sororities, that last year the idea was to get married.

"I think my husband is a very nice guy. But I was too rushed with the house – probably feeling inadequate as a home-maker – and had to be dependent on the progress of his career. Basically, I began to think I could develop as well on my own. It was selfish thinking, which I'm not too proud of. But too many women are still dependent on men's careers. As long as the money is coming in, they will stay married. It's the path of least resistance. They suppress their own feelings – no, I don't mean lesbian feelings necessarily – just their own feelings about themselves and their husbands, in order to stay on in a marriage, to hold the family together. In this society, women are pressed to do it. But it's too hazardous to depend on someone else's career."

Betty's background made her exceptionally wary of dependency. Both her grandmothers and mother had to assume the economic responsibility of raising their families; the specter of finding herself in a similar position was remote but real to Betty. Equally influential in her desire to be inde-pendent, though, was the admiration she had for her grand-mother – a successful small businesswoman who established and ran a bakery, "and got everybody through the Depres-sion," and her mother, a union president. "I'm so proud of that," Betty said. "I grew up with the idea that women had a lot of control – *needed* a lot of control. I very much had that heritage. My grandmother married an Irishman and she raised all of her kids Presbyterian." She laughed delightedly. "And my mother married a Polish Catholic and she marched all of her kids down a Presbyterian church aisle, to be baptized.

"Now, looking back, I think the one thing that bothered me most about marriage was that I never felt it was my own money. I always felt as if I were on a dole. My husband was good about money – he was not inclined to make me feel that way at all. I managed the money. But I just didn't feel good about it.

"I just assumed I would have babies. For all the lip service it isn't really considered a worthwhile job in the community. It is all well and good to say women should stay home and take care of their children, but our society isn't willing to pay for it.

"By the time my husband had gotten through grad school, I was used to sort of following him around, waiting for the next step.

"But there was a lot more to it than that. We were a swinging couple," Betty said in her quiet, modest way, "because my husband wanted to be so modern. I think for practically every one of those, it is the man who wants to do it, and no matter how the woman protests in those seminars and things, about how much she enjoys it, I think it gets to be a drag for women. Women have other things to do."

Betty read my thoughts: she didn't look like a swinger. "I'm a very socially oriented person." She smiled. "But it becomes a great game of challenge – who's going to top the other. I think my husband took a lot of punishment. I think it was a foolish role we were in. Politically we have always thought alike. I don't know where we were at that time. I just moved out before I thought of anything else."

But not before she had established her foothold in the job market. "It was bound to happen. Well, in the context of my grandmother and mother, it was just a natural thing to do. I was looking in papers. And somewhere along the line, I got a shorthand book. And I did an awful lot of looking, a lot of probing. Then I met a guy from college, and he said, what you do is take the Federal Service Entrance Exam. From there on it was easy. But I tell you," she met my eyes squarely, "I talk to women who want to do what I did, and I talk to them again a week later, and they haven't even called to find out when the Federal Service Exam is given. Something as simple as that first step. People are so strange!"

Betty buttered a piece of French bread thoughtfully, and then continued: "We moved to a big house in the suburbs. You see that a lot. I often think that happens a lot – buying a big house. So we split up when we had just about made it.

"Tim and I never discussed splitting. We never talked about it – we were so polite about the whole thing. I just started telling him that I was looking for an apartment and made it very obvious. He made sure he was away from the house the night I moved. After that we did have some confrontations over the phone. I would get furious. The more feminist I got, the more angry I got. Before that, I just took it for granted that women took care of themselves, and that it was all right. We should stay friends, and not be crude about it. And still," she gave a small shrug, "as much as my consciousness has been raised, I still don't see these things the way the girls do.

"I talked to the kids about moving out. Everyone was in his niche, so I figured that could just continue. I got an apartment downtown where I could walk to work. At that time, I was working long hours, staying late, for a study we were doing. It was convenient for working late and on week-ends."

When the study was over, Betty looked around for some social life, saw a woman's center, and went in. "They had seminars. It was the first time I had been exposed to feminism. Then we formed some CR [consciousness-raising] groups. We marched on one of those strike days. Somebody said, 'Oh, they're just a bunch of lesbians.' I must say I looked for them. Thought I could pick them out," she laughed.

"Then a friend introduced me to Esther as someone who would be just right for me. So – I was curious. I was a very sexual person, and I was out of patience with men at this time.

I think I always used men as a convenience – was very manipulative with them. Esther is very different," she said with a trace of a smile. "She is shocked by me. I must say, in some ways I felt stronger and more independent with men. As a heterosexual woman, I felt more mobile. After all, men are going to do you in, so you can go out and do them in first. But I don't think you can do that with women when you are a lesbian. You can't be as flippant. It's a much heavier trip. Of course, there is a whole area of nonfeminist lesbians who are into male-female role-playing, who are out to make conquests, but even they tend to settle down into relationships more than men, I believe.

"Did I think about it much before I crossed over?" she repeated my question. "I don't know. It was such an easy thing. Especially for a married woman. I've thought about that – how it was the most natural thing in the world. I think a lot of the younger women, the ones who have never been heterosexual, think it is a heavy trip. Yet it wasn't. I don't know, it's hard to explain. You don't concentrate on it.

"Everybody needs relationships. They shouldn't be afraid of a relationship, whether it's heterosexual or homosexual. Some people seem to think a lot of the people they see at work or around don't have a sex life, but it's there. There is practically always somebody in the wings, back home, somewhere. Of course, there are vast differences in people – personality, temperament. There may be a few who are asexual. It's hard for me to say whether a lesbian relationship is better. It is for me. But I don't know if it is in general. It's better for me at this time.

"A unified community? Yes, that is an interesting word that you use. I think that it is, in the sense that people feel like more of a church group. They are taken in – in the same way a church takes in a new member. I think that is the way that it is. You have certain biases, basic premises, right there. You have things in common, so you don't have to start from step one.

"And I see feminism as very much like a religious thing. It is the overwhelming facet of our lives. But I don't want to idealize it. There are some very unkind things going on. And in the world I know, politics, law, finance, government, the successful women appear generally to be the heterosexual ones. They identify with men so closely that they incorporate the whole male value system, such as their attitude toward achievement. And if they are wives and mothers, they have to have the most successful husband and children. I know – I was there. They are the ones who want to do men in when the system backfires on them. As we gain more from men, it becomes easier to feel friendship toward them, to wish them well.

"I see that achievement orientation with the older lesbians, too. They incorporated the ideas of men, every facet of men, long ago. And the part of me that still wants to achieve is the heterosexual woman. The part that wants to concentrate on relationships, on values, is feminist, lesbian. Of course, there are young men too who are incorporating a lot of the feminist value system. That is what the feminist revolution – the woman's movement – is all about."

"Would I ever go back to a heterosexual life?" Betty sighed and thought a moment. "There is a certain attractiveness to that old dependent, family existence. I find that I am nostalgic for some things with Tim. On the other hand, when I go back, in a few minutes I am out of patience, irritated by the same things that separated us.

"I think for most of us who turn away from a male orientation, we stick. Not many move back. Once you've crossed over, that's it. But I don't know – I don't think homosexuality is inborn. I don't think that you are just naturally gay, and I don't think it is any kind of inhibition or taint. Maybe there are women who move back and forth. And who's to say? I might eventually. I've lived long enough to know that we all go through stages.

"But I doubt it." Betty folded her napkin with an impish grin. "Esther and I look at those little old ladies together, and say, 'Well, there we go!' Someday we can travel. We only have a couple of years now until our last kids leave.

"Besides, Esther and I now have this tremendous background of women – it's our whole lives. And I couldn't share that with any man," Betty concluded.

And I thought of what the other women who had crossed over after they were forty had told me: that they could not have gone on alone and had such a rich and full life as they have found with their loved lesbian partner.

15. Out of the Myth a New Life

VIRGINIA HODGE

"It is a long baptism into the seas of humankind, my daughter. Better immersion than to live untouched . . . "

TILLIE OLSEN
"O Yes"

"I guess I reconstituted myself," she said.

"You mean changed or made yourself over?" I asked. "But why was it necessary to do that?"

"In order to survive," said Jinny.

"It was a choice, and I saw it very clearly as a choice, the only one I had. A choice between the violent self-hatred of depression, and maybe even death, and great inner change, hope and renewal. Sometimes the moments when I made choices were hardly noticeable. Other times they were momentous. Often I couldn't see the positive side of the choice – the choice of survival and renewal. All I seemed to have strength to do was to say no to depression or death.

"At one point I was standing by my window," Jinny said, "and I was thinking, it's eight floors down. That choice isn't hard. But finally I said, 'No! I will survive!' I didn't see any way in which I could. But, I thought, I will. Just survive. Not even because life was worth living. But I will survive until the end of my life just because that is the thing to do. It's what life demands of me."

I was dumbfounded! Virginia Hodge depressed to the point of suicide? The woman I had known twenty years before as the consummate foreign service wife: skilled hostess; disciplined volunteer worker; conversant in the language of every country she served in; acquainted with key people; sensitive to local culture and customs; involving her children as well as herself in local activities. Unthinkable! Yet here she was, at fifty, as far from her former life as could be imagined; the newly appointed director of admissions for a Washington, D.C., Children's Hospital, alone and dependent entirely on herself. What had happened?

I gazed more closely at this old friend I had not seen in years. She looked fit and comfortable in navy pants and a beige sweater, and there was a change in her, quite apart from those made by the passage of time. In fact, she seemed younger in the relaxed way she walked across the light, airy living room of her eighth-floor apartment and sank into the sofa, with one leg tucked under her and an arm stretched casually along the back cushion. I remembered her contrastingly quick, tight movements, dashing after her children or rushing off to a meeting. Her face, too, seemed more in repose, softened by her thick, sandy hair tied loosely back. But her blue eyes were quick and bright as ever; her high forehead correctly signified a shining intelligence.

"But you don't seem depressed now," I said.

She smiled at my confusion. "I've never been more at peace with myself. I have a sense of wholeness now."

"But why? How?" I wanted to know.

"Well," Jinny said thoughtfully, "I had this massive sense of guilt and failure that terrible things had happened to my family because I hadn't been strong enough. That it was my fault. The way of Christianity, of the Puritan conscience, said I must try harder. So I tried harder and harder."

Of course! I knew that Jinny's grandparents were Congregational missionaries, her religious upbringing of New England origin. Her conscientiousness sometimes used to make me feel like a slacker when we were young foreign service wives together in the little provincial capital of Dacca, then East Pakistan, now Bangladesh. Daily life for us in the tropics, with small children, was difficult in ways we were unprepared for. But we took enormous pride in coping.

"Don't you think trying hard is the answer?" I asked.

Jinny shook her head. "Finally, willpower is no good. The way of therapy or religion or conversion is that you must try *differently*. Not follow a determined road, but find a new creative way. And that is what I did – I found a new creative pattern. Not easily, or all at once," she added. "I had to overcome years of alienating my thought from myself. And I needed help."

I always associated rigorous intellectual endeavor with Jinny. When I knew her best, she was deeply concerned about basic questions of economic, social, and political affairs. Both she and her husband had been excellent students, members of the honor society Phi Beta Kappa at Oberlin College, which they attended as married undergraduates.

"There was a tremendous wartime pressure to marry," Jinny recalled. "But we were very, very young, and very immature." Their well-honed intellectual competitiveness overbalanced their emotional development, which stagnated, and they carried on in the same manner from their student days to their married life abroad.

"Your Bill said something one time to me in Dacca," Jinny said. "I don't remember the words exactly. There had been a little interchange between Max and me, and Bill put his arm around me and said to Max something like, 'Take care of her.' And I thought, Bill's the first person who *really* saw something was cracking. And yet I really wasn't facing it. Didn't for many years. I was in the usual rut, 'What should *I* do – so *he'll* change? We need to talk to someone.'"

She turned her head away for a moment, staring out the window at the magnificent, sweeping view of treetops and far-off buildings.

Great pride had been in her way too, she admitted – not wanting to acknowledge failure at anything, least of all marriage. "In my family people *didn't* fail at marriage."

Jinny and I were drawn together in Dacca, not only because of our mutual interests and the fact that there were so few Americans in this then sleepy Asian outpost, but because of the several parallels in our lives. We both were born in 1926, married when we were in college, had three children (Jinny had a fourth later), two boys and a girl of exactly the same ages. Our two eldest, born in 1950, made up two-thirds of the first grade class in the Dacca-American school. In other words, we were typical of our generation: early marriage, several children.

Also, we both had pioneer grandparents and were raised on that American version of stoicism, the lonely existence that Adrienne Rich captures so beautifully in "From an Old House in America":

> Isolation, the dream
> of the frontier woman
> levelling her rifle along
> the homestead fence
> still snares our pride . . .

Jinny's experience validates those lines. "I was the shock absorber for the kids in all the moves. Max concentrated on his career. My whole heritage supported this view. My maternal grandmother followed my grandfather to South Africa. My mother has traced our family back to 1631 in Maine. My paternal grandmother moved from one farm to another, taking one Appalachian type house after another and fixing it up, because that grandfather, though a magnificent farmer, could never stay on one farm. He would build up one and move on. So what's new? I'm moving about with kids, lucky to be higher up the social scale."

"I know. In Dacca I felt like a pioneer, too," I said. "The fact that I had kept the kids alive and whole – that was like a test and I had passed it. Not until that plane lifted off for home and I looked down on that Ganges River delta did I let myself think how hard it had been."

"Definitely." Jinny agreed softly, "Dacca was that for me too – a test."

She handed me her photo albums, with pictures of her grandparents in South Africa, and we speculated about what life really was like for those pioneer women. Both Jinny's grandparents kept fascinating diaries. Their papers are donated to the Harvard and the Talladega College libraries, but some of the passages relating to their personal affairs are pasted over.

"Can you imagine wearing those clothes," Jinny said, pointing to a picture of her grandmother in an 1880s high neck, long-sleeved, ankle-length dress certainly more suitable for a tea party in Boston than for crossing the Transvaal by ox-cart. "Victorian ladies did not sweat," Jinny noted, "so Grandma changed her clothes three times a day, hanging her petticoats on bushes to dry."

I thought of a picture I have of my little Swiss grandmother, wearing a long cotton dress with spotless white collar and cuffs, carrying two pails of milk from the cow she had just milked, across the muddy barnyard of an isolated ranch in Idaho. Images like that get in the way of women's ability to assess their true feelings. We go on following the skeleton of a pattern – a myth other women made. Our material benefits are so demonstrably better than our grandmothers' were, but how little we know about the rest of their lives: their recognized place in the family when it was a work unit, their feelings of worth about the work they did.

"The first time I had time to lie back and think about these things," Jinny said, "was when I was in the hospital for nearly a month, alone, in Boston." Her children were with her parents or friends, her husband in Washington, D.C. "Really, it was more a chance to feel. My tendency is to think and to try to put it into intellectual terms. But I was too weak and exhausted to think logically. For the first time I let myself *feel* hurt – *feel* that the marriage wasn't working, that the kids were in trouble." Through her teenage children, Jinny experienced every anguish of the 1960s.

"Lying there, so weak I had to be helped across the room, I thought a great deal about courage: what it was, what it takes to keep going when you are weak, the physical courage to keep going. I began thinking about my ancestors." And she began to reshape the myth of their lives, letting the reticence and prudishness and pride go, and reaching deep inside herself instead to find the courage and honesty that were also a part of their legacy, what she needed most.

"And something wonderful happened," she let out a happy sigh. "That fall I felt I got my own roots back in New

England. It was a beautiful autumn. I was driving back and forth between my parents in Royalston, Massachusetts, and the schools where the kids were. As I drove across the Mohawk Trail, I realized that this was the country that made my people. This was where they became Americans, in this rocky jungle.

"It was the first time that I had been alone in years and years and years. In this lovely autumn weather I drove slowly, and I saw what these people had done. A lot of the New England countryside has gone back to brush. My people hacked their way through this. I thought, they are grim, they are harsh, they are not as fun-loving as in other traditions, but I am a WASP and I'm glad. When you asked what made it possible for me to leave my marriage and to change, part of it was this knowledge of the grim determination of those Puritans."

But stern New England grit is not the only ingredient of Jinny's personality, as she first discovered when she learned foreign languages. "I'm much more emotionally open in Greek. I can cry, I can get mad." She flung her arms wide in a gesture of amazement. Intrigued by the differences she saw in her own actions, and by the uncharacteristic ways she felt when she spoke a foreign language, Jinny characteristically began to ask why.

She took a course called "The Theory of Personality" at Pierce College in Athens, Greece. "This just opened up everything. All my experience with languages, my ideas, began to jell." Her excitement over her ideas about language and personality was urging her forward.

"I read an article by Dr. Paul Kolers of Massachusetts Institute of Technology in 1968 in a copy of *Scientific American*," Jinny remembered, "It was just what I had been trying to say. So I wrote him – asked if I could go to see him. *This was me – the independent woman emerging.* He answered that I could come talk to him. I was vaguely thinking about a master's thesis. When I talked to him, he said, '*Do it!*' And so I sat down and started writing for admission to the graduate departments of psychology of several universities."

"I should imagine," she wrote, "that to any committee on admissions to graduate study, a forty-three-year-old housewife, twenty years out of college, must present fairly substantial justifications for her interest in further education, particularly when requesting financial aid . . . it would be dishonest to deny that part of the reason is the need to 'find' myself, to establish my own identity as a human being, part of the 'over forty' crisis, I guess. My undergraduate degree was in sociology, with some sort of social work as my career plan. It took me only a few months after getting my degree to know that what I did *not* want to do was social work. It has taken me eighteen years to figure out what I *did* want to do."

What might her research in psychology and the theory of personality development lead to? "I already have a 'derived' career – that of foreign service wife," she explained. "However, I have every intention of trying to forge a primary career of my own." And then she added, "In all likelihood, my husband will be assigned to Washington, D.C., for the next four to five years. These years offer me the only opportunity I will have to attend regular, nearly full-time classes. If I am not able to do this now, there will not be another opportunity for many years." The now-or-never tone of her application came from her feeling of whirling on somebody else's merry-go-round, with no strength to say she needed to get off for a bit to regain her balance.

Yet she was edging toward her independence in small ways, learning to be on her own. "Just that experience of going to school early in the morning in Athens was important, I realize now," Jinny said. "My classes were downtown, where there was no place to park. I would drive to the back side of Mount Lykabettos and walk over the ridge and down the slopes into the city. There was Athens all laid out before me – so beautiful! At first I couldn't enjoy it. I wanted to share it with my family. Why won't they come and see this? Finally one morning I said to myself, 'They are not going to come and they are never going to see it. But why shouldn't I?' So I did it for a whole year. I walked down into Athens in all seasons. It was pure joy walking down that mountain – and going to classes, having my mind stimulated again."

Jinny's husband was assigned back to the States as they had anticipated, and Catholic University offered Jinny a scholarship with full tuition plus twenty four hundred dollars, but only if she enrolled as a full-time student. "This offer was the end of the era of money for research," Jinny explained. "I remember just sitting there in my chair and going gulp, gulp, gulp, and saying to them, 'I'll do it. I'll go full-time.' I was scared out of my wits. Had to take graduate statistics. Never even had advanced math."

Jinny repeated the words so many women have said to me about their school or work during a time of crisis: "It was an absolute lifesaver."

Her family troubles grew worse. "But I would get into the car in the morning and go to those classes, and I loved it," she declared. "I recognized I was getting out of the house. Volunteer work would have been the same. But with this, there was light on the horizon, there was sun. A goal for *me*. And I said to myself, 'You don't really have to have an A + at this point in your life. You have had a full life. If you get C– in all of your classes, *I* will give *me* an A.'

"The great advantage of my age was experience to bat theories against. Everytime somebody brought something up, I could see the relevance or the irrelevance of it. And I found I had read so much – this huge background. I would get so excited. I would come home and deal with whatever problems I had to, and then read and fall asleep over my books. For the first time, I was me. Nobody at the university knew I had kids! A precious year!"

Then, fully aware that it might be the wrong decision to make, but wanting to make one final try to preserve many years of marriage, Jinny agreed, after one year in Washington, to accompany her husband to South Africa. The pull was strong. On the ship out, she read her grandfather's diary, in which he wrote in 1890, "Our attitude means that we are not going to survive here."

"He meant, of course, the whites' attitude toward the blacks," Jinny said. "He felt it was wrong. Eventually he had to leave the mission – he was too controversial. After that he worked for awhile with a League of Nations group looking into contract labor in the mines. I read Grandpa's report on that, too. Unless you live in a society like South Africa, you don't realize how much you have to think about the quality of your daily living, how often you violate your own principles each day. And if you do stand up for your principles, what are you doing to your children?

"I soon decided to seek out the Quakers. I had attended Quaker meetings off and on since college. Basically I like their form of worship, liberal philosophies, social action, and the fact that their official title is The Religious Society of *Friends*. We had interracial meetings. People from Soweto came to our meetings and some of our meeting went to theirs. One woman there became very important to me, helped me to find strength.

"I went to discussion meetings and became an activist. The reason I joined the Quakers in South Africa was that they gave me a group, a support group. And because I felt they were so small and needed so much. One person mattered. And I wanted to say, 'Here I stand with this group!'

"Sunday is a very family day in South Africa. Gorgeous climate. Everybody is playing tennis, swimming. We had this big garden with fruit trees and a pool. And servants. People would come over for Sunday lunch. I would go off, first, to this not very nice part of town for meeting and come back and feel a bit left out of it. At the same time, I saw that my family was getting on with their own lives. They were handling them.

"The Quakers were holding evening meetings to study social action – you might even call them consciousness-raising groups, except that I don't like the term. We had them at night. I would drive alone. Women didn't do this in South Africa. But I finally decided, Fine! I am just going to go. *And I am not going to be afraid!* And I drove everywhere, all sorts of places, all by myself. I wasn't going to live under this shadow of fear. One night I thought there was going to be a tribal fight in our garden. I went out and talked to both groups of Africans. Other small things. But I gained a great sense of physical courage there."

Jinny attended the University of Witwatersrand in Johannesburg, and did all of her research, testing groups of English-speaking and Afrikaans speaking students, for her doctoral dissertation. Then, not quite a year after her twenty-sixth wedding anniversary, she left South Africa, ostensibly to settle their youngest daughter in boarding school, knowing that the differences between her husband and herself were so deep and damaging that staying together would destroy them both.

The kind of courage she needed now was to decide to make the break. One of her children had brought her up short. After witnessing a family fight, he said, "Mom, you were vicious!" "That," said Jinny, "was when I stopped thinking what's wrong with my husband, and began thinking, what's wrong with *me*. It was a crucial point. I thought, I am being a horrible person. The only way I will be a better person is to get away from this man. Living with him, I cannot do what I want to do or, more important, be what I want. It's *me* I have to live with for as long as I live.

"I remember lying in bed with what was utter, complete panic, my heart pounding. Several years later, my brother recalled that he had never seen such a nervous person as I was when I came back from Africa. I would drop things, I would break things, I would bump into things. I was black and blue all over. I was disoriented, psychologically and physically.

"I went to see our family doctor, who has taken care of us for years. He had to give me some antihistamines for my hay fever and I went back for a refill. I remember saying to him, just sort of in passing, flippantly, 'You know, I've debated taking them all.' And I'll never forget – he had been sitting at his desk writing a prescription, and he wheeled around directly at me, and started to talk.

"I was there an hour. He said, 'I get so damned mad at these men. My waiting room is full of wonderful women like you who are taking this career crap from these men. Women who are trying to run their families, who are trying to take care of their children. And these men are making their lives miserable.'

"I dissolved," Jinny sighed. "He said firmly, 'I think this is serious. I want you to see a psychiatrist and I want you to go today!' You read how you should investigate these psychiatrists. Why, I was in no shape to investigate! I realized I had made a suicide threat. I thought I was flip. He knew I was not. And he sent me to an analyst who, my doctor said, personally lived the kind of healthy life he wants for his patients. A very kind man. A trustworthy man.

"At first," Jinny said, "all I knew was that this man was helping me. That's why I didn't go to a women's group. I believed him when he confirmed the seriousness of the family doctor's diagnosis of depression. I'd lived with it too long not to understand I couldn't handle this alone.

"But contrary to all the myths about psychoanalysts," she declared, "he didn't grab hold of me and keep me in therapy. He insisted that I think long and hard before making a commitment to active change – not only in the way I felt about myself, but about the way I behaved. This analysis was no ego massage. It demanded more commitment of time, money, honesty, courage, and physical pain than anything else I have ever done. If I had realized the pain and time involved, I *never* would have had the courage to make the commitment. Throughout all the therapy this man demanded of me the very best that was in me. Although he would never in a million years – being a traditional psychoanalyst – use the terminology, he did what Quakers say is the goal of life – to see that of God in every person. My experience strongly puts the lie to the charge of anti-feminism of his profession. He insisted that I could be independent and strong. Only then would I be freer and more able to feel myself as a woman!

"In addition, he maintained the strongest ethical code of professionalism – never swerving from the path of therapeutic loyalty to the goal of my independence."

The cost of Jinny's commitment to long-term psychoanalysis and to her own independence meant years of living at an economic level that was the starkest contrast to her former life in the foreign service. She found a tiny apartment in Washington, D.C., "in an old neighborhood. The building was deteriorating," she said. "I bought a secondhand bed and a secondhand card table and sat on my footlocker; I had two footlockers. That's all I had for a year. I bought frozen food, saved the metal trays for dishes, and bought one knife, fork, and spoon at Woolworth's. Nothing more. No radio, record player, vacuum.

"It was so bleak – November and December. We had ten more inches of rain than normal. It rained and rained and rained. And I remember thinking, even the weather is against me. I felt suicidal a couple of more times. It was each day at a time – just getting up. I read the want ads for a job. Finally found work as a receptionist at the YMCA. A very bad winter.

"What was becoming clear," Jinny continued, "was my inability to say goodbye. My fear of being alone. My fear of being independent.

"Then one day I went to the Hirshhorn Art Museum, I don't know why. I'm not a museum-goer. It had just opened. I have never enjoyed art particularly, but I can remember wandering through, concentrating on the art, particularly the brass sculptures. And it all came through to me. Then I sat on the terrace and watched the children. There was a sense of peace."

Without any plan to do so, she got into her car, drove to her husband's apartment, and told him her decision to leave was final. "That decision liberated me." Jinny declared. "I said, 'I will live my own life!' And I will never forget the strength that flowed back into me. I remember that spring, the cherry blossoms. It was like a convalescence being over. All my perceptions were clearer. Each piece of the cherry blossom was beginning to come into focus. My body felt so different. My feet didn't touch the ground. I was having minor hallucinations – not the scary kind. I was buoyant. I ran with some young people across a lawn – it felt like swimming in a dream – and I remember one young man said, 'You are so beautiful.' And later I thought, here I was forty-fiveish. It was that sense of physical liberation. I lost weight and changed my hairdo. And started using my full name – Virginia.

"Finally I had made a completely independent decision. But this one was the culmination of many, many small ones. Having to do it because it is right. Each tiny experience adds to the whole – the walk in Athens, moving to that first tiny apartment." Jinny moved along in her jobs also: to a computer firm; then to night admitting officer at Sibley Hospital; to bed controller at Children's Hospital; and now to her new position there as director of admissions. She works "with a calm smile," as the hospital newsletter reported, "as the liaison between the doctor and the patient (sometimes in the midst of a stormy session)."

Jinny has earned her credentials as a professional woman late in life. Only a dissertation away from a Ph.D., she is now not so sure that is what she wants – studying for it served its purpose. It kept her afloat; it was her means of intellectual self-preservation. Now she is happily involved in her very demanding administrative responsibilities.

"Seeing me independent and resourceful was what my children needed," Jinny said as she closed the photo album. "My reward has been to see them grow. And to know that they all are very close to each other now.

"In some ways I feel so lucky. How could I have done all this if the children had been little?

"*And I never lost faith or trust in men.* This seems to me to be why I so often don't feel comfortable with my 'sisters.' So many of them have had such terrible experiences. And while many women have inspired and helped me, the crucial people in my life have so often been men. I *expected* my mother and sister to support me in having to break up my marriage, but my father and my brother did too. And even my brother-in-law and father-in-law understood."

When Jinny's father-in-law died, not long ago, I remember how deeply moved she was to receive from him a small inheritance accompanied by a beautiful letter stating his appreciation of her fidelity and devotion to him and his wife.

"And more surprising," she continued, "the man whom I

left accepted my decision with respect!

"My professors and my two doctors were men who insisted over a number of years that I *could* reconstitute myself, and they rejoiced with me when I did. When I couldn't hope, *they* hoped for me.

"One of the things you need is a support group, over a long period of time, to maintain you. That is what my Quaker group does for me – both the men and the women in it. You cannot hope alone. In our Quaker group we are all hoping for each other. It is a searching group. In the silence of the Quaker meeting you go down deep in yourself and you find the word of God in yourself. It isn't conscience. It's something else. When I was most suicidal, my doctor said, 'Is that the heritage you want to leave for your daughter?'

"Nobody can take a hand-me-down family myth, though," Jinny concluded. "It's an expanding universe, and we have to recreate those old myths for our new needs. Once when I was very low, I read the psalms, and they didn't help much – they were not what I was looking for. Then I tried reading them aloud to myself and I heard Grandpa's voice from the pulpit, which I had heard many times as a child. And I thought, 'All I know is that the universe is beneficent and there is someplace in it for me.' That is what my religion has done for me. And psychoanalysis let me know people are good too – both men and women.

"I have some kind of core faith that the world is good. That is why I say I am lucky. I don't think I ever lost faith in the possibility of something better. Whether *I* could find it or not, I wasn't sure. Life struggles. That is what it is there for. It is some basic biological urge – to survive. And I *will* survive." Jinny reached over and clasped my hand. "I will survive until the end of my life. And the thing is," she laughed, "I come from a family that lives a very long time."

Virginia Hodge definitely is a triumphant survivor – in radiant bloom. Her roots are strong now. She has worked back through myths and misconceptions to affirm the strength in her heritage and in herself.

Part Six

Women Supporting Women

"Those who have no friends to open themselves unto are cannibals of their own hearts."

FRANCIS BACON
Quoted by Francine du Plessix Gray in
"Friends: A New Kind of Freedom For Women"

The Strengthening Tie of Trust

Considering that women are trained from infancy to offer up themselves, instead of their accomplishments, in competition with each other for the rewards in life ("Come here, darling, and let me comb your hair so you will look as pretty as Mary Jane."), they have maintained an amazing amount of trust between each other. One woman befriending another is the small bud that has blossomed into women's support groups and old girl networks that crisscross the country. But before some of us could join them, we had to jettison a lot of our dependency on men and our jealousy of other women.

I was lucky to have had my first monumental attack of jealousy over another woman rather early in life. It cured me from that form of competition and saved me a lot of pain and trouble later on. Rather, I should say that the other woman cured me. I was a junior in high school, and Ellen took the idol of my life away from me: she married my brother, Watson. Ellen asked me to be a bridesmaid at their garden wedding. Everyone worried about rain; I worried about whether I could go through with it. Watson had bought me my first watch, and my first radio. He taught me to ice-skate and he took me riding in his Ford V-8. He let me sit by the drummer when his orchestra practiced in our basement. Late at night he often came in with a quart of chocolate ice cream that we split between us. Without him, my world would shrink. I would have to be on my own. The moment the wedding vows were over, and Watson kissed Ellen, I hitched up my bridesmaid gown and bolted for the house. In the kitchen, I sobbed so hard that the matron of honor, who found me, was frightened. But Ellen won me over. She gave me lists of books to read, and took me to the movies – listened to all of my hopes, and heartaches, and made me question myself. Watson went out to play golf, and Ellen and I settled into a conversation that has been going on for thirty years.

My mother drew support from other women, too. She had a

*telephone network that we teased her about, but I'm sure it was
her lifeline. Her group activities ebbed and flowed with her
changing needs: her Schoolmasters' Wives, Literary Guild, a
bridge club for a short time, and, longest of all, her national
women's organization, the P.E.O., but, on the whole, she was
not much of a joiner. Like most women, Mother's associations
with other women tended to group and regroup in answer to
the needs of others: her family, a sick friend, or a short-term
community project.*

*But from her example I was able, without really realizing it,
to set up a support system for myself wherever I went, like
throwing up a temporary scaffolding to build my house. I counted
on women. In Asia, and England, and here at home, I would
have been lost without them. Those who are not locked into
nine-to-five jobs, who are attuned to the tone of voice, as well as
to the words said, are on call for the endless emergencies of life.
If they were not there to respond, who would? A social worker?*

*The most complete responder I know is my friend Jane Weld.
Her home is a haven for those who are temporarily out of the
race, felled by illness or fatigue or frightening loneliness.
Otherwise they would be in hospitals or other public places.
Jane also runs an early-warning system for her husband and
other busy males. ("That young man is* not *incompetent. His
wife is ill and they need help." "No, John, I will not pick out a
necklace for you to give her. You take her with you and have a
few days' vacation.")*

*Jane and I have a one-to-one support system that is not
ritualized or weighted down by an organizational super-
structure. By phone, before breakfast, we hold short briefings
on a needs basis: sometimes every day running for a week,
sometimes not for months. At lunchtime we may call for a staff
meeting of two.*

*Large formal groups do not appeal to us as they do to most
men. My father's life was filled by them. He was an active
member of a good percentage of the professional and civic
organizations (usually all male) in Seattle. His groups met for
breakfast, they met for lunch, and they met for dinner. The only
one that I remember having anything directly to do with our*

family was the "Hole-in-One" Club. He became an instant member of it that memorable day when his drive off the seventh tee at Meadowbrook sent the golf ball into a beautiful arch. My mother, brother and I watched it sail up, over, and down directly into the cup on the seventh green. I was caddying for him, and we all got a free dinner at the clubhouse. Other than that, his clubs did not have much affect on us.

My husband has kept his male communal bonds with a group of poker players since he was a boy. Not the same group, of course – there seems to be an international order of poker players. Wherever we are, he soon is a regular member of the local game. But it sometimes seems that he has not much noticed the change of faces behind the stacks of poker chips.

Years ago, when Bangladesh was East Pakistan, General Ayub Khan, the president, was overthrown in a military coup, and we Americans were confined to our quarters. The Bengalis were to be off the streets by eight o'clock. These restrictions were enforced for about ten days. Bill did not mind missing work, but came his poker night and a gnawing restlessness drove him out after curfew. At the house of his Bengali host, the game was in progress.

"But how did they all get there? Were there enough to make up a game? The finance minister has been thrown in jail. Isn't he a member?" My questions tumbled out to Bill the next day.

"They had someone sitting in for him," was Bill's laconic reply.

"Who?"

"Didn't catch his name."

"And Ayub Khan? I heard he's disappeared. Maybe fled to Switzerland. What happened to him? What did they say?"

"Didn't say. There was a replacement. Damned good player, too."

If one of Bill's poker partners would happen to turn up unannounced at our door, with a touch of amnesia and no wallet on him, Bill might be hard put to place the man without a hand of cards and a pile of poker chips in front of his face.

My mother, on the other hand, instantly recognized my Great-Aunt Martha that rainy night she rang our front doorbell

*and stood there, thin as a rail, with nothing on but a coat over
her nightgown and a pair of shoes without stockings. Her red-
dish hair was cut short in a jagged bob, and her face was white.
"Margaret, help me," she whispered. "I've run away."*

*"How she got to our house, I'll never know," Mother said
later. "The convalescent home was a good hundred miles away.
All she had in her pocket was a nickel and three pennies. But*
convalescent home!" *She spat the words out. "Martha went in
good faith because Harry convinced her she needed a rest.* He
knew! *Just wanted to get her out of the way. She lost thirty
pounds! The things they did to her!" Mother never divulged
just what they did. It never occurred to me to ask, so potent was
the message: beware of men, who have the power and money,
and want to get you out of the way.*

*Mother nursed Aunt Martha back to health. For months she
would not let Harry near her. I heard the story dozens of times,
and tales of witches in Hansel and Gretel and Rapunzel paled
beside that episode and the other stories Mother told me about
Great Uncle Harry – for the drama did go on.*

*I used to wonder at it all while I listened to the restored and
vigorous Aunt Martha admonish Mother: "Do it, Margaret!
Get that painting done. Let the ironing go. You have talent,
damn it! Do something with it! Virgil can cook his own dinner –
he's not a child."*

*How much Aunt Martha's encouragement helped Mother
decide to go back to school, I don't know, but I suspect it was
considerable. They were always on the phone when I wanted to
use it.*

*Later, when I was in college, Aunt Martha did get a bit dotty.
Who knows why? But it was in a friendly sort of way. She
heard voices that gave her warnings she passed along to us.
When Mother came home from the hospital, still weak from her
appendectomy, none of us was at home to help her out. So Aunt
Martha would drop over to make her a cup of afternoon tea.
"And she used to say," Mother laughed, (for she loved to tell
the story), " 'Now I've put just a little bit of poison in this cup
of tea for you, Margaret. You'll scarcely notice.' "*

"Good grief, then what did you do?" I asked on cue.

"Why, I just looked her in the eye and said, 'Now look here, Martha. Did you really put poison in this tea?' And she answered, 'Why, no, of course not. It was just a joke. You know I've thought of poisoning myself, but I won't, and I wouldn't do that to you either, Margaret. You're my friend."

"And you trusted her and drank the tea?"

"Of course," Mother replied. "Where would we be in this world without trust?"

Could be dead from an overdose of it, I used to think. Now I understand that my mother was a risk-taker for good reason. Trust, she always said, brings out the best in people. It gives them the courage to do the right thing. It means that someone believes in you and is reaching out. It helps you keep sane. Women's support systems are built on trust. That is a fragile tie, tenuous and easily broken.

Men, in contrast, have an ancient history of strong organizational banding together, but from what I have been able to observe, they are not too concerned about individual members. Women's banding together has been less structured, more one-to-one. But our bonds are crossing and strengthening. So if anyone is thinking of pushing herself into a late bloom, or of saving her own life, I would say, get thee to a woman's group. They will recognize you there.

16. Twelve in a Group and Three in a Shop

"O We have desperate need of laughter!"

BEATRICE LLEWELLYN-THOMAS
"To Puck"

When Irene, a friend of many years, visited me in Washington, D.C., and bought twenty-eight yards of fine imported cotton dress material to take back to a member of her study group in Seattle, it occurred to me for the first time that this "bunch of mostly doctors' wives," as she described them, might not be up to what the name of their group implied.

"Well, we really did start out as a study group," Irene mumbled when I pressed her.

"And then?" I persisted.

"Well, we were all about fifty." There was an edge of protest in her tone. "All wives at home. None of us were, I guess you could say, intellectually up to the mark. So Jacqui and Mara thought it would be a good idea if seven or eight of us got together to study a lecture series offered in the newspaper." She fiddled with her reading glasses. "You know how it is," she said.

I did indeed. My mother belonged to a women's study group in the 1930s called the Literary Guild. The only times I ever begged her to let me help with the food were when she was hostess for one of their meetings. I would squeeze into the corner of our breakfast nook, as far out of sight as possible, diligently arranging thin strips of pimento and bits of parsley on the heart- and diamond-shaped open-faced sandwiches, hoping my mother's friends would not notice me when they slipped into the kitchen to exchange whispered confidences.

Once I nearly stopped breathing when I saw a gray-haired family friend snatch a dishtowel to stifle her sobbing while my mother patted her shoulder, saying, "There, there, my dear. I'm sure he will come back. He's just having a little fling. You know how men are." When I started reading novels I caught on to the romantic plots right away. The events in *Tess of the D'Urbervilles* didn't surprise me a bit.

"So what happened then?" I asked, getting back to Irene.

"This little group began meeting in 1974," she explained, warming to the subject now. "None of us was actively involved in the women's movement." She stressed the point: "This was not a consciousness-raising group. I think that the first lecture we studied was called, 'The Future of Man.' It was about cloning.

"But at the second or third meeting, one of the women walked in and sat down and burst into tears. She was at a crisis point with her husband. You don't go on talking about cloning or environmental problems, or whatever, at a time like that. We did what we could to help her. And then we began talking about this need we all felt to make some changes in our lives. That's how the study part went by the board. Generally our problems are what to do with ourselves now that our families are gone, or how to survive a divorce."

The same questions persist, I thought, but now the answers are beginning to be different. Even in the farthest northwest corner of the United States, in Seattle, a city chosen by many polls as the most livable in the country, least battered by urban problems, and extolled by many writers for its beauty and lack of frenzied pace – even in this idyllic setting, women face the old problems of broken marriages and loneliness; how to develop a sense of worth; how to make a livelihood when they are suddenly on their own; and how to get back into the mainstream of life after the isolation of being a full-time wife and mother. The difference now is that they are talking about these things, not on a confidential one-to-one basis only, but to each other. They have moved from whispering in twos and threes in the kitchen to talking together in the living room. A sense of trust between women is sweeping across the country.

As Irene confirmed: "Women are less backbiting and much more supportive of each other now."

"But what," I wanted to know, "has that got to do with the twenty-eight yards of material you bought?"

She laughed. "Well, right away it was pretty obvious to our group that we needed to figure out ways to launch each other into some new activities that were more fulfilling than just being housewives, or that would make money, preferably both. We needed that kind of help a whole lot more than we needed that lecture series. The dress material is for the first one of our group that we launched. Before she was married, she had been a dress designer. We talked her into going back to designing. Like all of us, she didn't have much confidence in herself. But we encouraged her. She made dresses for several of us; she is good. We gave her a push and she went to a couple of specialty shops. They were glad to take what she designed and made up. But she was trying to do all of the sewing herself – it was nearly killing her. The group told her that was a pretty foolish way to do it, that she should hire others to do the sewing. So she got up her courage and did, and ended up selling her clothes to some of the most stylish shops in Seattle."

"Did you launch any others?"

"Oh yes. One woman started a plant shop. Another, who was always treasurer of women's clubs, took a refresher course in bookkeeping. She got a job working winters in a ski shop as a bookkeeper. The shop closed during the summer, leaving her free to be home with her kids. Then there is Mara, a former professional dancer from New York who started dance exercise classes.

"Our only failure so far," Irene sighed, "was with one who took a part-time receptionist-typing job against the group's advice. As so often happens with that type of job, the work-load increased and when she found she was expected to be a full-time assistant for two rather than one employer, she caved in. It was terribly hard on her morale. Now the group is trying to pick her up and relaunch her."

The next summer, when I visited Irene in Seattle, her group

gave a wine and cheese get-together for me at Shirley Johanson's beautiful home on the edge of Lake Washington. We lounged in deck chairs on her wide patio – even though she had the house listed for sale; she cannot afford to keep it up now that her husband is gone. "Probably the last time we will meet here," someone said. "And this is probably the last sunny day we'll have this summer," another quipped, alluding to Seattle's notoriously rainy weather – and also to keep the tone light. Sentimentality gets short shrift in this group. Without being flip, they try to strike a humorous note. No one is allowed to take herself too seriously; they know that a little laughter often is as great a balm as a good cry – not that they deny tears. It's the balance that they strive for.

As they came in, dressed in pants or shorts or cotton skirts and sandals, walking freely, an attractive and natural-looking group of women, I thought of how my mother's group at this age, or even younger, were corseted, in mind as well as in body. The openness of Irene's group was as refreshing as a summer breeze. While they were catching up with each other, I ran down to the small pier at the foot of the lawn to dip my feet into the cold water of Lake Washington once again. I had first sailed on this lake with my brother, skinny-dipped in it on moonlight nights, swam and canoed with dates, and in that freshness of youth, I learned the subtle stratagems of competition between women for the attentions of men. It was a long and hard lesson to deal with.

When all the group had arrived, I asked them if they had any rules. "Only one," several answered. It is that no woman is ever to indulge in any sort of a putdown of another member.

The group has also set a limit of twelve members as the maximum number possible for general conversation.

"There is just a neat closeness with this group," Marilyn said. "Every one of us has problems. It's a great comfort to know that. We've had little fights and little peeves, but they have passed."

"I just want to say that this is the most supportive group of ladies I have ever seen in my life," echoed Mary, a tall, graceful, white-haired woman in a tennis dress. "Not only are they supportive, they are frank. If you have a problem, they are not going to sympathize with you unless they feel you really need it. I think they make a very honest assessment of what is going on."

"We have to warn you," someone chimed in. "Mary is the nicest person in the group."

"No," Mary protested, "it's just that you all have such a great sense of humor."

"You have to!" Jacqui responded. "We are going through a shattering time."

"It's true," another said. "You have to learn how to laugh at yourself. One of our original members couldn't open up, which you have to do before you can laugh. We asked a speaker over, someone who had been through the women's program at the university, to give us some ideas. We all got out pencil and paper to jot down our problems. And this member just went into a spasm. She wasn't ready to say, 'I'm sure crapping this up, or things *aren't* working.' She was still keeping up a facade."

"Have you ever noticed," Mara interjected, "that all exercise charts cut off at fifty? After fifty, consult your physician."

"Don't worry, girls," Shirley shouted above the laughter, "I'm going to find a big old house and get a housekeeper and her husband, and when we all grow old we can live there."

"Sure," Marilyn piped up, "you'll put me on kitchen duty."

"Well, you've always wanted to cook," Irene reminded her.

"I *love* to cook," Marilyn said. "We've spent a great deal of time in this group trying to find some little business that will fill all our needs. But nobody wanted to do the food bit." There were groans all round. "Soup on Wheels she wanted," someone moaned.

Marilyn ignored them. "We pursued every idea. We found a little house owned by city hall. Looked at it to fix it up for a soup and salad place. We invited the city manager of Bellevue to talk to our group about what was really needed here. He encouraged us. We got very excited, were making lists. But the house was really run-down and we realized we would really be in for it. Then we got someone's brother-in-law to come down and tell us how much it would cost to move it, which we would have had to do. When we went into the financing, it was too much for us. Then we thought we would open a pub. A good idea, but someone beat us to it."

"You can see how we all are looking for a foot in the outside world," came a comment from the far side of the patio.

"Say, who is keeping the store this afternoon?" Irene asked. "I see that you're all here."

"Yep." Marilyn lit a cigarette. "We closed it to come to the meeting. We're the bosses, you know."

"The store?" I inquired.

"Munks, Old Main: European Antiques and Gifts," they told me. "On Main Street in Bellevue. The idea for that kind of a shop started here in our group."

There are three of them – Marilyn, Shirley and Jeanne – who own and operate Munks, Old Main. Marilyn Leyse teaches half-days in a learning disability school, Shirley Johanson is a private duty nurse, and Jeanne Wissler is a freelance interior decorator.

"We all need each other," Marilyn said. "We couldn't do it alone."

Until recently, Marilyn and Jeanne had not worked outside of their homes since before they were married. Shirley never had used her nursing degree. Now, having brushed up their old skills, they all work part-time for wages so that they can put the profits from their business back into it.

"Shirley and I needed to make money and make it quick," Marilyn emphasized. Both are divorced from doctors, Marilyn with three children and Shirley with five. With no social security or retirement plans, and with child support soon to stop, they have to make the most of their remaining working years. Unlike widows who grieve, divorced women are angry. "Anger is energy," one of them observed. "It gets the juices flowing."

"We're displaced homemakers," Marilyn said with a faint

Missouri drawl. Brown-eyed, with an animated face, she can make a person laugh through her tears – a born storyteller and mimic, talking with wide, sweeping gestures. "The group was terrific when I was going through my divorce," she told me. "My psychiatrist said, 'You know, Marilyn, that divorced doctors' wives are just not accepted in the community. The community looks to the doctor and the wife is soon forgotten.' And I could say to him, 'Well, I have friends now, and they are *my* friends, and a lot of them are doctors' wives.'" She crossed her legs with a "so there" flourish. "Although I am naturally a relaxed person, I was walking on TNT. So it was terrific to be able to go to the group and hear these gals talk about their feelings.

"We quickly realized that *everybody* had a problem. All of us had kept everything inside." Her voice dropped to a whisper: "We just *didn't* talk about it." Then her face lit up with her generous smile. "Without the females in my life, I think I might have gone down the tube. Of course, I may be strong like my mother, but who knows? The new thing is that women are open. It is hard to talk about yourself. But it's even harder to know who you are if you are all by yourself – unless you're mirrored off someone else. In the group you get some good concepts of yourself, some good vibes. It really is a support group.

"I brought Shirley into the group. [Everyone has to be invited by a member.] Jacqui introduced her to me because she was going through a divorce, and here I am, the old expert. We clicked. Well, who wouldn't with her? So I said she should come to the group. She said she didn't want to. I said, 'Shirley, you'll love it, and you need it *now!* What to do until the lawyer comes.'"

Shirley, blonde, with a deep tan and friendly blue eyes, is a Canadian by birth. An outgoing person who never meets a stranger, she likes to keep active and busy. "Shirley is the cleaner; she comes to my house and starts cleaning the counters," Marilyn said. "That's the nurse in her."

"The divorce was a bad thing, an awful thing in a way," Shirley sighed, "but I think I was stifled. I think I was in a role and wasn't my own person. I guess I was trying to maintain a smooth and happy home and that wasn't my real self. I was so busy with all these kids, or, rather, made myself busy with them, that when finally they were all raised, like most of my friends, I looked back and thought, my God, is this all there is? Being a housewife is dull, dull, dull.

"But then women can swing into something different, whereas men are still stuck in their job roles. I wouldn't want to be a man growing up today and having a family and putting them through school, the financial pressure. Men don't have it easy."

I must have looked surprised, because Shirley explained, "I know, not everybody agrees with me. But I feel sorry for the fellows. Men have had to be the macho – couldn't shed a tear, break down and say how tough it is. But that's the way our society is. Men keep everything in and won't say anything. Now in our little group we are all very open with each other, which is really a help. Women will talk and be very supportive of each other. We are all learning a little more. Each one of us is smartening up.

"Men have been in the same things all their lives. A tough, competitive world. With families, they got responsibility just boom, boom, boom. Now they have reached their peak. I think some of them can think they are gods, but they have a pretty hard row to hoe. They put on a pretty good front at the office.

"Doctors are under tremendous pressure to keep up. I'll tell you, these nurses today are damned smart. Those gals, a lot of them could be doctors, they are so well trained. It really is impossible to keep up with all the changes. Those young nurses and young doctors are on the way up. It's like the corporate ladder: they bring in a sharp young wheel and give the fellow who built the company the shaft without much compensation for what he has done. Men under the pressure of younger people moving up don't have the same physical stamina to keep up that the younger ones do. I don't know if men can face it, when they're at their peak, that it is not going to go on like this anymore.

"Whereas with us, with women, we're not so tied up. We have done one job, raising our families – now maybe we can go on with something else. Still," she smiled wryly, "if you take these guys at fifty-two, who are making sixty thousand dollars, and took their medicine or whatever away from them, and put them out, and said, 'Go make a living,' they would have a pretty hard time. Like here we are, just starting a career. So, I don't think it's fair."

Motivated by their urgent need to make money and build for their futures, Shirley and Marilyn began to talk over possibilities together. Marilyn longed to get into business. Her mother had always worked, and later in life, with her father, started their own accounting firm. Just starting her teaching at this stage in life would not provide her with very much financial security, Marilyn realized. Private duty nursing was more profitable for Shirley, but she felt limited by schedules and long hours and there was no retirement plan in private service.

"I would say, 'How about a catering business?' " Marilyn recalled, "and Shirley would say, 'Yuk!' " (Marilyn's desire to cook is so strong that even now, with her teaching and running the shop, she caters an occasional party or dinner for her friends.)

At this time, Shirley was redecorating her house, a common activity of women in crisis: clear out the old, rearrange, make a new setting, a new start. She called an old friend (not in the group) Jeanne Wissler, a freelance decorator, to give her some ideas. "She has a terrific flair," Shirley said.

"But I'm not such a social being," Jeanne claimed. "Shirley knows half of Bellevue and Marilyn knows the other half." Tall, creamy-complexioned, with large brown eyes and a radiant smile, Jeanne is the quietest of the three women. Her good taste and air of elegance may have come down to her through the French ancestry on her mother's side. After Jeanne was grown, her mother opened, and still operates, an antique/gift shop in Tacoma, Washington, from which the women took their shop's name of Munks. (They shared orders when the minimum amount was too high for Munks,

Old Main to carry alone.) Jeanne is married (her husband is in real estate) and they have one daughter.

"I had always thought about having a shop," Jeanne said, "but I didn't want to do it alone." So she decorated occasionally for friends, bought an old piece of furniture, refinished it and sold it through her mother's shop.

"Then I decided I should do something more," Jeanne said. "I was just spinning my wheels at home. So I answered an ad in the paper for a manager at a fabric shop. You had to send your picture in with your application. I got the job, but it was hard." She let out a long breath. "I had to sell and I'm not very good at that. I just couldn't push people, I would try to guide them. Oh, how I dreaded Saturdays. A woman would drag a poor man in and he would grump and fuss. Men don't want to be dragged into fabric shops on Saturdays. They were always grumpy. They had to assert themselves in some way, so they would say, 'I don't like that.' And the woman would say, 'Then what *do* you like?' 'Well, I don't know.' Then the man would mumble and I would think, 'Oh, my god, they're going to get in a fight.' And they did. I just hated it.

"The other gal in the shop, everytime I turned around she was selling something. She would sell, sell, sell. I couldn't understand how she could sell and I couldn't. We had a little chart on the wall, of sales made by each of us. I couldn't look at it. I tried to be a good sport when she would say, 'Well, how have we done?'

"When the other gal had customers who couldn't make up their minds, she would say "– Jeanne mimicked her brisk tone – 'O.K. There's got to be a decision made here.' She didn't care. And, by gosh, they did – they made a decision and bought it. I couldn't do that. I worked eight months and I tried to like it, but I discovered that I just wasn't a salesperson."

About this time, Shirley, who can no more pass a house for sale or rent without looking at it than a bee can pass by a rose in bloom, stopped with Jeanne to look at "a darling little house on Main Street." It was a frame house typical of the Northwest, two stories, with a long porch with turned rail posts, a dozen blocks from the old whaling station at the end of Lake Washington. When a floating bridge linked Seattle to Bellevue in the early 1940s, and then another even more direct bridge was built later, the business district of Bellevue moved away from its waterfront location to large, modern shopping squares. Then, in the middle 1970s, the restoration movement hit Bellevue's Old Main: brick sidewalks were laid, copies of old gas lamps lined the street, and small businesses, many of them run by women, moved back to revive the small town atmosphere so many people regretted Bellevue's losing. Now people stroll from shop to shop, stopping to chat with proprietors.

Irresistibly drawn to the little house on Old Main, the three women rented it for one month, just to keep it off the market. "We kept thinking there must be some business that we can get into there that will be fun, plus a challenge," Shirley recalled. "We got real excited and talked about how we could really do something."

"Sat and drank coffee and smoked," Marilyn added. "We wanted Irene to consider going in with us. She's so stable. But she was off being a bailiff."

"Quite a group of us met to talk about it," said Jeanne. "We just didn't know whether to take the jump. We didn't have the money."

"Up until the last day of our rent, we didn't know what we were going to do with it." Shirley laughed.

Then they hit upon the idea of opening an antique store. The group encouraged them. They knew that in this plastic world of mass-produced ersatz furnishings there is a great longing for pieces of individual beauty and distinctive craftsmanship. People do not want their homes to look exactly like their neighbors'; it makes them feel like automatons. And since new houses and apartments are becoming more efficiently uniform, the interiors are the only places left in which to create a setting reflecting one's individuality.

Antiques, the women reasoned, will always be sought after also because they evoke memories of our past, made tangible in a pewter candlestick, a porcelain platter, a mahogany secretary. Used things have what poet and historian Robert Graves calls *baraka* – a charm or power acquired from long use either by an individual or a community. Anything from a cooking pot to a Queen Anne chair can have *baraka*.

Women, the ones responsible for furnishing and maintaining homes, always have been fascinated by houses, furniture and accessories. "From way back, I've been interested in decorating," Shirley said. "I liked my grandmother and grandfather's old things. I could walk into a room and take it all in very quickly. I toyed with the idea of interior decorating, but knew nursing was first. Then, a couple of years before we opened the shop, I took an adult education course in interior design."

For Marilyn, it was her mother's influence: "She collected antiques ever since I can remember. Our house was full of them. I grew up with antiques and love them. The nice accents I have in my house are what I inherited. Also my aunt was in the business. And I have a background in selling. I worked in a dress shop and I worked in Penny's. Business – owning your own – is part of my background. It really appeals to me – to be in my own business. To be my own boss. But I don't like to do things alone." Neither does Jeanne. She would not have considered opening a shop by herself. But with two congenial partners, the venture held great appeal. Wendall, her husband, gave her his whole-hearted support. "Without his help and encouragement, I couldn't have done it," she said.

So, at a time ripe for all of them, three women with complementary talents and overlapping interests joined to form a small business. Their first problem belied the old saw about marriage being an equal partnership: they had no credit rating on which to borrow money. They might as well have been eighteen years old, for all their years of experience doing the buying and paying the bills for their families counted. Instead, of course, they were fiftyish matrons bristling at being treated as irresponsible nonentities.

"Nobody in the community really encouraged us," Jeanne recalled. "Bankers don't take any chances. We didn't know until the last minute if we could do it. It was not really a very big thing, but it was a big thing for us. Everybody told us it would be three years before we made any money. That discouraged us all." (They turned a profit the first six months.)

"But we do get tickled about things that would drive us crazy if we were by ourselves," Marilyn said.

"Like the small business seminar," Jeanne laughed. "One man gave us a very serious talk about how banks were in business to serve you. Of course we had all been turned down by them. None of us had any money. We began giggling, like you did in junior high – we couldn't stop. He said, 'You know, just tell them that if they won't meet your interest rates, you will go somewhere else.' That broke us up. Imagine us, just telling the banker we'll take our business elsewhere. No experience. No money. No credit rating. So the seminar didn't help us a lot."

They had decided that the minimum they could start the business with was five thousand dollars each. Jeanne took a personal loan from her parents, Marilyn was able to raise hers with a providential small inheritance from her mother's estate, and Shirley determined to make another round of the banks.

"The Small Business Bureau wanted an arm and a leg for a loan," she said. "I was indignant. So I walked into this bank, shaking, but trying to put on a brave front. Went to the loan division, but they wouldn't give it to me."

Jaw set, she took on another bank. "I tried to sound very sure of myself, which I wasn't, like I really knew what I was doing, which I didn't, so that they would think I was a good risk. Finally, a girl I talked to in the loan department listened. I think she knew my situation, and I think that she might have been in the same position. She has now moved to a big executive position. She might have been the one who helped my loan go through.

"I finally got a personal loan with only my car as collateral. Felt pretty proud of myself. A man can call his banker and ask him for certain terms. I had to do it with no income. We had a lot of hard lessons."

Now, a year later, Shirley and her banker are on a first-name basis and she *is* asking for terms. Persistence paid off. She is learning to read the fine print of contracts and feeling good about her growing business acumen.

"The little house on Old Main was a mess but darling." Shirley picked up the story of their beginning, told as a comedy rather than a tale of woe, because they were in it together, determined not to let anything get them down. The house was old and had not been cared for for years, with plywood walls full of nail holes. They ripped out the worn-out straw matting covering the old plank floors. A dead mouse was in the toilet that rocked on a loose piece of flooring. "It's going to fall through the floor anyway," said the plumber. They chucked out debris of years.

"Shirley's juices run when she's cleaning up," Marilyn said. They painted woodwork and covered the walls with blue plaid fabric that Jeanne selected, tore up the straw matting and rushed off to a garage sale for a carpet that had been ripped up from a house. They bought the carpet for five dollars, and wrestled it down a rockery and into the station wagon. "We've developed muscles like Russian athletes."

"A very snippy young woman" from the telephone company insisted on a deposit and information about their marital status. Shirley got hostile. "We all shifted into high gear," Jeanne recalled, "and just ran for inventory. We would hear about something and go." – auctions, estate sales, garage sales, pieces of consignment.

"Jeanne has the eye, and Shirley loves to shop," said Marilyn. "We grappled furniture up the stairs. I would run out on the street to see if I could find somebody to help us get a piece up over the banister.

"One day they drove me way out to this wholesale pottery warehouse for that gray pottery with blue stripes that has a salt-glazed look. You wouldn't believe it." She rolled her eyes upward. "'Be sure to bring flashlights,' Jeanne said. No lights in the place. Fumbling for the pottery, dirt falling in our eyes. Grab a piece off the shelf with the flashlight and take it over to a window to look over for chips and cracks. Find a box to put the stuff in piece by piece. No one helping us. Once in a while, a shout from some old guy up front, 'How yuh girls doin' back there?' Three hours!" Marilyn threw up her arms. "'My god, is this what we're going to have to do for everything?' I asked them. For no amount of money would I go back."

Jeanne continued: "Marilyn wanted to have a party so badly, so we had an opening with wine, strawberries, cheese, and Mara from our group made baklava for us. More people than I have ever seen – jammed. It was a success. We sold quite a few things before we opened."

"We were so green," Marilyn said. "Our shop officially opened the same day as the Old Main Street opening. Hundreds of people dripping through with ice cream cones. And Jeanne sitting there counting money! But in all of our experience we have lost only one thing, a little alabaster box, from shoplifting. No big deal."

Unpretentious as the three women are, they do not pretend to be expert businesswomen, as was plain to anybody who too the trouble to notice. One who did walked in on their first day of business. "A young man in a funny hat," Jeanne remembered. "I was trying to add up the day's receipts on a little crank adding machine and moaning, 'It doesn't balance, it doesn't balance.' He said, 'I'll help you.' And I said, 'Who are you?' He said, 'I'm an accountant. I work for Best Pies Company,' and he reached over and picked up from somewhere, I don't know, the slip that was missing. And there it was, it balanced. He brought in doughnuts and a cocoa cream pie and showed us how to count our money."

"He's darling, terrific," Marilyn agreed. "He's still with us. Set up our books. Did our taxes. Since he met us, he quit his job. We pushed him over the brink and he's out on his own. He says it's the best thing he's ever done. People trust each other on this level of business."

Another samaritan simply appeared one afternoon and they never saw her again – a young woman from New Orleans. "I'm in advertising," she said to Jeanne, who was trying to get a layout for an ad. "I will help you. I need the right kind of pen and mat paper." Jeanne dashed out to get supplies with her. "We had to meet this deadline and we were all frantic. She took off her jacket and I'll bet she stayed three hours and did the layout. We said, 'Can't we give you something?' And she said, 'No, I'll be back,' and left.

"We've met some lovely people," Jeanne concluded, "and we have a lot of repeat customers."

"But it would drive us crazy if we were trying to do it all alone," Marilyn said.

"We all get along," Shirley agreed. "I just don't know how one person runs a shop, it takes so much time. I think we all thought we would have more time for ourselves than is working out. Some days I go home and think it is too much. Then something happens one day, a good buy, a good sale, and I feel pretty proud."

As well they should. At a time of life when most people are thinking that retirement is not too far ahead, these women are just getting into the mainstream of life, starting from scratch, working six days a week and sometimes more.

"Well, if you've lived under somebody's thumb, you don't know what you can do," is Marilyn's cheerful outlook. "Jeanne and I," said Shirley, "can be very much all business. Marilyn comes in and is a real joy." Women working together!

They seldom go out to lunch: "That's all uptown." They have a coffee pot, Jeanne's jar of Ovaltine, and some crackers, and they sit around a table at the back of the shop. The atmosphere is very home-like, even in the front room, where the plaid curtains match the wall fabric, a wingbacked chair sits next to a table with a pewter candlestick and a crystal bowl filled with flowers, and a French armoire stands open with old china on its shelves.

Often a customer will say, with an air of surprise, "Why, this used to be a little old house." Marilyn always replies, "It still is a little house. It is very old and so are we."

Sometimes, after closing, Marilyn, Shirley and Jeanne go into the front room of the shop, sit down, and pour a glass of wine, raising their old cut-glass goblets in a toast to each other – small businesswomen who learned, with pain and laughter, that three women working and bluffing their way together can beat the odds in the "real" world far better than one broke woman alone.

17. How We All Changed (and Are Changing)

"Those dear old ladies,
All in their eighties,
Tackling St. Paul."

CHRIS PROUTY ROSENFELD

Chris brought the news. She had been to visit her aunt in Pasadena, California. One morning, Aunt Mabel took Chris along to her Central Christian Church discussion group. The meeting, as usual, was held in the apartment living room of one of the members, in a retirement complex. There a dozen women, all octogenarians or nearly so, were sitting on the sofa and extra folding chairs, gathered to discuss the teachings of St. Paul. Cookies and coffee were on the side table. Fumbling for their glasses, the women, each in turn, read a passage from the Bible. They had been raised on these words. But St. Paul, they had been hearing recently, had some very unfair attitudes toward women. They reread him and decided that it was true. In some fundamental ways, he was very out-of-date.

Three thousand miles away, in Washington, D.C., my Poor House Writers group heard Chris's account with joy – another confirmation that women in groups all over the country are discussing old attitudes and questioning accepted authorities. Women in church groups or study groups or social groups are responding to the changing concepts emerging from the women's movement. They are viewing themselves differently. And they are discovering that, all along, women have been good, strong people, not the limited, second-class human beings some authorities made them out to be. But building up their own confidence to act on this new self-acceptance is difficult for women to do by themselves. It is hard to be a late bloomer alone.

Like a baby learning to walk, we will dare a little more and go a little farther when we are sure there is a steadying hand nearby to catch us if we start to fall.

So, to help hold each other up, Timmy and I formed our group, the Poor House Writers. Elaine Reuben, the former director of the Women's Studies Program at George Washington University, where we were graduate students, gave us the idea. We are as mixed a lot as anyone could turn up – a dozen of us, in our twenties and thirties and forties and fifties; single, married, divorced, and widowed; working at paid jobs and at unpaid jobs, full-time and part-time. We are united by our feminist philosophy and by our commitment to write about feminist issues and feminist history. "The group," Rosemary wrote, "changed our lives around."

Rosemary is our youngest member, the notetaker, and the historian we count on to keep us up-to-date on the fast accumulating historical research on women.

Age differences do not divide us. Nor do our very different backgrounds. But it took time to build the trust that we now have, not only because we began as virtual strangers, but because each of us spoke with the special language of our own generation. Now we have built a common vocabulary enriched by the shared experience of our various lives. It worked, Rosemary believes, "because we all started out believing that trust between women was possible."

Some of us do not see each other in between our monthly meetings, so we send cryptic postcards, newspaper clippings, articles, and hurriedly copied quotes we want to share. Communication is our passion. "I think our group is wonderfully different and wonderfully the same," Isolde, a working writer and editor, and widow in her fifties, wrote. "Some of us are just beginning careers, some in midstream, some accomplished. And probably with each new effort, each of us relives the cycle from feeling like a raw beginner to turning out something one feels tolerable about. That's rather in the nature of writing, I think, but never mind, there is always a friend or two who is at whatever spot we are. Then it seems neither so lonely nor so permanent a position."

Looking through the written record of our two years' existence, I am surprised at how many rebuffs each of us experienced, how many wrong turns we took – all jotted down in a rather matter-of-fact manner – my idea for a book on pioneer women in Alaska that was turned down, all our rejection slips, returned manuscripts, and fruitless job interviews. Each of us alone, mulling over the bad news in our separate kitchens, might have been too discouraged to go on trying. Instead, we share our failures and help each other remove, without too much pain, the old dead blossoms of our false tries.

We spur each other on, not in a spirit of competitiveness, but with a deep caring. "If I ever become a 'writing writer,' to use Tillie Olsen's words," Terry wrote, "it will be because of the Poor House Writers. If anything will save me from the silences that have claimed so many other women, it will be the love and support of all of you." Terry's great-grandmother was the poet laureate of Wisconsin. Terry, now in her twenties, works forty hours a week as a secretary, plus two nights a week as a salesperson behind the jewelry and cosmetic counter at Sears Roebuck. She was in graduate school when the exciting, frightening realization that she wanted to be a writer spun her into a "crisis of confidence." Our group encouraged her to find a new thesis topic and a new advisor. She is going to bloom. "The fact that you published your first major book at fifty," she told me, "gives me hope."

Writing master's theses in Women's Studies occupied some of us for a fairly long time (though not all of us were or are in that program). Technical problems and dry spells in our writing were often overcome because of our Poor House Writers' discussions. And we celebrate each degree earned. "I love our rituals," Timmy noted, "cake and wine and flowers for special times, like a graduation or a book acceptance. It's a continuity with female ritual of the past, used in a new way."

But writing, as Barbara observed, "is a solitary task, and it is easy for me, working alone, to doubt my vision." Trained as a biologist, Barbara, mother of three children, has just started back to work, teaching high school science and math, and is working on a biography of Anna Howard Shaw, the suffrage leader. For her, the Poor House Writers is important because it gives her "an opportunity to express my opinions in a small, supportive group before I try them out in front of a larger, less sympathetic audience."

Our other Kris, with a *K*, joined us as a student/activist. "The group," she said, "quietly revived a long-ago abandoned goal – to be a writer. Within six months I finished my thesis, and within a year I won a book contract. I bought my own big dictionary, and my mother recalled I had written my first book at age eight – on paper bags 'bound' with grocer's twine. Poor House Writers reached for the child's lost dream and kindled it with real hope and ambition again. It takes a special environment to learn to walk as an adult beginning writer."

"I'll bet we cry every meeting," Judy said. But she means with joy – the happy tears of relief for having succeeded after some fierce struggle to express and thus change ourselves. We combine smiles on our faces with tears in our eyes, like the time Judy read us the first portion of her autobiographical article, "On Being Physically Different."

"I felt so vulnerable," she said. "It was a difficult piece for me to write, a very personal piece – what it was like to be born with cerebral palsy. Yet I wanted to share it with all of you as a group, because I valued your comments and reaction. I trusted that if the piece were too personal, too boring, too poorly written, or whatever, the members of Poor House Writers would let me know that in a caring way, but with honesty. The members of our group have never indulged in false flattery. They also do not display any envious ripping apart of other members' work. Criticism has always been done in the most supportive manner when someone shared her work, and yet there has been criticism when needed."

Judy, now in her thirties, worked in a factory for ten years before she achieved the confidence to test her intellectual abilities by attending first a junior college, then a four-year college. Six years later, she earned her M.A. at San Jose State College in California. The Poor House Writers' latest celebration was for Judy's contract and her ten-thousand-dollars advance for her book on the history of lesbians.

"The Poor House Writers is the only group that I have ever belonged to that is both predominantly straight (heterosexual) women, and also has a feminist focus," she noted. "Most of the feminist or women's groups that I have ever belonged to, or been a part of, have been at least half lesbian – whether the lesbians were out of the closet or not, I was at least aware that they were lesbians. There was a comfort in numbers, but always a strain or tension between the heterosexual women and the lesbian contingent. Here, in the Poor House Writers, there is no tension that I can feel at all about our basic differences, and there is a focusing on the similarities in ourselves. I value that a lot."

We all do. "There is such faith and trust, each for the other," Rosemary wrote, "that I feel I am letting down the entire group (as well as myself) if I don't have something written for a meeting."

We are more alike than we are different. When Elizabeth took the settlement money from her divorce for one last fling to visit all the places she had always wanted to see, from California to Paris, before she settled down to earn her living, the romantic in us understood. And hoped for her safe arrival home.

But hoping for each other is not all we do. We push when pushing seems appropriate. Sharon, a mother in her forties who works twenty hours a week for the journal *Feminist Studies* and is deeply involved in the women's movement, shoved me up in front of a podium to speak to a professional group for the first time in my life. Sharon is a connector: she connects people and events. And she took me out to breakfast to explain exactly why my speaking to the Chesapeake Area Group of Women Historians was logical and necessary for me and for them. Certainly such reasoning would never have occurred to me.

Other viewpoints enlarge our vision. Timmy, a journal keeper, a mother in her thirties, and the editor of the poet Michele Murray's journals, sees the process of writing as being as interesting as the result. She persuaded me to include myself in this book, a technique that I, trained to be an "objective" historian, would never have attempted without great encouragement.

We are helping each other change our lives by changing our attitudes toward ourselves, and toward what we are capable of doing. The stereotype of women in informal groups such as ours is the same as the one of women talking on the telephone: they must be gossiping, engaged in a competitive exchange about the central concern of women – men. That is a myth perpetuated by the media and by the romantic novel. As one person I interviewed put it, "Women have other things to do." They are as varied in their natures and in their interests as men. And, like most human beings, women have a tremendous need for work that is satisfying, sustaining, supportive, and practical. What they do not have in the same degree as men is the experience and the skills of the modern marketplace. These are what they are talking about in their groups, what they are helping each other develop.

But, in the process, I hope that we do not become stratified with our new associations and locked into organizational rigidity. The old female grouping on the basis of need seems to me more humane. We change and we grow. A role that sustained us yesterday may thwart us today. Giving up old ways is what releases us for new beginnings. Being able to say, "That was fine for then, but times have changed, and so have I," is a potent message to oneself.

And there is a magical power in naming oneself. Say to yourself, I am a writer, or a specialist in Oriental carpets, or a scientist, or a superb tour guide, or an artist, or a scholar, or a communications expert, or whatever work is closest to your heart, and something inside of you shifts gears. You can almost hear them mesh into a new and satisfying purr.

It is hard, of course, to cast off old, inappropriate names. Isolde and I feel that our group hastily misnamed ourselves. She and I grew up in the depression years, when "going to the poorhouse" was a real fear that permeated everyone's consciousness. So Poor House Writers carries unpleasant associations we cannot shake. "Furthermore," Isolde pointed out, "I think there is a good chance many members of our group are going to do so well that the name will sound ironic and insensitive." But now we have vested interests in the name: a great gold, white and purple banner with blue letters on a white panel, which we carried in the July 9, 1978, Women's Equality Day March to the U.S. Capitol. We have property. And tradition: Poor House Writers has been our name for more than two years.

Tangible goods and traditions have always weighed women down. But now that we can talk about those things, and in the talking, honestly, to each other about how they affect our lives, we can do away with goods and chattels, and names, and traditions, and attitudes that no longer are beneficial to us. St. Paul does not have the last word. We do. Women, here and now, in the twentieth century, are naming themselves and moving into fuller lives of their own choice. We are the late bloomers of history.